Barcode in Back

GENDERED JOURNEYS, MOBILE EMOTIONS

Gendered Journeys, Mobile Emotions

Edited by

GAYLE LETHERBY
University of Plymouth, UK

GILLIAN REYNOLDS
Coventry University, UK

ASHGATE

Published by
Ashgate Publishing Limited
Wey Court East
Union Road
Farnham
Surrey, GU9 7PT
England

Ashgate Publishing Company
Suite 420
101 Cherry Street
Burlington
VT 05401–4405
USA

www.ashgate.com

British Library Cataloguing in Publication Data
Gendered journeys, mobile emotions
1. Travellers - Psychology 2. Feminist theory
I. Letherby, Gayle II. Reynolds, Gillian
910.1'9

Library of Congress Cataloging-in-Publication Data
Gendered journeys, mobile emotions / [edited by] Gayle Letherby and Gillian Reynolds.
    p. cm.
Includes bibliographical references and index.
ISBN 978-0-7546-7034-6
1. Voyages and travels. 2. Women. 3. Emotions I. Letherby, Gayle. II. Reynolds, Gillian.

G465.G4615 2009
910.4082--dc22

2008040984

ISBN 978 0 7546 7034 6 (hardback)
eISBN 978 0 7546 9272 0 (ebook)

Mixed Sources
Product group from well-managed
forests and other controlled sources
www.fsc.org Cert no. SGS-COC-2482
© 1996 Forest Stewardship Council
FSC

Printed and bound in Great Britain by
TJ International Ltd, Padstow, Cornwall

Contents

Notes on Contributors

Mike Barnsley has travelled extensively in Old and New Europe and North America and has visited Asia, Australasia and South America for business and pleasure. His mode of travel has varied from planes, helicopters, trains and boats to cars, motorbikes, bicycles, hitchhiking and foot according to available time and money (and who was paying the bills). His passion is motorcycling, which has been undertaken in North America and Europe. He owns a customized Harley and he wants to get out and ride.

Mike Esbester's doctoral research, at the University of York, explored sociocultural aspects of safety education for British railway workers between 1913 and 1939, including the use of print media and photography to convey messages, and the ways in which safety was used as a form of discipline by the railway companies. His wider research concentrates upon the cultural history of transport and mobility, focusing on the railways. Since October 2006, Mike has worked at the University of Reading, on the project 'Designing information for everyday life, 1815–1914', which explores how information intended for daily use was designed, received and used.

Rachel Grant is a textile artist. After graduating from Buckinghamshire Chilterns University College in 1999 she returned to the city of Stoke-on-Trent where large-scale 'regeneration' had just begun. Combining her role as mother and artist, she discovered the importance of daily walks and their relevance to her practice. Walking familiar routes repetitively offered the opportunity to observe, record and respond to the rapidly changing urban environment. Rachel has exhibited widely in gallery locations as well as being involved in a number of public realm related commissions.

Stephen Handsley is a Senior Lecturer in Health Studies at De Montfort University. With a background in sociology and health, since returning to education in 1995, he has taught in a number of higher education institutions. Prior to this, he was company director for a transport company which, at the time, reflected his keen interest in travel and subsequently, its relationship to the social construction of identity. His research interests include public health, sociology of death and dying, mental health and ethnicity and health. Stephen has published widely on aspects of mourning and funerary culture; public health; health impact assessment, research methodology and identity.

Zannagh Hatton graduated with an Honours Degree in Sociology and Criminal Justice from the University of Plymouth and added this to a pre-existing Psychology degree. Undeterred by geographical isolation, the demands of two children, eight chickens, plus a variety of animals *and* a busy working life, she undertook further academic studies and obtained an MSc in Social Research followed by a PhD. Zannagh's work has predominately allowed her to pursue her passion for research into the psychosocial world of what she describes as 'Naughty Boys' together with her enduring interest in how people travel and use varying modes of transport.

Robert Hart has enjoyed an entire lifetime's career in driving trains. His particular passion, though, remains firmly in the Age of Steam. He considers himself fortunate to be able to continue with this passion on a regular basis, especially as the skill of driving or firing such engines becomes more scarce, and therefore more valued. His model railway is already established and waiting in the sidings for his eventual retirement from paid employment.

Jonathan Kington has had a lifelong interest in natural history and its conservation. At the age of 46 he was offered a place at Staffordshire University, based on previous experience. Returning to education after 30 years proved to be a steep learning curve; university life was difficult to adjust to and very hectic! But after three years of mixed emotions he graduated with a BSc Hons in Ecology, of which he is very proud, and is currently embarking on a Masters (MSc) course studying Biological Monitoring and Recording. Using a campervan, he travels extensively whenever the opportunity arises.

Debra Langan is an Assistant Professor of Sociology and a Faculty Associate at the Centre for the Support of Teaching at York University, Toronto, Canada. She specializes in the scholarship of teaching and learning, critical social psychology, families and intimate relations, and qualitative methodologies. Her experiences as a taxi driver fostered a street sense that she has found invaluable in her subsequent endeavours as a waitress, a probation officer, a prison caseworker, a consultant on community protocols to improve responses to violence against women, a teacher in higher education, and a mother (who is continually driving kids around!).

Gayle Letherby is Professor of Sociology at the University of Plymouth. Her writing and research projects are varied but connected by interests in gender and power and in all things methodological. Much of her work is also linked to autobiographical concerns with travel and transport being one good example of this. The phrase 'have backpack will travel' is relevant in both her work and leisure time. Gayle's work in this area has been nurtured and sustained through her relationship with her dear friend Gillian Reynolds with whom she wrote *Train Tracks: Work, Play and Politics on the Railways* (Berg 2005).

Jen Marchbank is Director of Explorations in Arts and Social Sciences at Simon Fraser University, British Columbia. She researches, publishes and teaches across disciplines on topics such as resistance to violence, student experiences of higher education and is currently working on 'mail order' brides. She is the editor/author of several books, including *Introduction to Gender: Social Science Perspectives* (with Gayle Letherby). Her interest in travel includes not only the experiential but also the social, environmental and economic impacts of tourism, labour migration and the interactions of people both travelling and at their destination.

Mike McBeth has been in love with bicycles from an early age; they provided an independent, inexpensive means of escape from domestic difficulties. His bike could get him to the safe haven of much-loved grandparents. He has never driven a car and his father's one attempt to teach him ended, perhaps inevitably, disastrously. He also discovered a cycling fraternity that was (and largely remains) overwhelmingly masculine – a continuing source of fascinated admiration for him as he grew into a gay man. Thirty years on, he commutes 22 miles on his beloved bicycle. Colleagues remain amazed that he does it. He cycles because he loves it, something that those not enamoured of the 'beautiful machine' seem unable to understand.

Phil Nicholls is Professor of Sociology and Educational Support at Staffordshire University. He graduated from Nottingham University in 1977, and completed a doctorate examining the history of homoeopathy in Britain in 1984. He has taught at Staffordshire since 1979. Apart from continuing work on alternative medicine, he has also undertaken research on disability. The way in which 'bodies' are managed is an issue in both of these areas and, more recently, partly because of a passion for walking of all kinds and a commitment to issues of access for disabled people, he has begun to develop a sociological interest in the analysis of movement, beginning with work on the body at leisure.

Karen Overton grew up in central New York. She has an undergraduate degree in Latin American and Caribbean studies and a Masters degree in Urban and Regional Planning. Both degrees were realized at The State University of New York at Albany. Karen lived in Mozambique for one year as director of Bikes for Africa. After returning to the US she settled in New York City and joined the staff of Transportation Alternatives. She founded Recycle-A-Bicycle, an environmental education and youth job training program, and developed it into a national model for social entrepreneurship. Currently, Karen works for Partnerships for Parks.

Andy Reynolds is a marine engineer who has stepped ashore on every continent except Antarctica. But his real passion is for travel of the human-powered kind: cycle touring from an early age, then white water kayaking, rock climbing, hiking and, increasingly over the past ten years, backcountry ski touring. He does these things not in pursuit of danger, but for the invigorating simplicity of days reduced to the basics of navigation, victuals and shelter; a little risk merely gives meaning to each decision.

Gillian Reynolds is a sociologist and Research Fellow with SURGE (Applied Research Centre in Sustainable Regeneration) at Coventry University. As a passionate advocate of lifelong learning, she facilitates a lively sociology group for her local University of the Third Age (U3A). She completed her doctorate exploring disability, work and identity at Staffordshire University in 1994. Her publications and research interests focus around issues of embodied identity, and the integration of theory and praxis in everyday life. She loves to travel. With her friend and colleague, Gayle Letherby, she wrote *Train Tracks: Work, Play and Politics on the Railways* (Berg 2005).

Jackie Rose has a BA (Hons) in Applied Social Studies and is currently working towards a doctorate in the Centre for Social Gerontology, Research Institute for Life Course Studies, Keele University. For this, her research interests lie in older people, community and arts engagement. Her most recent publication is 'Connecting Cultures and Learning for Life: the Bridge International Youth Project' in *Personalised Learning: Taking Choice Seriously* (2008), edited by M. Webster (Educational Heretics Press). She is the reluctant driver of a very small car, enjoys walking and is passionate about improving public transport in the UK, especially for future generations.

Keith Sharp is Dean of the Faculty of Education, Humanities and Sciences and Associate Pro Vice-Chancellor at the University of Gloucestershire. He is a sociologist with interests in evolutionary psychology, social theory and deviant identities. He is the author, with Sarah Earle, of *Sex in Cyberspace: Why Men Pay for Sex* (Ashgate 2007). Keith has a passion for fast cars, although is currently on a break and driving a boring, but economical, diesel hatchback. His friends say he can bore for England on the subject of air travel.

John Shiels is a retired university teacher. He started to hitchhike because of financial necessity but the places he saw, people he met and experiences he had made hitchhiking intrinsically interesting as well as a method of getting from A to B. As a child and young man John rarely travelled far and his first experience of flying was in his late 40s. Yet, whether on foot or in the air, on a bus or a train he always finds travelling interesting in itself and enjoys the journey as well as the arriving.

Kim Stevenson is a Senior Lecturer in Law at the University of Plymouth and is Co-Director of the SOLON research project – an inter-institutional collaboration that facilitates and promotes interdisciplinary research on crime and bad behaviour. Her research interests include historical aspects of the criminal law, sexual offences, sexuality and violence. She is currently examining aspects of these within the broader context of transport and travel.

Jo Stanley is a writer, lecturer and facilitator specializing in the creative representation of lifestories, with a particular interest in spatial mobilities' impact on how people can change identity. She especially works with marginalized communities such as female and gay seafarers, and black working-class elders. Her recent books include *Hello Sailor: The Hidden History of Gay Life at Sea* (Pearson Education, 2003). Currently she is Honorary Research Fellow at the Centre for Mobilities Research, Lancaster University and curator of the travelling exhibition, Hello Sailor!

Carole Sutton's recent research interests are in the area of the sociology of the body and sport. She is particularly interested in non-elite or leisure sports participation, which initially emerged out of her own experiences of road running. Her emerging research includes a methodological interest in the contribution of autobiography to research. Current research is focused on a study of non-elite road running communities. How individuals engage and understand their running as an embodied activity, one which involves travel through different physical and social environments, as well as the personal development of the individual running body.

Margaret Walsh is Emeritus Professor of American Economic and Social History, University of Nottingham. Her main areas of research have been American business and transport history, the American West and American women's labour history. She has published *Making Connections: The Long Distance Bus Industry in the USA* (2000) and *The American West: Visions and Revisions* (2005). She guest-edited the gender issue of the *Journal of Transport History* (2002). She is currently working on 'Women and American Automobility since 1945'.

Ruth Waterhouse has spent her adult life as a Sociology teacher in Higher Education. She was born in Oldham, Lancashire in 1951 and has been travelling, one way or another, since then. She learnt also that journeys never take you far away from yourself; that, like the snail in the picture books, we carry our homes with us. As a Methodist minister's daughter, she learned how to form a sense of belonging to every new town or village to which her family moved. As she gets older, Ruth carries these childhood journeys inside her.

Drew Whitelegg has had a lifelong fascination with aviation. Growing up two miles from De Havilland's Hatfield factory, he subsequently fused this interest with a concern for labour and work. He holds a degree in Economic and Social History and a doctorate in Geography. He is the author of *Working the Skies* (NYU Press, 2007), an examination of airline cabin crew, as well as numerous articles on them appearing in *Gender, Place and Culture*, *Antipode*, *The Journal of Transport History* and *Southern Cultures*. He currently works at Emory University, Atlanta.

Helena Wojtczak BSc (Hons) worked as a railway guard for twenty years from the age of nineteen. She is now a freelance women's history researcher, an author and publisher, and an occasional tutor at the University of Sussex.

Acknowledgements

As editors of this collection we have several people to thank. From proposal to completion – as is usually the way – quite a while has passed and we hope that in that time we have not forgotten anyone who has helped us along the way. First and foremost, we owe huge thanks to all of our fellow contributors, without whom of course there would be no book. We are grateful to all of them for their willingness to write 'honest' accounts and for their forbearance with editorial demands and delays. One of the chapter authors – John Shiels – has also helped immensely by casting a constructively critical eye over the text, despite the occasional 'breakdown' in network capital. Thanks to Neil Jordan, Carolyn Court, Pam Bertram and others at Ashgate for pushing us towards a less boring title than our original suggestion and for patience and support throughout.

As ever, it has been a joy to work together. The editorial process has sometimes been a little fraught, not least because of the geographical distance between us, but we are happy to have been able to further indulge our interest in travel and transport and in auto/biographical writing. It has also provided us with many hours in which to deepen our friendship.

Gayle Letherby and Gillian Reynolds

Preface
Gendered Journeys, Mobile Emotions

Gayle Letherby and Gillian Reynolds

We were inspired to bring together this edited collection following our experience of researching and writing *Train Tracks: Work, Play and Politics on the Railways* (Letherby and Reynolds 2005). It was during that time that one day, in particular, stands out. As often happened, we were travelling together on an early morning train. On the table between us were scattered papers and documents; we were on our way to work. Later we wrote in *Train Tracks*:

> Working together on the 7.04 from Stoke-on-Trent one Monday morning we were sharply reminded of one persistent gender stereotype …
>
> SCENE: Gillian and Gayle sitting opposite each other at a table. Each is reading through some (different) notes. Gayle's large work diary is on the table. The Train Manager walks down the train and Gayle says 'tickets, Gillian'. As he clips the tickets the following exchange takes place:
>
> Train Manager: Good morning, having a 'Girl's Day Out' are we?
>
> Gillian: No.
>
> Train Manager: Oh, I'm sorry. I thought you were together.
>
> Gayle: We are, we are going to work together.
>
> We feel sure that this exchange would not have taken place if we were two men. Just as we assume that doctors, solicitors and artists are male (and put 'lady' or 'woman' before such a noun if the job is undertaken by a woman), we 'naturally' assume that all commuters are male and that women remain more 'appropriately' in the private sphere ... (Letherby and Reynolds 2005, 152).

This encounter (and others throughout the project) made us reflect on the interconnections between the concepts of gender, travel and emotion and in this book we, and the authors of chapters herein, focus further on these interconnections. In this preface to the book we outline our understanding of key concepts; make some preliminary links between them and briefly outline the structure of the book.

Gender is of course much more complex than just a focus on 'women' and 'women's issues': it is about social and cultural expectations, behaviours and relationships built upon and framed around differences of sex. Thus a true understanding of gender has to consider both femininities and masculinities, the range of ways in which these can be expressed and the interrelationship between gender and other signifiers of social difference (such as age, class, 'race', dis/ability and sexuality). In addition our gender is not merely something that we 'have'; not a fixed given but rather needs to be understood more fluidly as something that is re/constructed. In paraphrasing Chris Brickell (2005, 32) we agree that:

> the gendered self can be understood as reflexively constructed within performances; that is, performances can construct … [gender] rather than merely reflect its preexistence, and socially constituted … [gendered] selves act in the social world and are acted on simultaneously.[1]

Travel is more than the concept of transport, or being transported from A to B in a box and/or on wheels, but less than an all-embracing concept of movement through spaces, or a euphemism for tourism: '[M]obility needs to be reconsidered as a multi-layered concept, rather than the mere accumulation of miles travelled' (Fay 2008, 65). A concern with travel is one aspect of the 'turn to mobilities' (Sheller and Urry 2006, Urry, 2004, 2007). John Urry (2004) emphasizes the need to separate out the nature of five interdependent 'mobilities' that form and reform social life:

- corporeal travel of people for work, leisure, family life, pleasure, migration and escape;
- physical movement of objects delivered to producers, consumers and retailers;
- imaginative travel elsewhere through images of places and people on television;
- virtual travel often in real time on the internet, so transcending geographical and social distance, and
- communicative travel through person-to-person messages via letters, telephone, fax and mobile phone (Urry 2004, 28).

Focusing on 'real' travel stories challenges the view that mobility is becoming an 'elusive theoretical, social, technical and political construct' (Cresswell and Uteng 2008, 1) and emphasizes that '[u]nderstanding the ways in which mobilities and gender intersect is undoubtedly complex given that both concepts are infused with meaning, power and contested understandings' (Cresswell and Uteng 2008, 1).

---

1 Where Brickell uses the word masculine or masculinity we have replaced this with gendered or gender respectively.

Traditionally, mainstream sociology (and social science more generally) took the masculinist route of 'rationality', which aimed to specifically exclude human emotion from analysis (e.g. Weber 1968). Emotion was felt to be 'irrational', or indeed the subject matter of other disciplines such as psychology. But as Simon Williams and Gillian Bendelow (1998, xvi/xvii) argue:

> the 'deep sociality' of emotions – offers us a way of moving beyond microanalytic, subjective, individualistic levels of analysis, towards more 'open-ended' forms of social inquiry in which embodied agency can be understood not merely as 'meaning-making', but also as 'institution making'.

We would further suggest, with Stephen Fineman (2005), that analyzing such 'sociality' of emotions is a fundamental and necessary part of any investigation that attempts to understand, as distinct from 'rationally' categorize, the social world. Furthermore, pointing out that the word 'emotion' comes from the Latin, *emovere*, meaning 'to move, to move out', Sara Ahmed (2004, 11) suggests that 'emotions are not only about movement, they are also about attachments or about what connects us to this or that ... What moves us, what makes us feel, is also that which holds us in place, or gives us a dwelling place.'

It is increasingly acknowledged that a full analysis of travel needs to include a consideration of both gender and of emotion. Tana Priya Uteng and Tim Cresswell (2008, 2) argue that 'understanding [travel] mobility ... means understanding observable physical movement, the meanings that such movements are encoded with, the experience of practicing these movements and the potential for undertaking these movements.' They add that each of these aspects of mobility – movement, meaning, practice and potential – has gender difference. In addition travel is also an emotional experience. Our emotional relationship with travel may be affected by feelings of nostalgia and affection or frustration and even anger. These responses may be prompted by our personal experiences as workers and/ or as passengers and/or by historical and current cultural representations of and political influences – including those that impact differently on men and women – on travel and travelling. Trains, planes, cars and buses are spaces and places within which we may have to engage with the emotions of others (see, for example, Letherby and Reynolds 2005; Sheller 2004). Although motorbikes, bicycles, small single-person crafts (in the air or on water) and travel by foot do not offer the same kind of space within which to move around in quite the same way, such travellers do engage more or less constantly with other travellers in the same spaces. Travel and travelling then not only prompt emotional reactions but also at times require the management of, and work upon, one's own emotions and the emotions of others (e.g. Hochschild 2003 [1983], Frith and Kitzinger 1998). Emotions are also gendered, either through the differing experiences of social identities, or through cultural expectations of the 'normal' display of emotions, such as 'weeping women' or 'angry (young) men'. In each contribution to this collection, readers will find the presence of emotion – sometimes overt and extreme, sometimes implicit or less overtly articulated – in addition to a gendered critique of the travel experience.

As we move/travel through this multi-disciplinary book we illustrate the process of making some connections between gender, travel and emotion and making sense of those connections. This book is based largely on auto/biographical reflections on gendered experiences of travel. Some chapters appear to be unrelated to the personal and only by relating the work to its author's biographical note at the beginning of the book does that connection become clearer. Other chapters clearly have overt connections with the author's experiences of everyday life. The book is divided into four main sections. Section 1: *Planning the Journey* includes three chapters each focusing on some of the background theoretical issues to a consideration of gender, travel and emotion. Section 2: *Moving Off – Autobiographical Perspectives* contains 15 short explicitly auto/biographical pieces in which authors reflect on personal experiences of gender, travel and emotion. Section 3: *Working on the Move* includes three chapters focusing specifically on travel workers' experience and Section 4: *Making the Journey – Travel and Travellers* features three chapters on travellers' experience. Finally, in *Destinations Unknown* we (the editors) reflect on what we have learnt, where we have got to and where else we might have to travel; both with reference to substantive and methodological issues and in terms of our editing experience.

References

Ahmed, S. (2004), *The Cultural Politics of Emotion* (Edinburgh: University of Edinburgh Press).

Bendelow, G. and Williams, S.J. (eds) (1998), *Emotions in Social Life: Critical Themes and Contemporary Issues* (London: Routledge).

Brickell, C. (2005), 'Masculinities, Performativity, and Subversion: a sociological reappraisal', *Men and Masculinities* 8(1), 24–43.

Cresswell, T. and Uteng, T.P. (2008), 'Gendered Mobilities: towards an holistic understanding' in T.P. Uteng and T. Cresswell (eds).

Fay, M. (2008), "Mobile Belonging': exploring transnational feminist theory and online connectivity' in T.P. Uteng and T. Cresswell (eds).

Fineman, S. (2005), 'Appreciating emotion at work: paradigm tensions', *International Journal of Work, Organisation and Emotion* 1(1), 4–19.

Frith, H. and Kitzinger, C. (1998), 'Emotion Work as a participant resource: a feminist analysis of young women's talk-in-interaction', *Sociology* 32(2), 299–320.

Hochschild, A.R. (2003 [1983]), *The Managed Heart: Commercialization of Human Feeling* (20th Anniversary Edition) (Berkeley: University of California Press).

Letherby, G. and Reynolds, G. (2005), *Train Tracks: Work, Play and Politics on the Railways* (Oxford: Berg).

McDowell, L. (1999), *Gender, Identity and Place: Understanding Feminist Geographies* (Cambridge: Polity Press).

Sheller, M. (2004), 'Feeling the car', *Theory, Culture and Society* 21(4/5), 221–42.

Sheller, M. and Urry, J. (2006), 'The New Mobilities Paradigm', *Environment and Planning A*, 38, 207–236.

Urry, John (2007), 'Mobility, Network Capital and Gender'. Paper presented to Gender, Emotion, Work and Travel: Women Transport Workers and Passengers Past and Present Conference, Greenwich Maritime Institute (GMI), University of Greenwich, London 22 and 23 June.

Urry, J. (2004), 'Connections', *Environment and Planning D*, 22, 27–37.

Uteng, T.P. and Cresswell, T. (eds) (2008), *Gendered Mobilities* (Aldershot: Ashgate).

Weber, M. (1968), *Economy and Society* (New York: Bedminster).

Williams, S. and Bendelow, G. (1998), 'Introduction: Emotions in social life: Mapping the terrain', in G. Bendelow and S. Williams (eds).

Section 1

Introduction: Planning the Journey – Theoretical Background

Gayle Letherby and Gillian Reynolds

Background Issues

In his recent book *Mobilities*, John Urry (2007, 8) writes:

> a generic 'mobilities' includes various kinds and temporalities of physical movement, ranging from standing, lounging, walking, climbing, dancing, to those enhanced by technologies, of bikes, buses, cars, trains, ships, planes, wheelchairs, crutches … Movements examined range from the daily, weekly, yearly and over people's lifetimes…[1]

Although this book does not include reference to all the forms of mobility that Urry lists (e.g. walking and cars are included, climbing and crutches are not), neither is his list exhaustive as reference in this book to trucks and caravans and so on demonstrates. The 'turn to mobilities' (Sheller and Urry 2006, Urry 2004, 2007) has been embraced across the social sciences and attempts to add to earlier work within transport studies, history and migration theory which 'tended to fix on particular kinds of mobility without considering mobilities itself in the wider context' (Cresswell and Uteng 2008, 5). This volume reflects the multi-disciplinary interest generally in mobility and more specifically in the relationships between travel, emotion and gender. It would of course be unwise of us to attach disciplinary 'labels' to contributors who themselves might disagree with our perception of their primary identification. But it is fair to say that this book includes contributions from academics who work within and between history, sociology, law, transport studies, gender studies, political science, social policy, geography and the arts. Furthermore, and in addition to its gender sensitivity, this collection includes attention to other aspects of difference and diversity.

Many of the chapter authors draw on personal experience and/or empirical work and all engage in analytical as well as descriptive reflexivity.[2] Additionally,

---

1 The rest of the quote includes reference to the other aspects of mobility that Urry (2004, 2007) is concerned with in his analysis (see Preface this volume.)

2 'As reflexivity can be defined as reflecting back on something, descriptive reflexivity is clearly a description of one's reflection. Analysis means breaking something down into

especially within Sections three and four (but also to some extent in Section two), contributors are concerned to make connections between their own theoretical considerations and those of others. Thus, it is important not to read this section as *the* theory section. Rather, the aim of authors here is to reflect back along the routes of previous work on gender and transport/travel, explore new avenues for making connections between emotion and gender and travel, and to begin that process by 'studying the map'.

Planning the Journey

Urry (2000, 50) notes that if people are forever moving around, then 'the distinction of home and away loses its organisational and ideological power and the home loses its ability to sediment women's work.' In Chapter 1, 'Gender and Travel: Mobilizing New Perspectives on the Past', Margaret Walsh effectively raises the question of whether this prevailing sociological view concerning the 'home-bound' nature of women's work and lives was ever quite as straightforward as it appeared. Indeed, understanding ways in which gender and mobilities are interwoven is undoubtedly complex given that 'both concepts are infused with meaning, power and contested understandings' (Cresswell and Uteng 2008, 1). As Tim Cresswell and Tanu Priya Uteng (2008, 5) argue, general observations of the masculinity of perceptions, as well as male domination, of travel 'have been hotly contested. Women have always been on the move. Mary Kingsley's explorations in Africa, however complicated by class and imperialism, remind us that women have constantly upset gendered expectations about who moves, how they move and where they move.' Clara Greed, however, points out that, contra the case of exceptional women such as Mary Kingsley, most equate mobility with physically travelling from A to B: 'Nowadays, the majority of people's journeys take place in crowded, busy, urban, and often fraught, physical surroundings. This is particularly true for women' (Greed 2008, 243). In these days of the 'global village' when almost no country is barred to the determined 'globetrotter', even the majority of longer-distance travel remains within the geographical 'localized' interior of North America and within Europe (Urry 2000).

Working from an historical perspective, Walsh begins by exploring the historical (and continuing) male (and masculine) domination of transport and travel histories and studies. Whilst establishing what is initially depressing news, she offers hope of change following the gradual growth of women as not just transport and travel consumers, but also as transport workers and as researchers in the field. As she says, 'There is a buzz about the concept of mobility that suggests an invigoration of the study of transport and travel.'

---

its constituent parts or elements and examining the relationship between them so analytical reflexivity involves comparison and evaluation. All individuals reflect on their lives and on the lives of others.' (Letherby 2002: 4.4).

Walsh's review of the focus in previous and current research identifies three promising areas for further research: personal mobility and the consumption of travel, gendered workers and the production of travel, and imaging gendered transport and travel. Each of these areas has the potential, she argues, to highlight issues embedded in the *process* of travel, rather than merely emphasizing the business of transport. In turn, such developments are vital in informing and improving policy or corporate decision-making.

In 'Emotion, Gender and Travel: Moving On' (Chapter 2) we, Gillian Reynolds and Gayle Letherby, begin the process of noting how the concept of emotion – heavily censored in the history of the social sciences in favour of 'rationality' – is clearly intricately, and in a most complex way, interwoven with both corporeal and imaginative travel. And since we already know that travel and movement are gendered in a plethora of ways, then so emotion and travel have a gendered facet. In a number of ways, we explore the assertion that emotions are not simply something 'I' or 'we' have; rather, it is through emotions that the 'I' and the 'we' are shaped, and even take the shape of, our contact with other people (Ahmed 2004). Thus, it is not just that travel/mobility shapes emotions but also that the emotions shape mobilities. Human movement is rarely simply movement: it engenders, and is embedded in, a whole raft of meanings.

In part, the meanings of movement depend on its juxtaposition with belongingness (Fay 2008). Narratives and discourses make cultural sense of movement. One of the ways in which we explore physical or imaginative movement is to note what is observable and representable on maps (Cresswell and Uteng 2008). As well as other visual representations that make the modern western world meaningful to us, such as television, photography, and the Internet, maps privilege sight over the other senses. Such emphasis upon the visual 'reduces the body to surface … and impoverishes the relationship of the body to its environment' (Urry 2000, 92). By contrast, a feminist consciousness seeks to integrate all the senses in a more democratized way (Rodaway 1994).

In Chapter 3, 'Mapping the Way? Maps, Emotion, Gender', Mike Esbester explores the intensely symbolic nature of maps, a whole variety of which we might use when planning a journey. Journeys always start from somewhere and Esbester's journey begins from a sense of belongingness in and around his home. His exploration illustrates some of the ways in which maps (as well as paths and various forms of transport technology) 'powerfully reconstruct the relations of belonging and travelling' (Urry 2000, 132). Esbester notes that 'maps are an interesting site at which emotional and gendered relationships are exposed for view.' Those emotional and gendered relationships include a review of ways in which a different kind of map is now being produced, often by women, which engages with concepts of meaning, locality and emotion.

References

Cresswell, T. and Uteng, T.P. (2008), 'Gendered mobilities: towards an holistic understanding' in T.P. Uteng and T. Cresswell (eds).

Fay, M. (2008), "Mobile Belonging': exploring transnational feminist theory and online connectivity' in T.P. Uteng and T. Cresswell (eds).

Greed, C. (2008), 'Are we there yet? Women and transport revisited' in T.P. Uteng and T. Cresswell (eds).

Letherby, G. (2002), 'Claims and Disclaimers: knowledge, reflexivity and representation in feminist research', *Sociological Research Online* 6:4, www.socresonline.org.uk/8/4/letherby.html.

Letherby, G. and Reynolds, G. (2005), *Train Tracks: Work, Play and Politics on the Railways* (Oxford: Berg).

Rodaway, P. (1994), *Sensuous Geographies. Body, Sense and Place* (London: Routledge).

Sheller, M. and Urry, J. (2006), 'The New Mobilities Paradigm', *Environment and Planning A*, 38, 207–236.

Urry, J. (2007), *Mobilities* (Cambridge: Polity Press).

Urry, J (2004), 'Connections', *Environment and Planning D* 22, 27–37.

Urry, J. (2000), *Sociology Beyond Societies: Mobilities for the Twenty-first Century* (London: Routledge).

Uteng, T.P. and Cresswell, T. (eds) (2008), *Gendered Mobilities* (Aldershot: Ashgate).

Chapter 1

Gender and Travel: Mobilizing New Perspectives on the Past

Margaret Walsh

Introduction

The history of transport and travel has been and remains primarily male-dominated. It is essentially an arena where male academics and enthusiasts prefer to discuss vehicles, machinery and large-scale enterprises (Walsh 2002, 2007). Despite a generation of research in women's history, few transport historians have expressed gendered concerns. Women may now work in transport but their forebears are remarkably unknown. As consumers of travel, women are often invisible. Considerations of gender as a relational concept in which men and women's actions and feelings are interdependent are deemed unimportant and the study of masculinity is rare. At the margins, however, a minority of academics have challenged the paucity of women and gender issues and have begun to integrate these into histories of transport and travel suggesting that some traditional ways of conceptualising human mobility may have to be re-interpreted.

Gender and Travel at the Turn of the Twenty-first Century

Traditionally, publications in transport history were written by mode of operation and were dominated by studies of railways in the nineteenth century. More recently, researchers have investigated motorized road and air transport, modes of travel popular in the twentieth century. Though this trend has widened the scope of historical research, it is the newer interest in mobility, a concept that engages with both everyday and long-distance social, cultural and human movement that may transform the area and make it more inclusive of gendered issues. The quarterly international journal, *Journal of Transport Geography*, launched in 1993 and the Transport and Mobility book series launched by Ashgate in 2000, offer a forum for research into social scientific approaches to mobility. The International Association for the History of Transport, Traffic and Mobility (T²M), founded in 2003, aims to move traditional transport history towards 'a history of mobility' whose content and borders are flexible (Mom 2006, ix). The sociological-based journal *Mobilities*, launched in 2006, looks towards a new paradigm in which a 'mobility turn' has already started to alter the social sciences. There is a buzz about the concept of mobility that suggests an invigoration of the study of transport and travel.

Gender, however, remains on the margins. All the new approaches to mobility are open to gender analysis. Yet remarkably little interest in gendered matters has been forthcoming. Some pioneering work in the older *Journal of Transport History* offered insights for future development (Stanley, Freedman, Muellner, Carter, Schmucki and Whitelegg, all 2002; Walsh 1996). Other interesting research has been published by non-specialists in transport. Trained in feminist theory, gender and women's studies, these academics perceive the world in different ways and ask different questions. Their perspectives need to be discussed because they are crucial to understanding the full range of travel activities.

In this chapter, three areas that have brought initiatives and new researchers into the history of transport and travel – namely, personal mobility, gendered workers and imaging gendered transport and travel – are examined for their potential to demonstrate that the activity of travel rather than the business of transport can be concerned with more than corporate behaviour and policy and planning decisions.

Personal Mobility and Consumption of Travel

Affluent women have always travelled, though their mobility was less frequent than their male counterparts. For twentieth century journeys at least the motorcar has been the mode of mobility that offered women most personal freedom and the United States has been the country where automobility reached its pinnacle (Federal Highway Administration 1997 and 2002; *Automotive Facts and Figures*). It was not, however, until 1991 that driving women were discussed in any historical detail. Then, in *Taking the Wheel*, Virginia Scharff (1991) established that some women, prior to 1930, were capable of managing automobile technology in the same way as they managed household technology. More women preferred to be passengers, but forward-thinking women did drive. The automobile was not a machine exclusive to males, even though most men behaved as though it was.

Although *Taking the Wheel* has become a classic in transport history, remarkably little gendered automobile research followed. Ten years after its publication Michael Berger in his comprehensive reference guide, *The Automobile in American History and Culture* (2001), could still remark that there had been 'surprisingly little scholarly study of women motorists.' It remained for a British scholar, myself, to take a closer look at gender and American automobility. Searching through federal government statistics, reports and conference proceedings I proposed a framework for examining automobile patterns that demonstrated when and why women closed the gender gap in driving by the turn of the twenty-first century. More detailed research in qualitative sources suggested how the suburban housewife of the 1950s realized that driving was becoming an essential part of her domestic role (Walsh 2005, 2007a, 2008; Kraig 1987).

If progress in discussing motorized gender travel has been slow in the United States, it has crawled elsewhere. International data, such as that published by UNESCO, suggest random trends, but research needs to be undertaken at the national and regional level by native language speakers. In Britain, Sean O'Connell (1998) analyzed driving patterns prior to the Second World War and found that class as well as gender impeded women from getting behind the wheel. Indeed, as late as the mid-1960s as few as 13 per cent of British women held a driving licence. Rising incomes, greater access to credit and the increased participation of married women in the labour force subsequently promoted female driving. Yet even in the early twenty first century only 63 per cent of women could drive in comparison to 81 per cent of men. The processes by which motorized mobility ceased to be associated with manhood in Britain are only beginning to be discussed by social scientists (Department of Transport 2006; Dobbs 2005; Root 2000).

Driving has not been the only means of personal travel. Historians have also paid some attention to travel by such communal vehicles as trains, buses and boats (e.g. Walsh 2000). In the same way as Virginia Scharff (1991) challenged historians to engender the car, Amy Richter (2005) disputed the dominant masculinity of the train. American women did venture by rail in the nineteenth century and their journeys changed train spaces by bringing a form of domestic courtesy into a public arena. White women at least learned to consider the train as a manageable type of mobile home, though their black counterparts faced considerable disrespect. Other women in the same era encountered class rather than racial hazards when challenging propriety by travelling by train in Germany (Muellner 2002). Only in the late Victorian era did enough women travel by train for recreation and work to become important rail consumers. Sociological research suggests more insights into recent female rail passengers, but there is ample scope for research on both earlier and recent female rail travel (Letherby and Reynolds 2005).

Historians have been more forthcoming about women's ventures at sea. They have examined the travelogues of women whose husbands worked overseas, and have discussed immigrants and lady explorers. In this long-distance waterborne setting historians established a female presence on ocean liners, often using the records of major British corporations like Cunard or the East India Company together with fragmentary information from diaries (Stanley 2004, 2004a and in this volume; Maenpaa 2004; Coons and Varias 2003; Druett 1991; Birkett 1989). More challenging interpretations of female passengers holidaying on cruise liners have been constructed by cultural historians and sociologists. Clearly they expected high levels of service, entertainment and comfort. The resulting friction encountered between passengers and female crew often regarded as domestic servants and belonging to a different class, is played out in the peculiar arena of ships, which are ambiguous spaces surrounded by water and perceived as borderlands, panopticons or heterotopias (Stanley 2002; Mather 2002; Zhao 2002).

Gendered Workers and the Production of Travel

Most workers in the transport sector have in the past been male and their workplace masculinity has conveyed rights and privileges. Increasingly in the late twentieth century, however, these men were joined by women. The general expansion of post-industrial economies in these years drew on both cheap unskilled female labour and professional and managerial women who gained qualifications following the enactment of equal employment opportunities. Some of these occupations have become feminized and have raised questions about the nature of women's work. Research on the nature of this diverse labour market has produced some stimulating and thought-provoking gendered outputs (e.g. this volume).

Traditionally, men dominated transport work. In analyzing the ways in which this heavy and at times long-distance labour shaped workers' lives, historians conscious of gender have focused not on trade unions and their activities, but on considerations of masculinity. How men perceived themselves in relation to their work had a direct impact on their families and their communities and was important in establishing gender relations. The culture of 'rough masculinity' dominated work in the maritime, canal and rail industries, at least in the eighteenth and nineteenth centuries (Wojtczak 2005; Coleman 1965).

Recent writing has drawn attention to the need to engender such male workers as well as to recover and dissect new patterns of female labour. Casual, strenuous work has long been associated with ports even in more recent times. In Liverpool in the interwar years dockworkers constructed their male identities around their role as breadwinners with an entitlement to spend part of their wages, whether or not they adequately supported their families (Ayres 1999). This 'tough masculinity' was outmatched, at least in terms of sexuality, by the culture of the 'whoring, drinking sailors' on nineteenth-century British sailing ships, who behaved in a larger-than-life manner. Some of the yarns about these maritime workers, however, were based on their water-bound existence as this gave them the status of 'otherness' when compared to land-bound British men (Burton 1991, 1999).

The railways, whether in Nigeria, Australia or the United States, gave men a different status. African men who had previously shared with their wives the income-generating roles increasingly sought to become the bread earners and to adopt a European-style family because they earned a steady wage on the colonial railways and because it gave them greater bargaining power with their employers. Their wives colluded with this male-provider image because it suited their family purposes (Lindsay 1998, 2003). In Australia, however, masculinity was defined in relation to steam trains where physical power, control over machinery, skill and stamina created a milieu of prowess and dominance. The introduction of the cleaner, safer diesel trains jeopardized rail workers' traditional authority and masculine pride (Taksa 2005). In the United States, railroad work created a diverse set of masculine practices which were developed around managerial efforts to control labour, skilled workers' attempts to gain autonomy and union endeavours to expand and gain stability (Taillon 2001). The deconstruction of men's work offers a new tool of analysis to understand how mobility can be gendered.

This newer approach to male labour in transport needs to be interwoven with the expanding presence of female workers. Historically, women in transport have been absent, primarily because they were in secondary positions that were deemed to be unimportant. In bus and train companies, for example, they held semi-skilled feminized positions like secretaries, ticket sales personnel, telephonists, filing clerks, ticket collectors and travel agents or unskilled occupations like cleaners and cafeteria workers (Wojtczak 2005; Matheson 2002; Walsh 1996). Women have continued to take these jobs at the lower end of the service sector hierarchy and in the past quarter-century have been joined by many peers in both old and newer transport areas. This rapid expansion of the female workforce has been fuelled by technology and the search for cheap labour. As travel and freight movement have become quicker and more flexible and electronic communications have reduced the tyranny of distance, firms have downsized and restructured their operations in a bid to be more competitive. They used information technology to search worldwide for cut-price workers, which have included women as well as men in developing countries. These women have become part of a large pool of miscellaneous workers with variable labour contracts and few labour rights.

In the maritime sector, major jurisdictional issues stemming from flags of convenience have badly affected female seafarers from developing and Eastern European countries. The growth of repeat short-term contracts in the cruise ship industry and the constant outsourcing of labour have produced a casualized workforce where women not only receive low wages, but have limited maternity benefits and family rights. Indeed, conditions have so deteriorated that many women who need to send money home only tolerate a few work contracts (Wu 2005; Thomas 2003; Zhao 2002).

For cabin crew, most of whom are young women, the growth of low-cost airlines in the 1980s and 1990s resulted in lower salaries, flexible employment, temporary contracts and deteriorating working conditions. The rise of transnational airline alliances facilitating crew-sharing and code-sharing has brought workers of different nationalities together. In their search to maximize profits, airlines have then tried to undermine not only the labour rights of the flight attendants, but even their professionalism by re-introducing the sexual titillation factor into hiring practices. Any improvements gained through labour legislation in developed countries have been seriously threatened (Whitelegg 2007; Women's Work 2003).

Call centres have expanded very rapidly and have become highly controversial forms of employment in the transport sector, being tantamount to contemporary sweatshops. In these sites dealing with tele-marketing and tele-sales large concentrations of young, predominantly female workers on fixed-term contracts and low wages sell passenger information, ticketing, banking details, hotel reservations and IT services. Lacking the social benefits and statutory rights of many of their predecessors in post-industrial economies, their work has become an alienating and debilitating experience. Even when some of this work became outwork, as with car rescue service, the conditions of labour have not improved significantly (Finke 2006).

The growth of logistics or 'supply chain strategies' that produce an integrated delivery of goods or services to the correct address, on time and at minimum cost, has stimulated another form of flexible work deemed suitable for cheap, particularly female, labour. Manufacturing has been replaced by logistics and retailing as the new form of production in many advanced economies. In the warehouses or distribution centres that manage the flow of goods by sophisticated technology, women have been employed in office work, packing and dispatch and are moving into driving. There are many opportunities for inexperienced, flexible and compliant workers and for 'perma temps' or workers who can be easily dismissed (Finke 2006; Mather 2005). Considered suitable for women with household responsibilities, this work has offered deteriorating pay and conditions and weak gender rights. Women have become part of a large pool of miscellaneous transport workers.

At the other end of the labour spectrum they have been joined by a smaller group of professional women who, having gained both qualifications and skills, have become managers and chief executive officers. By the 1970s and 1980s women in the American intercity bus industry served in all categories of management, in both bus companies and urban transit systems. They were most visible in planning, marketing and finance and in personnel relations. No longer could public transport be considered a single sex arena. In areas as diverse as airport planning and management and transport engineering, women were responsible for producing transport services. Their progress in those workspaces where the application of equality legislation was transparent was often quicker and smoother, but managerial women who demonstrated competence and who could organize their domestic commitments became well established. Women also gained executive office in the rapidly expanding tourist industry. Much research needs to be undertaken on these businesswomen examining whether their managerial styles and values differed from their male counterparts (Women Trailblazers in Transportation 2007; Walsh 1996).

While the face of transport has become more feminine in the late twentieth century some areas had already been feminized. On planes and cruise ships women were not only hired because their labour was cheap, but also because they brought their nurturing characteristics to the job. These domestic virtues together with their sexuality were commercialized either to provide a different form of competition in specific travel sectors or to gain high levels of customer satisfaction. Labour historians have paid much attention recently to flight attendants in that the juxtaposition of caring and service sector work on airlines has become crucial to understanding the gendered nature of women's work (Boris 2006; Cobble 1999, 2004). Focusing on air travel, Kathleen Barry (2007) and Drew Whitelegg (2002 and this volume) add greater depth and nuance to an understanding of women's contributions to servicing commercial flight. Both discuss the interaction between flight attendants' attractive appearance and their efforts as workers and trade unionists to gain respect and to acquire recognition of their professional status in being responsible for passenger safety. Whitelegg (2007) moves beyond the issues of sexual exploitation and labour rights to understand the ways in which the spatial dimensions of work on planes is important in balancing the female life–work conundrum. This aspect of workplace mobility has changed remarkably since the introduction of 'stewardesses' in 1930s because of the expansion of air travel, the advent of budget airlines and the impact of 9/11.

Airlines have not been the only travel site in which emotional labour has been analyzed. On cruise liners female workers were required to serve passengers courteously and demonstrate that they were doing so to their employers. Historical research has documented how women who worked on British liners in the late nineteenth and early twentieth centuries were expected to wait on and be caring of passengers whether they were invisible below deck or whether they were stewardesses (Stanley 2004, 2004a and this volume; Maenpaa 2004). A century later, women recruited from all parts of the world were also exploited to ensure the entertainment, relaxation and comfort of passengers on modern cruise ships in the international leisure travel industry. Funloving passengers were not concerned that these seafarers worked long hours in cramped quarters for low pay. They were expected to smile and be cheerful. More vulnerable than cabin crew because of the length of cruises, the problems of personal exploitation and the dependence on tips to supplement wages, these workers suggest a more textured insight into emotional labour (Zhao 2002).

Deconstructing men's labour to assess how masculinity has brought particular values both to the workers themselves and to their social environment raises challenging issues that can recast transport history. The growing numbers of women employed in the contemporary international transport and communications industry has suggested the need to analyze female workers in earlier years, whether in manual or executive positions. Labour historians, viewing the increase of the female participation in the workforce worldwide, have perceived transport as an area in which women invest nurturing characteristics. In some ways this emotional labour shares in the expectations placed on women more generally in the service sector, but in other ways it has its own dynamic. There remain many exciting avenues to follow, both for historians and sociologists.

Imaging Gendered Transport and Travel

The vision of gender and mobility also offers great potential for researchers, but the trajectories of viewing women and men as travellers have very different origins and employ both economic and cultural analysis. Much recent work focuses on advertising and media representations, but literary and sociological studies offer further fruitful ideas. Diaries and journals documenting journeys have become a sub genre for those in English Studies and bring with them alternative styles of analysis. The tourist gaze now features as a means of examining travel practices especially in sociology, but these practices might well be changed by being viewed more frequently with gendered eyes. Interdisciplinary interlinking can bring new dimensions to images of travel.

Advertising, important throughout modern times, became the common means of communication and persuasion in the twentieth century. Companies producing travel services, and manufacturers of motorised vehicles or bicycles, relied heavily on advertising for their sales. Their early promotions were functional in describing journeys and their price, or talking about the mechanics of vehicles. Once colour printing enhanced pictorial copy, advertisements became more suggestive of consumers' needs and desires. Then women not only became the targets of travel agents, but their bodies were used suggestively to promote both scheduled and special services and to make vehicles attractive. As standards of living rose in westernised societies after the Second World War and consumers became more discerning, this advertising became more sophisticated and nuanced in both its style and its target audiences (Marchand 1985; Schudson 1984; Williamson 1978; Ewen 1976).

The car has featured heavily as an object of desire. Often in the twentieth century women have been used in advertisements to eroticize cars, to influence male purchasers and to persuade women to drive. When historians have addressed this phenomenon, they have tended to analyze images from the perspective of the car manufacturers and designers and their advertising agencies. Here the masculine dominance of car culture has prevailed in the ways in which women have been represented, even in the late twentieth century when women have moved towards equality. Cultural historians and those who analyze pictures for their consumer value have paid much more attention to deconstructing advertisements and negotiating their feminine stereotypes as ways of understanding modern society. Their insights range from the positive representation of women as independent persons to the more frequent negative portrayal of women as sexual objects, as consumers who prioritize fashion, beauty and comfort or as incompetent drivers. The use of cars in films and in popular music has only served to heighten such associations (Lees-Maffei 2002; Behling 1997; Gartman 1994; Bayley 1986; Lewis 1980). More historical research could usefully suggest thought-provoking ideas about how women fitted into visions of car culture.

Railway and airline advertisements have provided another visual source for historical analysis. Some innovative work has suggested that much more can be achieved. Drawing on French cultural theory to underpin his theoretical framework, Ralph Harrington (2004) proposed that images of holiday travel portrayed by the largest British railway companies in the interwar years gave women agency and a measure of economic power. Whether working-class or middle-class, women perceived the attractive figures in the posters as a means to enjoyment and as a symbol of the significance of the vacation.

The advertising campaigns of airlines have been more renowned for their sexualized use of women's bodies. Their messages, as with car commercials, were directed primarily to men who, in the early years of commercial flight, wanted reassurance. Cabin crew were then trained nurses and were perceived as maternal figures. Once planes became safer and more comfortable, men wanted charm as well as composure in their hostesses and then with the advent of jet planes they desired youth, glamour and titillation. Such sexist slogans as 'Fly me, I'm Margie' or the wearing of hot pants or mini-skirts only disappeared when equality legislation insisted that older and less visibly attractive women were also to be hired. Indeed, visually, the female flight attendant has been used both to epitomize sleek, fast-moving air travel and to embody the 'natural' qualities of womanhood. Only research demonstrating the high degree of safety training required, the domesticated service nature of the work, and the concept of emotional labour have offered a reality check on sexualized airline advertising (Whitelegg 2007; Barry 2007; Lyth 2005). The use of these advertisements has created both challenges for traditional historians, who feature pictorial media primarily as illustrations for text, and opportunities for those academics who embrace feminist scholarship and cultural studies.

Their literary colleagues offer further possibilities of analyzing gender by placing mobility and its vehicles in their discussion of popular and canonical texts. In *Driving Women* (2007), Deborah Clarke investigates women's relationship to the car in women's fiction in order to generate new ways of thinking about American culture and American configurations of gender. By examining how cars can shape female space, suggest female identity, and restructure female agency, she suggests new perspectives for approaching fiction written by and about women and thereby offers fresh avenues for interdisciplinary work. Alisa Freedman (2002) also provides insights into literary texts when she analyzes *The Girl Fetish*, a short novel published in 1907 in the influential Japanese journal, *Taiyo*, to discuss gender and class relations on the daily commute on electric trains in Tokyo. She argues that these trains became spaces for observing the actions and appearances of others and that trains had become symbols of the modern city. For an earlier period, Beth Muellner (2002) uses autobiography to investigate the gendered and class spaces on nineteenth-century German railways.

Sociologist Ian Carter also used novels to contest traditional scholarship on mobility. He turned to crime fiction to dissect the constrained position of women on trains and show how this raised issues about gender, class and modernity in Britain (2002). He challenges his readers to rethink fertile sources for research (2001), as do some sociologists who focus on tourism, past and present. Though their theoretical work may cause difficulties for those outside the discipline, their more empirical materials, frequently emphasizing consumerism, discuss the ways in which people travel (Letherby and Reynolds 2005). There is much scope to investigate how travelling for pleasure has been and remains gendered and the upsurge of interest in the cultures of tourism, as distinct from purveyors of tourism, promises yet other opportunities for research (Baranowski and Furlough 2001; Aron 1999; Rojek and Urry 1997; Urry 1990).

Conclusion

In 2002 the special gender issue of the *Journal of Transport History* anticipated exciting years ahead when gender as a tool of analysis became central to research in transport history. Five years later in 2007, a conference held at the University of Greenwich, 'Gender, Emotion, Travel and Work: Women Transport Workers and Passengers Past and Present', provided an arena to stimulate more discussion, as indeed does this book. The pathway to work that is sensitive to gender, however, has not been smooth; nor has it been actively encouraged by mainstream historians working on travel. It has never been discouraged, but most academics or museum specialists who publish such work have felt more comfortable in alternative arenas, where issues focusing on gender or women are considered highly significant. Mobility studies may offer more potential for considering the human dimensions of travel. The dynamic is present; some of the themes and authors discussed here suggest the potential, but it will take a concerted effort by many researchers to raise the gender profile.

References

Automotive Facts and Figures (continued as *Motor Vehicle Facts and Figures*) (1934–2004).
Aron, C.S. (1999), *Working at Play. A History of Vacations in the United States* (New York: Oxford University Press).
Ayers, P. (1999), 'The Making of Men: masculinities in interwar Liverpool', in M. Walsh (ed.).
Baranowski, S. and Furlough, E. (eds) (2001), *Being Elsewhere. Tourism, Consumer Culture, and Identity in Modern Europe and North America* (Ann Arbor: University of Michigan Press).
Barry, K.M. (2007), *Femininity in Flight: A History of Flight Attendants* (Durham, NC: Duke University Press).
Bayley, D. (1986), *Sex, Drink and Fast Cars: The Creation and Consumption of Images* (London: Faber & Faber).
Behling, L.L. (1997), 'Fisher's Bodies: automobile advertisements and the framing of modern American female identity', *The Centennial Review* 41:3, 515–28.
Berger, M.L. (2001), *The Automobile in American History and Culture: A Reference Guide* (Westport CN: Greenwood Press).
Birkett, D. (1989), *Spinsters Abroad: Victorian Lady Explorers* (Oxford: Blackwell).
Boris, E. (2006), 'Desirable Dress: Rosies, sky girls and the politics of appearance', *International Labor and Working Class History* 69 (Spring), 123–42.
Burton, V. (1999), '"Whoring, Drinking Sailors': reflections on masculinity from the labour history of nineteenth century British shipping', in M. Walsh (ed.).

Burton, V. (1991), 'The Myth of Bachelor Jack: masculinity, patriarchy and seafaring labour' in C. Howell and R. Twomey (eds).

Carter, I. (2002), 'The Lady in the Trunk: Railways, Gender and Crime Fiction', *Journal of Transport History* 23:1, 46–59.

Carter, I. (2001), *Railways and Culture in Britain: The Epitome of Modernity* (Manchester: Manchester University Press).

Clarke, D. (2007), *Driving Women: Fiction and Automobile Culture in Twentieth Century America* (Baltimore: Johns Hopkins University Press).

Cobble, D.S. (2004), *The Other Women's Movement: Workplace Justice and Social Rights in Modern America* (Princeton: Princeton University Press).

Cobble, D.S. (1999), 'A Spontaneous Loss of Enthusiasm: Workplace Feminism and the Transformation of Women's Service Jobs in the 1970s', *International Labor and Working Class History* 56 (Fall), 23–44.

Coleman, T. (1965), *The Railway Navvies. A History of the Men who Made the Railways* (London: Hutchinson).

Coons, L. and Varias, A. (2003), *Tourist Third Cabin: Steamship Travel in the Interwar Years* (New York: Palgrave Macmillan).

Department of Transport (2006), *National Travel Survey*, 'Driving Licences', published at www.statistics.gov.uk/socialtrends35.

Dobbs, L. (2005), 'Wedded to the Car: women, employment and the importance of private transport', *Transport Policy* 12, 3, 266–78.

Druett, J. (1991), *Petticoat Whalers: Whaling Wives at Sea 1820–1920* (Auckland: Collins).

Ewen, S. (1976), *Captains of Consciousness: Advertising and the Social Roots of Consumer Culture* (New York: McGraw-Hill).

Federal Highway Administration (Department of Transportation) (2002), *Highway Statistics* 2001 (Washington DC: US Government Printing Office).

Federal Highway Administration (Department of Transportation) (1997), *Highway Statistics Summary to 1995* (Washington DC: US Government Printing Office).

Finke, S. (2006), 'Women, Work and the Changing Transport Industries', unpublished paper, Economic History Conference, Reading, UK.

Freedman, A. (2002), 'Commuting Gazes: schoolgirls, salarymen, and electric trains in Tokyo', *Journal of Transport History* 23, 1, 23–36.

Gartman, D. (1994), *Auto Opium: A Social History of American Automobile Design* (New York: Routledge).

Halsey, A.H. with Webb, J. (eds) (2000), *Twentieth Century British Social Trends* (Houndmills: Macmillan Press Ltd).

Harding, R., Jarvis, A. and Kennerley, A. (eds) (2004), *British Ships in China Seas: 1700 to Present Day* (Liverpool: National Museums).

Harrington, R. (2004), 'Beyond the Bathing Belle: images of women in inter-war railway publicity', *Journal of Transport History* 25, 1, 22–45.

Horowitz, R. (ed.) (2001), *Boys and their Toys? Masculinity, Class and Technology in America* (New York: Routledge).

Howell, C. and Twomey, R.J. (eds) (1991), *Jack Tar in History: Essays in the History of Maritime Labour* (Fredericton, New Brunswick: Acadiensis Press).

Kraig, B. (1987), 'Women at the Wheel: a history of women and the automobile in America' (unpublished PhD thesis, University of Washington).

Lees-Maffei, G. (2002), 'Men, Motors, Markets and Women' in P. Wollen and J. Kerr (eds).

Letherby, G. and Reynolds, G. (2005), *Train Tracks: Work, Play and Politics on the Railways* (Oxford: Berg).

Lewis, D.L. (1980), 'Sex and the Automobile: from rumble seats to rockin' vans' in D.L. Lewis and L. Goldstein (eds).

Lewis, D.L. and Goldstein, L. (ed.) (1980), *The Automobile and American Culture* (Ann Arbor: University of Michigan Press).

Lindsay, L.A. (2003), 'Money, Marriage and Masculinity on the Colonial Nigerian Railway' in L.A. Lindsay and S.F. Miescher (eds).

Lindsay, L.A. (1998), '"No Need … to think of Home"? Masculinity and Domestic Life on the Nigerian Railway c. 1941–61', *Journal of African History* 39, 3, 439–66.

Lindsay, L.A. and Miescher, S.F. (eds) (2003), *Men and Masculinities in Modern Africa* (Portsmouth, NH: Heinemann).

Lyth, P. (2005), '"Think of her as your Mother": Airline advertising and the stewardess, 1920–80', unpublished paper.

Maenpaa, S. (2004), 'Women below Deck: gender and employment on British passenger liners, 1860–1938', *Journal of Transport History* 25, 2, 57–74.

Marchand, R. (1985), *Advertising the American Dream: Making Way for Modernity 1920–1940* (Berkeley, University of California Press).

Mather, C. (2005), 'Women Working in Logistics', Preliminary Research Findings, ITF Conference 22–23 September, www.itfglobal.org/women/wconf2005.cfm.

Mather, C. (2002), *Sweatships: What it is Really Like to Work on Board Cruiseships* (London: War on Want).

Matheson, R.M. (2002),'Women and the Great Western Railway with specific reference to Swindon works' (unpublished PhD thesis, University of West of England).

Mom, G. (2006), 'Editorial', *Journal of Transport History* 27, 1, ix–xi.

Muellner, B. (2002), 'The Deviance of Respectability: nineteenth century transport from a woman's perspective', *Journal of Transport History* 23, 1, 37–45.

O'Connell, S. (1998), *The Car in British Society: Class, Gender and Motoring, 1896–1939* (Manchester: Manchester University Press).

Richter, A.G. (2005), *Home on the Rails*: W*omen, the Railroad and the Rise of Public Domesticity* (Chapel Hill: University of North Carolina Press).

Rojek, C. and Urry, J. (eds) (1997), *Touring Cultures. Transformations of Travel and Theory* (London: Routledge).

Root, A. (2000), 'Transport and Communications' in A.H. Halsey with J. Webb (eds).

Scharff, V. (1991), *Taking the Wheel. Women and the Coming of the Motor Age* (New York: Free Press).

Schmucki, B. (2002), 'On the Trams: women, men and urban public transport in Germany', *Journal of Transport History* 23, 1, 60–72.

Schudson, M. (1984), *Advertising the Uneasy Persuasion: Its Dubious Impact on American Society* (New York: Basic Books).

Stanley, J. (2004), 'Go East Young Women (but not often). Inter-war British Indian Line stewardesses' in R. Harding, A. Jarvis and A. Kennerley (eds).

Stanley, J. (2004a), '"Wanted Adventurous Girls": stewardesses on liners, 1919–1939' (unpublished PhD thesis, Lancaster University).

Stanley, J. (2002), 'And after the Cross-dressed Cabin Boys and Whaling Wives? Possible futures for women's maritime historiography', *Journal of Transport History* 23, 1, 9–22.

Taillon, P.M. (2001), '"To Make Men Out of Crude Material": Work, culture, manhood and unionism in the railroad running trades, c. 1870–1900' in R. Horowitz (ed.).

Taksa, L. (2005), '"About as Popular as a Dose of Clap": steam, diesel and masculinity at the New South Wales Eveleigh railway workshops', *Journal of Transport History* 26, 2, 79–97.

Thomas, M. (2003), '"Get Yourself a Proper Job Girlie": Recruitment, retention and women seafarers', Symposium, (Seafarers' International Research Centre, Cardiff University), 25–40, www.sirc.cf.ac.uk/publications.

Urry, J. (1990), *The Tourist Gaze* (London: Sage).

Walsh, M. (2008), 'Mobilising Gender: Women, work and automobility in the United States', *History* 93, 2 (forthcoming).

Walsh, M. (2007), 'Gender in the History of Transportation Services: An historiographical perspective', *Business History Review* 81, 3, 545–62.

Walsh, M. (2007a), 'At Home at the Wheel? The woman and her automobile in the 1950s' (London: The British Library). Also available at www.bl.uk/ecclescentre

Walsh, M. (2005), 'Gender and American Automobility', www.autolife.umd.umich.edu.

Walsh, M. (2002), 'Gendering Transport History: retrospect and prospect', *Journal of Transport History* 23, 1, 1–8.

Walsh, M. (2000), *Making Connections: The Long-distance Bus Industry in the USA* (Aldershot: Ashgate).

Walsh, M. (ed.) (1999), *Working Out Gender: Perspectives from Labour History* (Aldershot: Ashgate).

Walsh, M. (1996), 'Not Rosie the Riveter: women's diverse roles in the making of the American long-distance bus industry', *Journal of Transport History* 17, 1, 43–56.

Whitelegg, D. (2007), *Working the Skies: The Fast-Paced, Disorienting World of the Flight Attendant* (New York: New York University Press).

Whitelegg, D. (2002), 'Cabin Pressure: The dialectics of emotional labour in the airline industry', *Journal of Transport History* 23, 1, 73–86.

Williamson, J. (1978), *Decoding Advertisements: Ideology and Meaning in Advertising* (London: Marion Boyars).

Wojtczak, H. (2005), *Railwaywomen. Exploitation, Betrayal and Triumph in the Workplace* (Hastings: Hastings Press).

Wollen, P. and Kerr, J. (eds) *Autopia* (London: Reaktion Books).

'Women Trailblazers in Transportation' (2007), Conference session at 86th Transportation Research Board Annual Conference, Washington DC.

'Women's Work' (2003), *Transport International Magazine*, 10 January, www. itfglobal.org/transport-international.

Wu, B. (2005), 'The World Cruise Industry: a profile of the global labour market', (Seafarers' International Research Centre, Cardiff University), 1–42 www.sirc. cf.ac.uk/publications.

Zhao, M. (2002), 'Emotional Labour in a Globalised Labour Market: seafarers on cruise ships', Working Paper Series 27 (Seafarers' International Research Centre (SIRC) Cardiff University), 1–28, www.sirc.cf.ac.uk/publications.

Chapter 2

Emotion, Gender, and Travel: Moving On

Gillian Reynolds and Gayle Letherby

Introduction

Emotion, gender and travel are, individually, all concepts much written about within our own discipline (sociology) and more broadly within the social sciences and humanities. In this chapter, as indeed in this collection, we draw on writers from various disciplines and consider some of the attention given to each concept. We focus on historical and recent connections that have been made between emotion, gender and travel and present our own suggestions of some of the ways in which they are interlocked in the complex process of everyday living.

On Emotion ...

Theoretical debates of emotion are many and varied, from the causes of or motivations to emotion (e.g. Lutz 2007; Milton 2005; Bowler 2005; Damasio 2000), or the ways in which emotions are represented in text (e.g. Tonkin 2005; Miller 2002), to the experience (e.g. Skinner 2007; Sedgwick 2003), or performance and display of emotion (e.g. Bauman 2005; Brickell 2005; Giddens 1991; Goffman 1967). What is patently incontrovertible is that – human beings *feel* and that those feelings are part and parcel of everyday social life. Yet until comparatively recently, emotions have been perceived as being largely located within the individual, as the 'stuff' of psychology and psychiatry. Mainstream sociology largely excluded the overt concept of emotion from theoretical discussion, except as an inference, or under another guise (Shilling 2002; Barbalet 2001; Hochschild 1998), for what appeared to be strong, academic reasons going back several hundred years.

René Descartes' comment, 'I think, therefore I am', is arguably the most famous, and most often quoted, theoretical speculation in the history of Western philosophy. Appearing first in his *Discourse on the Method* in 1637, Descartes implies that 'thinking, and awareness of thinking, are the real substrates of being. And since we know that Descartes imagined thinking as an activity quite separate from the body, it celebrates the separation of mind, the "thinking thing" ... from the non-thinking body ...' (Damasio 2006, 248). Such 'dualism' of mind and body, with the 'rational' mind taking theoretical precedence over the (conceptually, both machine-like and passionate) body, set an agenda for researchers and theoreticians for much of the succeeding three hundred years, being largely adopted as the very foundation for epistemological understanding in most Western disciplines relating to humanities.[1]

Conversely, the less well-known and less fêted 'you are, therefore I am' is an ancient African proverb. In contrast to the inward-looking individualism embedded in Descartes' 'discovery', this African philosophy focuses on interpersonal relationship as the very source of our awareness of self-existence. When 'I think, therefore I am' and 'you are, therefore I am' are juxtaposed, we can detect the clash between cultures and thus the undeniable presence of cultural influence on the nature of the philosophy of being and feeling.

'We feel', says Arlie Russell Hochschild in her now-classic 1983 work, *The Managed Heart: Commercialization of Human Feeling* (2003[1983], 17):

> But what is a feeling? I would define feeling, like emotion, as a sense, like the sense of hearing or sight. In a general way, we experience it when bodily sensations are joined with what we see or imagine. Like the sense of hearing, emotion communicates information. It has, as Freud said of anxiety, a "signal function". From feeling we discover our own viewpoint on the world.

This viewpoint is not simply a theoretical device – it feeds and is fed by our everyday, moment-by-moment lives. Michael Hardt (2007) argues that there is an epistemological correspondence between the power to act and the power to feel the emotion, the 'affect'. Taking the perspective of 'affects', he suggests, does not mean we assume that reason and passion are the same thing, but rather that they work together on a continuum in our thinking:

> One way of understanding this complex set of propositions ... is simply to say that the perspective of the affects requires us constantly to pose as a problem the relation between actions and passions, between reason and the emotions. We do not know in advance what a body can do, what a mind can think – what affects they are capable of. The perspective of the affects requires an exploration of these as yet unknown powers ... [It is] an ontology of the human that is constantly open and renewed (Hardt 2007, x).

Emotions *shape* the 'surfaces' of both individual and collective bodies. In terms of traditional academic, conceptual, theoretical and gendered hierarchies, however, emotion:

> ... has been viewed as "beneath" the faculties of thought and reason. To be emotional is to have one's judgement affected: it is to be reactive rather than active, dependent rather than autonomous ... [T]he subordination of emotions also works to subordinate the feminine and the body ... Emotions are associated with women, who are represented as

---

1 Although Chris Shilling (2002, 13) suggests that Hobbes' analysis of the relationship between the passionate nature of individuals and the problem of social order exerted a greater influence on the foundations of sociology.

"closer" to nature, ruled by appetite, and less able to transcend the body through thought, will and judgement ... The Darwinian model of emotions suggests that emotions are not only "beneath" but "behind" the man/human, as a sign of an earlier and more primitive time (Ahmed 2004, 3).

As Oakley (1981: 38) notes, women have historically been characterized as 'sensitive, intuitive, incapable of objectivity and emotional detachment and ... immersed in the business of making and maintaining personal relationships'. Women are considered naturally weak and easy to exploit and, as the subordinate sex, women's psychological characteristics imply subordination – i.e. they are submissive, passive, docile, dependent, lack initiative, are not able to act, to decide, to think and so on. From this perspective women are more like children than adults in that they are immature, weak and helpless (Oakley 1981, Evans 1997). If women adopt these characteristics they are considered well-adjusted (Miller 1976, Oakley 1981) (Letherby 2003).

Despite the theoretical subordination of emotions, the early 'Grand Theorists' of sociology did allocate an 'absent presence' to emotion:

> All of the nineteenth-century founders of sociology touched on the topic of emotion ... Max Weber elucidates the anxious 'spirit of capitalism' ... [and] questions what passes for 'rationality'. Emile Durkheim explores the social scaffolding for feelings of 'solidarity'. Karl Marx explores alienation and ... implies much about resentment and anger (Hochschild 1998, 2).

Thus, for the early social theorists, emotions had to be conceptually and analytically separated from thoughts and either re-negotiated as representations of objectivity (such as 'spirit of capitalism', 'solidarity' or 'alienation') or dismissed altogether from theoretical parameters. In the ancient Greek philosophy of Kant, so influential in the thinking of Durkheim and Weber in particular, emotions are subjective – forms of 'unfreedom' and 'determination' (Seidler 1998, 195). As social theory grew and matured, states Victor Seidler, the disdain for experience as 'personal' and 'subjective' went hand in hand with the disdain for emotions as sources of knowledge; the distinction between reason and nature in terms of knowledge and experience was (and frequently still is) reproduced (see also, for example, Hardt 2007; Williams and Bendelow 1998).

Within contemporary Western cultures the conceptual hierarchies of reason and affect have become even more complex (Ahmed 2004; Evans 1997; Oakley 1981). Sometimes, for example, '[t]he hierarchy between emotion and thought/ reason gets displaced ... into a hierarchy between emotions' (Ahmed 2004, 3). Some emotions are perceived as signs of weakness, others as signs of cultural cultivation. The 'cultivated' emotions are elevated above the others that are perceived as 'weaknesses'. All are then worked on, to improve or to eradicate, and also 'managed', in order to enhance productivity and/or profit.

Sara Ahmed (2004, 92) suggests that many emotions work 'performatively not only as the intensification of contact between bodies and objects, but also as a speech act.' Such speech acts constitute what Judith Butler (1990), following earlier theories of the philosopher John Langshaw Austin, refers to as 'performative utterances' – statements that do not simply say something, but have symbolic or actual actions embedded within them. These utterances are made manifest by citing norms and conventions that already exist in any given culture: cultural signs and signifiers (see also, for example, Brickell 2005 for a useful critique of Butler's theories, especially in relation to masculinity).

These signs begin to 'stick' through repetition over time. The repetition has a binding effect between words and also blocks the words from acquiring new cultural meanings. Thus, to the words 'woman' and 'emotional', an association is formed with the words 'weakness' or 'irrational' (see above). This association between the words is concealed and '*it is this concealment of such associations that allows such signs to accumulate value*' (Ahmed 2004, 91–2 original emphasis). Furthermore, whilst some emotions are seen as irrational, weak and therefore to be ignored in any analysis of human interaction, other emotions are seen as rational and 'cultivated'. 'Cultivated' emotions may be represented as better than reason or rationality if they are accepted as a form of intelligence, as skills that can be used in the life project, or as the 'finer qualities' of humaneness (Illouz 2001; Lupton 1998): 'if *good* emotions are cultivated, and are worked on and towards, then they remain defined against uncultivated or unruly emotions, which frustrate the formation of the competent self' (Ahmed 2004, 3; emphasis added). A demand by employers for employees to manage these 'good emotions' constitutes what Hochschild (2003[1983]) describes as emotional labour: the commercialization, or capitalist colonization, of human feeling.

In our contemporary times, where we are thrust into an almost constant variety of social roles and situations, we spend much mental time asking ourselves, 'What should I be feeling in this situation?' (see, for example, Whitelegg 2007). Yet, according to Hochschild (2003 [1983], 190), in cultural practice we have begun to place an unprecedented value on spontaneous 'natural' feeling: 'we are intrigued by the unmanaged heart and what it can tell us. The more our activities as individual emotion managers are managed by organizations, the more we tend to celebrate the life of unmanaged feeling.' We also still search, she suggests, for a 'solid, predictable core of self':

> people turn to feelings in order to locate themselves or at least to see what their own reactions are to a given event. That is, in the absence of unquestioned external guidelines, the signal function of emotion becomes more important, and the commercial distortion of the managed heart becomes all the more important as a human cost (Hochschild 2003[1983], 22).

Stephanie Shields (2002, 85), however, provides a useful rejoinder to this cultural turn in the world of emotion. She points out that:

[w]hile much is made of getting in touch with one's true feelings, the aim of getting in touch is to get in control ... [The 'ideal' emotion] is especially evident in positive images of masculinity, the raised eyebrow, the quiet snarl, the explosive "yesss!" all signal that strong feeling is present and that it is controlled and directed by the experiencer.

Emotions, in summary, define the way we respond to our social, built or created environment (Milton 2007). They involve a way of understanding the world and are directed or orientated towards an object, although this does not assume that the object has a material existence, for 'objects in which I am "involved" can also be imagined [or, indeed, remembered]' (Ahmed 2004, 7). This two-way reciprocal movement of emotion is summarized by Hochschild (1998, 6), who sees emotion as a 'means by which we continually learn and relearn about a just-now-changed, back-and-forth relation between self and world, the world as it means something just now to the self.' Emotion thus consists of *both* feeling *and* meaning, as something that 'combines bodily processes and cultural interpretations' (Milton 2007, 62). A useful way of sociologically exploring emotions, therefore, is to conceptualize them as 'existentially *embodied* modes of being which involve an *active* engagement with the world and an intimate connection with both culture and self' (Williams and Bendelow 1998, xvi) (original emphasis). With this in mind sociologists and others have begun to 'bring emotions into' their deliberations, not least in the study of health and illness and intimate and familial relationships (Hunter 2001; Duncombe and Marsden 1998; Hochschild 1990; James 1989) and the social research process (e.g. Letherby 2003; Lee-Treweek and Linkogle 2000; Ramsay 1996).

Bendelow and Williams (1998) suggest that because emotion lies at the intersection of many fundamental dualisms in Western thought such as mind and body, nature and culture, public and private that are currently under critical scrutiny and seen as limiting the understanding of social scientists, a study of emotions offers significant analytical strength. Margot Lyon (1998, 52) reinforces this perception: 'Emotion has a central role in bodily agency, for by its very nature it links the somatic and communicative aspects of being and thus encompasses both social and cultural domains ... This 'being-in-the-world', this grounding in reality, is fundamentally linked to the material aspects of our bodies.' Emotion, she argues, 'has a social ontology. That is, the experience of emotion, which involves both physical and phenomenal dimensions, has also a social-relational genesis' (Lyon 1998, 55). If emotions have social-relational beginnings, constitution and consequences, then other key sociological concepts such as gender are also interwoven into the complexity of the analysis.

On Emotion and Gender

Stephanie Shields (2002, 44–5) suggests that, like other stereotypes, dominant ideas about emotion can be powerful filters of information that the individual takes in about the world. Stereotypes, she says, fall into the category of 'everyone knows that …'. These stereotypes might be beliefs that 'too much emotion is immature', or the expressing of emotion is 'irrational': such truisms of emotion are often gendered in that they are connected to beliefs about what is 'typical', 'natural' or 'appropriate' for one sex or the other. Shields demonstrates these truisms in a quote from a book written two psychologists in the 1930s. We feel the quote is worth repeating in full for its historical relevance and as an example of cultural stereotyping:

> In modern Occidental cultures, at least, the typical woman is believed to differ from the typical man in the greater richness and variety of her emotional life and in the extent to which her everyday behavior is emotionally determined. In particular, she is believed to experience in greater degree than the average man the tender emotions, including sympathy, pity, and parental love; to be more given to cherishing and protective behavior of all kinds. Compared with man she is more timid and more readily overcome by fear. She is more religious and at the same time more prone to jealousy, suspicion, and injured feelings … Her moral life is shaped less by principles than by personal relationships, but thanks to her lack of adventurousness she is much less subject than man to most types of criminal behavior (Terman and Miles 1936, 2; quoted in Shields 2002, 50–1).

As Shields (2002) points out, the writers provide no corresponding description of the typical man – 'he is the standard and the woman is what he is not.' This is perhaps not surprising in that historically, men dominated academic settings and created a male 'scientific' culture characterized by male concerns and grounded in an academic machismo. Women were largely ignored in traditional approaches to knowledge and when considered at all judged against masculine 'norms'. Women's experiences and concerns were not seen as authentic but as subjective, whereas men's were seen as the basis of the production of true knowledge (Smith 1989). Here then human equals man and woman is considered in relation to man and as a deviation from his essential humanity: 'she is partial man, or a negative image of man, or a convenient object of man's needs' (Westkott 1990, 59). As Simone de Beauvoir (1972 [1949], 18) puts it, women were defined as 'other' to the male norm:

> Humanity is male and man defines woman not in herself but as relative to him; she is not regarded as an autonomous being … she is simply what man decrees … She is defined and differentiated with reference to man and not with reference to her; she is incidental, the inessential as opposed to the essential. He is Subject, he is the Absolute – she the other.

Yet, to suggest, as does the Enlightenment vision of masculinity, that men are 'rational' whilst women are 'emotional' is a simplistic notion that fails to come to terms with the power of a dominant white heterosexual masculinity within modernity (Seidler 1998, 195). Victor Seidler argues that within modernity emotion is deemed to be a threat to male identity:

> men would often choose to live without emotions at all, treating them as 'distractions' that take them away from the path of reason. It is acceptable for women to be emotional, for this only confirms their weakness, and shows that they need men to be independent and self-sufficient, rocks that can be relied upon (Seidler 1998, 195).

When men and women (or boys and girls) are asked what they know about emotion, most research findings suggest very few gender differences; Shields (2002) maintains, however, that differences do begin to emerge in correlation with the level of social context that is embedded in the given research question. The less information that is made available about a person, the more both sexes will rely on emotion stereotypes: 'People are very knowledgeable about the stereotypes, and this stereotype knowledge is evident even at a very young age' (Shields 2002, 29). Such stereotypes are an important part of learning the practice or performance of gendered behaviour. It emerges, then, that when emotion and gender are intertwined, what we are exploring is less an unequivocal concept of gendered emotion, and more a concept of stereotypical speculations of masculine/feminine emotions (not to be confused with male/female differences).

Implicitly affirming such an analysis, Deborah Lupton (1998) concedes that emotions structure ideologies of gender as well as cultural practices; our experiences of emotions are reciprocally shaped by the capitalist organization of culture. There is a 'forwards and backwards' movement going on. The concept of gender is no mere backdrop to people's lives and the way they see themselves: it is an intrinsic part of the broad social landscape that all of us negotiate on a daily basis (e.g. Halford and Leonard 2006; Evans 1997). Thus, exploring shared beliefs about emotions 'reveals what gender means, how gender operates, and how gender is negotiated in our relationships with others' (Shields 2002, 41). The emotions that travel and travelling engender, as well as the gendered stereotyping of emotion, and the management of emotion and emotional labour undertaken by travellers and travel workers are therefore affected by masculine and feminine expectations and identifications. Taking gender and emotion seriously, then, also produces different perspectives on any analysis of movement.

On Travel ...

Movement (and especially travel by modern mechanical transport) 'generated one of the most distinctive experiences of the modern world, restructuring the existing relations between nature, time and space' (Urry 2000, 56). It is a reasonable question to ask why we have chosen to use the concept of 'travel' here, rather than 'movement', as suggested by John Urry. Although the concept of travel is traditionally associated within the humanities disciplines with the masculinist (albeit in that sense, hotly contested – see, for example, Cresswell and Uteng 2008) theories of tourism, we arrived at its use more or less via a process of elimination of other concepts.

Using, for once, the more vague concept of 'travellings', Urry (2000, 49) notes that they are 'constitutive of the structures of social life – it is in these mobilities that social life and cultural identity are recursively formed and reformed.' This then begs the question: why not use 'transport', or join the current obsession[2] with the concept of 'mobilities'? The former is clearly too specific: we certainly move around a great deal by transport, but to limit our analyses to that would be to ignore, for example, all kinds of moving around on foot.

The concept of mobility, on the other hand, 'involves the physical movements, which are observable and representable in maps and models … Mobility also involves the meanings associated with movement – the narratives and discourses that make movement make sense culturally … And mobility involves practice – the embodied and experienced aspects of moving' (Cresswell and Uteng 2008, 6). Urry (2000, 49) notes that '[M]obilities, as both metaphor and as process, are at the heart of social life and thus should be central to sociological analysis.' This means that any sociology that claims to explore movement and mobility instead of structure and order, must focus on the 'corporeal, imagined and virtual mobilities of people' (Urry 2000, 18). Our difficulties with using this concept for our purposes here are that its parameters are broadly defined to include imaginative, communicative and virtual travel (as well as corporeal travel of individuals and physical movement of objects) (see Preface, this volume). In addition (although this book includes reference to train, air and motorized travel), we are not entirely concerned with hypermobility which denotes individualized transport spanning wider and wider distances (Adams 1999). Rather, we are mostly concerned with the aspect of 'mobility' that focuses on the individual and social experience of travel (broadly defined) from both the perspective of the traveller and the travel worker, which sometimes *may* include the physical movement of objects (in the case of truck-driving). Thus, we are concerned with how 'mobility also happens "within"' and acknowledge that '[t]he layers of meaning of mobility are not merely a question of movement but of the making of particular identities, relations to the world and affective attachments with which subjects are implicated in the world' (Fay 2008, 77).

One splendid – but perhaps unexpected – example of travel in a (very) social context is dancing, for which we draw heavily upon Tim Cresswell's work, *On the Move* (2006). Cresswell claims that the history of the eradication of superfluous motion in dancing came to the fore in 1920 (during that period – most notably in 1929 when the Irish Dancing Commission was founded – the movements of Irish step dancing were also standardized and re-validated, arguably through the historical influence of Catholic priests – see, for example, Haurin and Richens

---

2 Eve Kosofsky Sedgwick (2003, 2) describes 'obsession' as the most durable form of intellectual capital.

1996). According to Cresswell, 200 dance teachers gathered in London to discuss the 'condition' of (especially ballroom) dancing in Britain. As he notes, '[t]he movement of dance seems, at first glance, to inhabit a different world from the movement of work. Work appears to be the realm of unfreedom and constraint, while dance is often thought of as a realm of freedom, pleasure and play' (p. 123). But the history of dance alerts us to the 'operations of an array of disciplinary practices and deep-rooted ideologies of mobility … [B]allroom dancing became enmeshed in beliefs about appropriate and inappropriate mobility' (p. 123). It is, for Cresswell, an account of the production of aesthetically 'correct' movement, devoid of the Othered 'degenerate' and 'freakish' *emotion-displaying* movement ingrained in the dance of African–American and Latin–American cultures. The history of ballroom dance shows how forms of 'correct' and 'appropriate' movement 'are produced in relation to "inappropriate" forms of movement through a complicated representational process … reveal[ing] the normative geographies that are at play in this process' (Cresswell 2006, 142).

One further, perhaps unexpected, example which exemplifies the connections between gender and travel is the queue. Throughout history, and across all cultures, women, more than men, have stood in queues: for food, for water, for medical help for their children, for public transport, by government decree, and so on. The 'queue' is perhaps the slowest and most frustrating 'journey' there is (Greed 2008, 249). At the most simple level, then, travel is about footsteps, real or symbolic, but for social scientists, at least, it cannot be legitimately disentangled from ideologies embedded in modes of production and consumption.

Movement of the body and/or mind through space and place can also be conceptualized as one of many 'spatial practices'. The story of spatial practices begins 'on ground level, with footsteps. They are myriad, but do not compose a series. They cannot be counted because each unit has a qualitative character … Their intertwined paths give their shape to spaces. They weave places together' (de Certeau 1984, 97). As the world has appeared to become more mobile, so the way we *think about* the world has become 'nomad thought' (Cresswell 2006) (our emphasis). For Cresswell (2006, 43), this effectively means that 'everything that has been at the heart of the history of sociology has changed or been made irrelevant due to an observable change in the world itself toward increasing levels of mobility.'

Travel, Gender and Emotion

It is something of a truism that moving around in time, space and place is an experience which is also often fundamentally different for women and men (see, among others, Walsh (this volume); Uteng and Cresswell 2008; Schmucki 2007; Halford and Leonard 2006). Some aspects of these differences are well-known and well-established and include:

- differential access to public transport (e.g. Grieco 1989, 2007; Fernando and Porter 2002, in relation to developing countries);
- the trip-chaining (combining a number of tasks within single trip, e.g. disposing of recycling waste at the bottle bank, calling at the supermarket, checking on an elderly relative, and picking up the children from school) and multi-tasking that are key features of women's travel (e.g. Greed 2008);
- gendered spaces and gendered politics within public transport (e.g. Reynolds and Rose this volume; Whitelegg 2007; Letherby and Reynolds 2005);
- the manifold relationships between the car and masculinity (e.g. Hatton, Sharp this volume; Best 2006; Davison 2004; Anger 2002; O'Connell 1998).

Narratives around travel and mobility play a central role in the constitution of gender as a social and cultural construct (see, for example, Walsh, Stanley, Stevenson, all this volume). Even the detailed aspects of mobility – movement, meaning, practice and potential – have embedded within them whole histories and geographies of gendered difference. As Tana Priya Cresswell and Tim Uteng (2008, 2) assert, 'Understanding mobility … means understanding observable physical movement, the meanings that such movements are encoded with, the experience of practicing these movements and the potential for undertaking these movements.' For example:

> The male body is culturally performed as a more mobile body, while the female body becomes more restricted and spatially circumscribed … Boys (at least until recently) often were accorded more freedom than girls to move around their neighbourhoods, to engage in unsupervised walking or riding bicycles to meet with friends, to go camping, fishing or hiking, or to ride on public transport. Such capabilities for mobility are deeply tied up with the production of white masculinity and its materialisation in particular kinds of embodied agency (Sheller 2008, 259).

> Particular hatred seems to be reserved for the 'school run', that is women taking their children to school by car. This activity only contributes to 15% of rush-hour traffic but it is widely condemned, for 'cluttering up the roads', a sentiment voiced no doubt by male commuters and businessmen who do not question their own right to use a car … The school run is portrayed in the media as being undertaken by rich lazy housewives in their '4 by 4' Range Rovers, although many families only own a cheap car and make major economies to keep it running … In reality, many women find it very difficult to get to work early in the morning, to ensure their children reach the school and childminder within a very tight morning time slot. If mothers do go by bus or train with their children during the rush-hour they may be accused of 'filling up the spaces' and slowing down the system, which is clearly not intended for them, but for commuters (Greed 2008, 248).

These quotes still (we think) encapsulate the connectedness of travel, gender and emotion at the beginning of the twenty-first century in Britain as, indeed, do all the contributions to this volume.

According to Cresswell (2006), mobility normally *appears* as a chaotic thing – chaotic in the sense that things that are moving are often chaotic in the way we experience them. Human movement, however, is rarely simply movement; it carries with it a wealth of meaning. It is this issue of meaning that remains largely absent from accounts of mobility, and important (both theoretical and subjective) connections are therefore neglected (Cresswell 2006). 'Meaning' is crucial to any analysis of movement. And 'meaning' is also fundamental to emotion. Although the theoretical practice of combining emotion and meaning is itself controversial (see, for example, Skinner 2007), exploring and managing those meanings of emotion, according to Hochschild (2003), can alert us to the contradictions in wider society that create strains and tensions and, we would add, pleasure and opportunities.

References

Adams, J. (1999), *The Social Implications of Hypermobility OECD Project on Environmentally Sustainable Transport* (Paris: OECD).

Ahmed, S. (2004), *The Cultural Politics of Emotion* (Edinburgh: University of Edinburgh Press).

Anger, K. (2002), 'Kar Krash Karma' in M. Brottman (ed.).

Barbalet, J. (ed.) (2002), *Emotions and Sociology* (Oxford: Blackwell).

Barbalet, J. (2001), *Emotion, Social Theory and Social Structure: a macrosociological approach* (Cambridge: Cambridge University Press).

Bauman, Z. (2005), *Liquid Life* (Cambridge: Polity).

Bendelow, G. and Williams, S. (eds) (1998), *Emotions in Social Life: Critical Themes and Contemporary Issues* (London: Routledge).

Best, A. (2006), *Fast Cars, Cool Rides: The Accelerating World of Youth and their Cars* (New York: New York University Press).

Bowler, P. (2005), 'Darwin on the Expression of the Emotions: the eclipse of a research programme' in K. Milton and M. Svašek (eds).

Brickell, C. (2005), 'Masculinities, Performativity and Subversion', *Men and Masculinities*, vol. 8, 1, 24–43.

Brottman, M. (ed.) (2002), *Car Crash Culture* (Basingstoke: Palgrave Macmillan).

Butler, J. (1990), *Gender Trouble: Feminism and the Subversion of Identity* (London: Routledge).

Clough, P. Ticineto with Halley, J. (eds) (2007), *The Affective Turn: Theorizing the Social* (Durham and London: Duke University Press).

Cresswell, T. (2006), *On the Move: Mobility in the Modern Western World* (Oxford: Taylor and Francis).

Cresswell, T. and Uteng, T.P. (2008), 'Gendered mobilities: towards an holistic understanding' in T.P. Uteng and T. Cresswell (eds).

Davison, G. (2004), *Car Wars: How the Car Won Our Hearts and Conquered our Cities* (Crows Nest, Australia: Allen and Unwin).

Damasio, A. (2006), *Descartes' Error* (revised edition) (London: Vintage).

Damasio, A. (2000) *The Feeling of What Happens: Body, Emotion and the Making of Consciousness* (London: Vintage).

de Beauvoir, S. (1972 [1949]), *The Second Sex* (translated by H.M. Parshley) (Harmondsworth: Penguin).

de Certeau, M. (1984) (transl. Stephen Rendall), *The Practice of Everyday Life* (Berkeley: University of California Press).

Duncombe, J. and Marsden D. (1998), '"Stepford wives" and "hollow men"? Doing emotion work, doing gender and "authenticity" in intimate heterosexual relationships' in G. Bendelow and S.J Williams (eds).

Evans, M. (1997), *Introducing Contemporary Feminist Thought* (Cambridge: Polity Press).

Fay, M. (2008), '"Mobile Belonging': exploring transnational feminist theory and online connectivity' in T.P. Uteng and T. Cresswell (eds).

Fernando, P. and Porter, G. (eds) (2002), *Balancing the Load: Women, Gender and Transport* (London: Zed Books).

Fernando, P. and Porter, G. (2002), 'Introduction: bridging the gap between gender and transport' in P. Fernando and G. Porter (eds).

Giddens, A. (1991), *Modernity and Self-Identity: Self and Society in the Late Modern Age* (Cambridge: Polity Press).

Goffman, E. (1967), *Interaction Ritual: Essays on Face-to-Face Behavior* (New York: Pantheon).

Grieco, M. (2007), 'Gendered Mobilities? Engaging the transport academy in repairing a traditional neglect', keynote paper presented to Cosmobilities Conference, Basle, September.

Grieco, M. (1989), *Gender, Transport and Employment: Impact of Travel Constraints* (Aldershot: Avebury).

Greed, C. (2008), 'Are we there yet? Women and transport revisited', in T.P. Uteng and T. Cresswell (eds).

Halford, S. and Leonard, P. (2006), *Negotiating Gendered Identities at Work: Place, Space and Time* (Basingstoke: Palgrave).

Haurin, D. and Richens, A. (1996), *Irish Step Dancing: a brief history*, www. geocities.com/aer_mcr/irdance/irhist [Accessed 24 June 2008].

Hall, D. (2000), 'The End(s) of Masculinity Studies', *Victorian Literature and Culture*, 28, 227–37.

Hardt, M. (2007), 'Foreword – what affects are good for' in P.T. Clough with J. Halley (eds).

Highmore, B. (ed.) (2002), *The Everyday Life Reader* (London: Routledge).

Hochschild, A.R. (2003[1983]), *The Managed Heart: Commercialization of Human Feeling. 20th Anniversary Edition* (Berkeley: University of California Press).

Hochschild, A.R. (1998), 'The Sociology of Emotion as a Way of Seeing' in G. Bendelow and S. Williams (eds).

Hochschild, A.R. (1990), *The Second Shift* (London: Piatkus).

Hunter, B. (2001), 'Emotion Work in Midwifery: a review of current knowledge', *Journal of Advanced Nursing* 34, 4, 436–44.

Illouz, E. (2001), 'What Role for Emotions in Sociological Theory?' in *Body and Society*, 7, 1, 97–102.

James, N. (1989), 'Emotional Labour: skill and work in the social regulation of feelings', *Sociological Review*, 37, 1, 15–42.

Lee-Treweek, G. and Linkogle, S. (eds) (2000), *Danger in the Field: Risk and Ethics in Social Research* (London: Routledge).

Letherby, G. (2003), *Feminist Research in Theory and Practice* (Buckingham: Open University Press).

Letherby, G. and Reynolds, G. (2005), *Train Tracks: Work, Play and Politics on the Railways* (Oxford: Berg).

Lupton, D. (1998), *The Emotional Self* (London: Sage).

Lutz, C.A. (2007), 'Emotion, Thought, and Estrangement: emotion as a cultural category' in H. Wulff (ed.).

Lyon, M. (1998), 'The Limitations of Cultural Constructionism in the Study of Emotion' in G. Bendelow and S. Williams (eds).

Lyon, S. and Busfield, J. (eds) (1996), *Methodological Imaginations* (London: Macmillan).

Miller, D. (2002), 'Making love in supermarkets', in B. Highmore (ed.).

Miller, J.B. (1976), *Towards a New Psychology of Women* (Boston: Beacon Press).

Milton, K. (2007 [2005]), 'Emotion (or Life, The Universe, Everything)', in H. Wulff (ed.).

Milton, K. (2005), 'Meanings, Feelings and Human Ecology' in K. Milton and M. Svašek (eds).

Milton, K. and Svašek, M. (eds) (2005), *Mixed Emotions: Anthropological Studies of Feeling* (Oxford: Berg).

Oakley, A. (1981), *Subject Women* (Oxford: Martin Robertson).

O'Connell, S. (1998), *The Car in British Society: Class, Gender and Motoring, 1896–1939* (Manchester: Manchester University Press).

Ramsay, K. (1996), 'Emotional Labour and Organisational Research: how I learned not to laugh or cry in the field' in S.E. Lyon and J. Busfield (eds).

Schmucki, B. (2007), 'Gendered Spaces – Gendered Places. Women, urban transport and walking in the 19th and 20th century'. Paper presented to Gender, Emotion, Work and Travel: Women Transport Workers and Passengers Past and Present Conference, Greenwich Maritime Institute (GMI), University of Greenwich, London 22 and 23 June.

Sedgwick, E.K. (2003), *Touching Feeling: Affect, Pedagogy, Performativity* (Durham and London: Duke University Press).

Seidler, V.J. (1998), 'Masculinity, Violence and Emotional Life' in G. Bendelow and S. Williams (eds).

Sheller, M. (2008), 'Gendered Mobilities: Epilogue' in T.P. Uteng and T. Cresswell (eds).

Shields, S.A. (2002), *Speaking from the Heart: Gender and the Social Meaning of Emotion* (Cambridge: Cambridge University Press).

Shilling, C. (2002), 'The Two Traditions in the Sociology of Emotions' in J. Barbalet (ed.).

Skinner, J. (2007), 'Emotional Baggage: the meaning/feeling debate among tourists' in H. Wulff (ed.).

Smith, D.E. (1989), *The Everyday World as Problematic: A Feminist Sociology* (New England: Northeastern University Press).

Terman, L.M. and Miles, C.C. (1936), *Sex and Personality* (New York: Russell and Russell).

Tonkin, E. (2005), 'Being there: emotion and imagination in anthropologists' encounters' in K. Milton and M. Svašek (eds).

Urry, J. (2004), 'Connections', *Environment and Planning D* 22, 27–37.

Urry, J. (2000), *Sociology Beyond Societies: Mobilities for the Twenty-first Century* (London: Routledge).

Uteng, T.P. and Cresswell, T. (eds) (2008), *Gendered Mobilities* (Aldershot: Ashgate).

Whitelegg, D. (2007), *Working the Skies: The Fast-paced, Disorienting World of the Flight Attendant* (New York: New York University Press).

Williams, S. and Bendelow, G. (1998), 'Introduction: Emotions in social life. Mapping the terrain', in G. Bendelow and S. Williams (eds).

Wulff, H. (ed.) (2007), *The Emotions: A Cultural Reader* (Oxford: Berg).

Chapter 3
Mapping the Way? Maps, Emotion, Gender

Mike Esbester

Introduction

Let me take you on a journey. Not as deep as that of Michel de Certeau (1984) through New York, certainly, but I will attempt to portray one of my everyday practices of space. From my house, to the west of Oxford, I will walk us into the centre of the city, noting the maps that we pass. Inside the house there are several: Ordnance Survey, street atlases, bits of maps printed out from the Internet, an atlas and – somewhere – copies of old maps. Leaving the house, we pass the car (which contains a road atlas of Britain, an A-Z and some Ordnance Survey maps of other parts of the country). We pass other cars and homes, which undoubtedly contain maps. We continue approximately 300 metres to the end of the street, where we turn left onto one of the arterial routes into Oxford. We walk for around 15 minutes, passing 12 bus stops, each with a schematic map of Oxford's bus routes. We also pass several 'you are here' maps: the first near the station, another by a car park and finally one by the Odeon cinema. In the space of approximately one mile we have moved from my house to the centre of Oxford: in doing so, we have passed at least 23 maps, 15 of which were on public display, intended to aid everyday navigation.

What does this show? That in 2008 maps are – for me at least – ubiquitous. I suspect that I am not alone in this and whether you actively notice them or not, whether you actively use them or not, you will be as familiar with maps, public and private, as this short urban walk suggests. But are maps more than 'just' wayfinding devices? Do they possess emotional content, or inspire emotional reactions? When I casually put this question to a friend, she resolutely denied it. They epitomize rationality: calculated, cold. Although, curiously, she did then list her responses to using maps, including frustration (when the place she wanted to find was not shown); anger (when she could not get to a place marked on the map), and satisfaction (when she did finally get to the place). Still, she maintained, how could maps be emotional or inspire emotions?

Yet it is clear that maps *are* an emotive subject. A number of brief examples suffice. In May 2005 the British Broadcasting Corporation changed the weather map used in television reports, provoking a barrage of complaints on a variety of grounds: aesthetic (the 'dull brown and beige background illustrates what appears to be a Britain a few months after a nuclear attack' ('Oracle' 2006)), political (to do with the relative size of Scotland to the south of England) and egalitarian (to do with the speed of scrolling and dyslexia). The schematic London Underground map by Harry Beck regularly inspires enthusiasm for its design. Contested terrain as represented on maps can result in tension between nations: Ramesh (2007, 31) recently noted in the *Guardian* accusations of 'cartographic aggression' between India and Pakistan over the Siachen glacier near Kashmir, claimed by both countries. Consider the pity, sorrow or anger provoked by maps of war, genocide or empire; or the pride induced by a map of the nation to which the viewer owes allegiance (Monmonier 1996, 88–90).

In this chapter I offer some brief thoughts on maps, gender, emotion and travel. This is an area which has not been considered widely; even the growing body of literature on gender and transport looks more at the interactions between cultures, technologies and mobility, rather than at the items such as maps that are perceived as 'incidental', but which support (or inhibit) mobility. However, given the frequency with which we interact with them, maps are an interesting site at which emotional and gendered relationships are exposed for view.

In considering the emotional content of maps, I am concentrating upon certain types of maps: symbolic representations of the physical environment, exemplified in Britain in the work of the Ordnance Survey. Of necessity, this excludes numerous types of map, all of which certainly inspire emotional responses. These maps have been – and in some cases, remain – crucial to the journeys that people undertake in life, whether involving physical movement or some sort of mental voyage. Thus, nautical charts – of both sea and stars – do not feature; celestial maps and mapping have also held religious significance, ensuring maps extend beyond terrestrial navigation of space and place, but are here excluded. Maps of the body (from Vesalius's 1543 *De Humani Corporis Fabrica* to the National Health Service's interactive 'Body Map'); satellite-dependent composite photograph maps (such as 'Google Earth', which allow the user to manipulate, select and view); schematic maps (the London underground); metaphorical maps ('the road map to peace'); fictional or imaginative maps (Treasure Island, Atlantis, the Garden of Eden, Lord of the Rings); site maps on websites; mind maps: all have similar elements, as ways of representing structures to people, aiding navigation, sharing information or values, clarifying. Yet space has (ironically) precluded their consideration here. The discussion that follows draws upon evidence from the late nineteenth century to the present day, and is anglocentric. I aim to show how maps have ambiguous emotional and gendered meanings, very much dependent upon the individual.

Mapping the Physical

Each of the 23 maps passed on our one-mile journey into Oxford had one thing in common – they were all, in different ways, attempting to render the space through which we were travelling in a way that would be meaningful to us. This section of the chapter discusses what maps attempt to achieve and the techniques they use. In doing so, it highlights the absences in these physical cartographies, including emotional absence.

Anne Humpherys (2002, 601) asks us 'Is the city knowable?' Maps certainly try to make space (or, at least, some parts of space) knowable. Using symbols for natural and built features, they are the cartographers' interpretation of what can be found on the ground. They also form part of governance and power, depicting administrative boundaries and items that often have no physical presence (Harley 2001, Wood 1993). According to Lynda Nead (2000, 26) the 'modern map ... compartmentalises, classifies and explains the logics of the metropolis; it lays out its boundaries and priorities.' Maps are thus physical-political. But this leaves little space for emotions or gender on the map itself.

Similarly, the idea that maps are objective writes gender and emotionality out of mapping. In the wake of the First World War, *The Times* (Anon. 1919, 11) reported that cartography was 'essentially independent' of political considerations, as mapping served 'the common interests of humanity.' It is necessary here to question whose humanity is being mapped. Doreen Massey (2005, 10) notes that 'the story of the world cannot be told (nor its geography elaborated) as the story of ... the white, heterosexual male.' If, as Paul Rodaway (1994, 136) suggests, modern western maps emerged as tools of power for political and/or economic purposes, then the paradigms and conventions which shape and constrain official maps (such as atlases, maps produced by government-sponsored agencies, or road atlases) to the present day have been established in a male-dominated environment.

As Pamela Gilbert (2004, 10) has observed, 'During the Enlightenment, maps came to embody the power of the objective, scientific gaze to construct – or reflect – an accurate description of the geographic environment.' This 'objectivity' has been associated with masculinist perceptions, in this case of the environment (physical and sociocultural). As a long body of literature attests, spaces and places are gendered; yet the ways in which these gendered spaces and places are depicted on official maps is difficult to discern – they are now so ingrained in our readings and understandings of cartography as to be virtually undetectable.

If gender is hidden in the most common forms of maps, then the treatment of physical features is similarly problematic. Maps did not – and do not – necessarily display 'an accurate description of the geographic environment' (Gilbert 2004, 10). Brian Harley (2001), Mark Monmonier (1996) and Denis Wood (1993) argue that maps are not simple representations of an objective reality, but rather are selective, showing only aspects of the reality that their (gendered) creators observe and wish to promote as significant. A variety of things are missing from geographical maps. At the most elementary level, there are objects which we would encounter in the world but are absent from maps: road signs, traffic lights and the like (Cantor 1977, 50). Wood (1993, 12) gives the example of 'white space' on maps, which seems to indicate 'nothingness' – but there will be something in that space if you were to go there (for example, grass and soil).

More significantly, *people* are missing from virtually all maps. Certainly maps show the cultural artefacts of people's interventions in the natural landscape – for example, buildings or agricultural patterns. Wood (1993, 71) makes the point that modern western maps are static: they do not show movement. As a result, lived space is missing: how people experience the environment is not portrayed on the map (Gilbert 2004, 23). According to Monmonier (1996, 122), maps show 'streets, landmark structures, elevations, parks, churches, and large museums – but not dangerous intersections, impoverished neighbourhoods, high-crime areas, and other zones of danger and misery.' These cartographic 'silences' become significant in the context of emotion: Keith Oatley (2004, 4) observes that '[r]eactive emotions occur when the appearance of the world as we assume it to be is pierced by reality.' Thus, emotional responses to maps can arise from the mismatch between what is experienced 'on the ground' and what is shown on the map. Making this point, a 1908 editorial in *The Times* (Anon. 1908, 11) argued that 'never yet did the possessor of a good map fail to study it in the fond fancy that something of the ideal presentation of reality would be his [sic] if only he would continue to pore over it.' This 'reality' was not that offered by the map, which fails to include emotions. Massey's (2005, 9) contention that space is 'a product of the relations-between, relations which are necessarily embedded in material practices which have to be carried out' suggests that the roles of women and men and emotion in constituting space is key – yet these aspects are absent from most cartographic representations of space.

Mapping the Emotional

Gillian Bendelow and Simon Williams (1998, xvi) contend that 'rational methods of scientific enquiry, even at their most positivistic, involve the incorporation of values and emotions.' Therefore understanding how people interact with their environment and with maps needs to embody an appreciation of the emotional content of these interactions. As Joyce Davidson et al. (2005, 3) observe, 'An emotional geography, then, attempts to understand emotion … in terms of its socio-*spatial* mediation and articulation rather than as entirely interiorised subjective mental states.' Although not considered explicitly by the authors in their book, maps are an important aid to this attempted understanding. In the following section, there are two strands to my examination of maps and emotions: how people feel *about* maps and how people's feelings are represented *on* maps.

Feeling about *Maps*

In 1941 *The Times* (Anon. 1941, 5) declared that a map 'arouses so much emulation, self-assertion, impatience, and other forms of human frailty.' However, the map in itself is not emotional: it provokes emotional responses on the part of the map user(s). The user has to invest the map with 'intellectual and emotional meaning' (Anon. 1908, 11). According to David Cantor (1977, 9) 'every seemingly minor aspect of our physical surroundings may be imbued … with a variety of meanings, because of the mixture of memories, habits and expectations with which we link it.' Lord Montagu (quoted in Anon. 1908, 11) observed that 'a well-designed map arouses thought, and is really capable of bringing pleasure, though it consists of but a sheet of paper with coloured lines, a dab of green, a streak of blue there.' Emotional responses to maps are thus conditional upon what the user brings to the map, including their gender, and what the user wants from the map.

The emotional responses generated by maps depend upon underlying reasons for consultation. These reasons are not always functional. Rather than simply working as a wayfinding tool, maps are aesthetic and imaginative objects. G.K. Chesterton (1901, 55) railed against functional map use, but admired the object as something that 'should be taken [on a journey] chiefly because it is such a particularly beautiful thing in itself.' It is not only the object itself that contributes to the 'timeless fascination of old maps', but also 'the stories behind them ... to day-dream about the people who owned it, where and why they used it and whether it served its purpose' (Wormley 1977, 2–3). Imagination therefore plays a significant role in some people's reactions to maps. Such emotional responses to maps escape the bounds of wayfinding or information provision: there is more to maps than 'practical' geographic use.

Even those approaching a map ostensibly for information could have an emotional response: during the Second World War *The Times* (Anon. 1941, 5) observed that, when trying to find places referred to in the news, the map 'is charged with sorrow for the suffering of others.' The map, then, can become a means of structuring the user's experience – structuring their perception of the environment, but also itself structured by the user's emotions. According to Davidson et al. (2005, 1), 'emotion has the power to transform the shape of our lives.' This is of significance: with the increasing ubiquity of maps since the nineteenth century (Gilbert 2004, 10) we can expect to have greater interaction with maps and hence more frequent emotional experiences.

People consult maps for a number of reasons, which intimately affect the nature of their emotional experience; these reasons can, broadly, be understood in terms of time (and space) – when (and where) the individual consults the map. Consulted after the event, the map can act as a strong emotional trigger, reminding us of past experiences: 'the sentimental joy of thinking what a splendid holiday it was' (Anon. 1941, 5). These events need not have been experienced directly, and need not be positive; an editorial in *The Times* of 1965 observed maps that transport people 'all the way down to those distant parts where in unhappier days they had atrocities' (Anon. 1965, 13). These emotions are not attached to the map *per se*, but rather to the (gendered and 'othered') notions of place that we hold (Harley 2001, 147).

The use of the map in the present is more obvious: frequently this is a use for action – for wayfinding. Beryl Markham (1943, quoted in Harley 2001, 150) understood the map as speaking to her, telling her '[w]ithout me, you are alone and lost.' Perhaps unsurprisingly, perceived deficiencies in maps have ensured a reliable stream of emotional responses: in 1893 'every one who has used the Survey maps at all has been annoyed by the frequency with which the section stops just in the middle of the route he [sic] means to take' (Anon. 1893, 9). Here the author followed the conventions of their time, unselfconsciously assuming the map-reader was a man.

It is likely that emotional reactions to maps reflect prevailing social and cultural attitudes that may encourage differing levels of familiarity with, and use of, maps in men and women. Thus, in 1960 *The Times* (Anon. 1960, 11) held that women were 'generally ready to admit that maps and all they stand for are a little too much for them … maps, from their point of view, come into the category of those things that are best left to others to cope with.' If true, it may simply have been a corollary of the 'masculinity of the map' – the culturally pervasive view that has potentially restricted women's access to and practice in map reading. Such supposed inferiority had not prevented Phyllis Pearsall from mapping London and producing the first 'A-Z' map in 1936.

Nevertheless, according to *The Times* (Anon. 1941, 5), mapreading could produce 'an almost purely physical contest', resulting in lingering discontent: 'whatever place on the map may be found the domestic harmony will be lost.' This was one of the points of slippage, where the stereotypical rhetoric of masculine mapreading and feminine map-nonreading broke down. Here, women were just as capable as men and men just as incapable as women at reading the map. Unconsciously, it was recognized that gender might not be key to using a map. Yet for all this 'domestic' discord, there is satisfaction upon finding your destination: 'Could the rewards of the practical and the theoretic life be more happily blended than in a triumphant verification of the monosyllable, "inn", when the sun is sinking and it is time for dinner?' (Anon. 1932, 11). Clearly, then, 'practical' map use and experiencing the environment embody an intensely emotional element, whilst being gendered in complex ways.

Maps also possess an emotional future – in planning a journey. This allows the physical form of the journey to be structured: *The Times* (Anon. 1931, 15) claimed that '[i]t is a great thing to be planning out the route, to be speculating on the landmarks and the landscape, to be sizing up the difficulties and studying the means of overcoming them.' It also allows for emotional preparation. Maps can mean 'the exciting joy of planning a holiday' (Anon. 1941, 5) through 'the promise of adventure they offer' (Anon. 1965, 13). This returns to the imaginative element of the map, making visible the contents of the map. *The Times* (Anon. 1973, 13) believed users to be 'glad' of maps which 'on a winter's night when study of a good map creates in the mind's eye an image of the ground it covers, [and] anticipation of pleasures to come.'

All of these temporal functions of the map – and their associated emotional responses – form a part of what Phil Nicholls (this volume) calls the 'ongoing process of negotiation with [the] environment.' The map user can perform all of these emotional activities whilst using the same map: 'the … [user] who has a soul will dote on his [sic] maps, cherish them, and thus keep fresh in mind past pleasures and the hope of future delights' (Montagu 1908, quoted in Anon. 1908, 11). Wood (1993, 7) summarizes this merging of time in the map and the responses

it can provoke: 'Past and future – neither accessible to my sense *on the ground* ...
come together in my present through the grace of the map' (original emphasis).

The idea of the emotionality of the past and future map, and the imagination
used to construct these emotions and meanings, suggest that maps enable a type
of travel without requiring the traveller to leave their physical location. It was
noted in 1919 that 'few people buy atlases with the intention of visiting every
country between their covers' (Anon. 1919, 11). Perhaps consulting the map in
the comfort and safety of the home lets people travel to these places that they
will never physically see. Nicholls (this volume) suggests that the experience and
emotion of travel can be consumed without moving, by viewing the map. This
may not result in the same experience or emotions as would be experienced were
the journey physically undertaken, but nonetheless it can be travel – emotional
travel. Certainly, remembering past travel through maps remakes the journey,
recomposing what has gone before and making it into a new journey. It is therefore
possible to unpack the static nature of the map.

In narratives concerning maps and map-use, women are largely present through
their near complete absence. Thus, the historical primary evidence cited until this
point has tended to generalize male experience, subsuming female experience into
a universal set of emotions. What is particularly interesting about this is that there
has been some very open expression of 'universal' (male) emotion – reaching
beyond 'masculine' emotions such as anger. So although '[t]he stereotype ...
that as compared with men, women are more emotionally expressive ... more
emotionally skilled' (Oatley 2004, 34) might still be commonplace, in practice
masculine emotion is not necessarily hidden from view. If men are expected to
perform as map-readers then they are more likely to leave traces of their interactions
with maps – including on an emotional level. Perhaps maps were – and are – one
area in which the expression of male emotion is 'allowed'.

Of course, the evidence for 'male' cartographic emotionality is problematic. On
a number of occasions male failure to use the map was implicitly associated with the
female. In 1915 it was suggested that the man who failed to understand maps was
likely to be 'bewildered and terrified' even in his own town, and the only way he
could 'find his way' was by 'humiliating recourse to the nearest policeman' (Anon.
1915, 9). Implicitly, these were feminine attributes, experiences and emotions: yet
they were associated with men who failed to understand maps. Male mapreading
identity was feminized more problematically in 1931, when the typical in-car
mapreader was described as 'an obscure creature, generally elderly and male, who
neither owns nor drives, but is allowed to sit by the driver's side' (Anon. 1931,
15). Although a mapreader, he was removed to a position of incompetence in the
'masculine' arena of driving and rendered powerless as a passenger: a situation
that at this time would largely have been associated with the feminine.

The Emotional Ambiguity of Maps

As the range of emotional expression discussed above demonstrates, our relationships with maps are by no means simple. Each person invests the map with their own meaning, something acknowledged in *The Times* in a view that '[e]ach man's [sic] journey remains his very own' (Anon. 1931, 15). Not only is this meaning individual, it is, as *The Times* clearly demonstrated, gendered. Further, within an individual this meaning can change according to the moment in time and to their immediate emotional state (Golledge 1999; Cantor 1977). Our emotional responses are thus ephemeral, providing an ambiguous means of understanding maps.

This ambiguity is increased as maps can be aesthetic, geographic and emotional simultaneously: 'an agreeable mingling of the scientific and the artistic' (Anon. 1960, 11). Whilst they may enable travel from departure point to destination, maps can also limit the journey, channelling the traveller's options or gaze in certain directions and obscuring other possibilities. And, of course, maps are renowned as difficult to use, from the 1863 comment that they are 'a sort of thing that no fellow [sic] can make out' (Anon. 1863, 8) to the view 100 years later that few 'can translate into the terms of real country and of distances the contours and scale of the enticing map before them' (Anon. 1963, 15). How we interact with maps would perhaps best be characterized as ambivalence: 'Maps ... encourage what psychoanalytic jargon rejoices in calling a love-hate relationship' (Anon. 1963, 15).

How we experience space cannot be fully comprehended through the geographic maps that have formed the basis for the discussion thus far. In 1932 this was given substance by Thomas Burke (1932, 17): 'Guide-books and maps are useless. Throw them away and wander.' This idea that maps were insufficient, in terms of the emotional experiences of and responses to space, was found implicitly in the *flânerie* (the act of strolling) of the nineteenth and twentieth centuries. Experiencing space without cartographic intervention created 'imaginary landscapes', superimposed on the physical landscape.

Feeling on *Maps*

In September 2007 the Ordnance Survey (OS) launched its online 'explore' facility, touted as 'more than just maps.' It allows users to plot a route onto an OS map and 'add points of interest and photos and share all this with the world' (Anon. 2007a). This permits the individual a small degree of expression of how they interact emotionally with the landscape that is mapped. Other initiatives have gone further towards creating 'emotional maps': ways of charting how people experience subjectively the spaces shown on geographic maps, and showing emotions, bodies and relations in space.

Emotional maps are not a recent phenomenon. The psychogeography of the Situationists in the 1950s and 1960s was an early example, in which the city's geography was experienced emotionally; Guy Debord's *Guide Psychogeographique de Paris* of 1957 re-arranged a cartographic representation of Paris to show emotional connections across the city. In the 1970s Tim Robinson attempted to map Arainn Island (off the west coast of Ireland) geographically, emotionally, and imaginatively. In September 2007 the New Museum in New York displayed a series of 21 maps of Manhattan, composed by artists to show 'a territory that is both real and imaginary ... fictional landscapes, utopian visions, private memories ... past, present, and future' (Anon. 2007b). Jon Adams' 'Alternative Platform' project aims 'to produce a map of personal [railway] journeys in the style of the network rail map', using 'events from passengers' own life stories' (Adams 2007).

To all of these efforts, meaning and locality is integral. Rachel Grant (this volume) has produced maps of viewing points for both her artwork and local physical features. Similarly, the organization 'Common Ground' encourages local communities to create parish maps, which portray events or places of importance to the community. It is interesting that these are 'unofficial' maps – maps that have tried (self-consciously or not) to escape the confines of 'objective' cartography and to engage with concepts of meaning, locality and emotion. Women, in particular, have often played an important role in the creation of such maps, perhaps reflecting their position as some of those otherwise disenfranchised by the process of 'official' mapping.

In the context of the representation of emotional responses to the environment, Christian Nold's emotion maps are of particular interest. Using monitors to detect changes in the body's physical state that can be linked to emotions, he has tracked volunteers as they experience their locale, before asking them to reconstruct their emotional journey superimposed on a geographic map as a series of coloured zones. His 2005–06 map of Greenwich represents 'a living space of human activity where people interact with their environment as well as each other to generate feelings and opinions' (Nold 2007). Rather than a geographic map, we can see points of emotional encounter. And the map itself becomes a part of this dialectic, as a thing of beauty and as a means of navigation (of emotions if not of geography) – it has been printed as a map for use in Greenwich. If, as Gilbert (2004, 20) contends, 'mapping often determines or alters the human practices within the territory it defines', then the use of Nold's map can only contribute to the emotionality of the mapped territory.

There is a danger that emotional maps are understood only as art. However, as with any other map this privileges the aesthetic over the representative: although emotions are subjective, they can be indicative of wider social perceptions, and they certainly contribute to structuring the reality of our experiences of an environment. According to Hochschild (1998, 6), '[l]ike other senses, hearing, touch and smell, emotion is a means by which we continually learn and re-learn about a just-now-changed, back-and-forth relation between self and world.' Nold has understood this in his emotional mapping; although conceived as art, he has been careful not to ignore the political implications of his work. Instead, Nold has acknowledged that the discussion of his maps is at least as important as the maps, particularly in relation to social policy formation, such as local regeneration schemes (Nold 2006) (see also Rachel Grant's discussion in this volume). Sensitivity to emotions, as represented on maps, can be just as valuable a tool in understanding our environment as geographic maps: both are representations of some facets of our individual realities.

Conclusion

In this chapter I have highlighted some of the reactions that we have in relation to some maps – from frustration to joy, sorrow to excitement – and the ways in which emotions are now being 'mapped' on to our physical surroundings. Despite common appreciation of the map as a mundane, flavourless – unemotional (as my friend suggested) – item, maps are clearly not insipid: they are emotionally complex, deserving further study. The world of maps, the world which we map, is changing, as new appreciations of the emotional are represented (by the likes of Nold (2006)) and as new technologies change our interactions with maps (through Global Positioning Satellites and Satellite Navigation).

These maps are comprised of many elements: physical and emotional, 'official' and 'unofficial', masculine and feminine. To express these as binaries is misleading, however, as maps are sites that can simultaneously take on – or have superimposed upon them – characteristics of both sides of any of these binaries. These are relational elements, mutually constitutive, of maps and mobility as of identities. How space, gender and emotions interact on – and in the use of – maps is clearly complex, and demands subtle readings. This chapter has only been able to make a start in this work – perhaps not mapping the way (too grand), but at least exposing the territory for others to find their own way through?

References

Adams, J. (2007), Artwork on the Regional Rail Network. [Online]. Available at: www.alternativeplatform.googlepages.com/home [accessed 24 September 2007].
Anon. (1863), ' Editorial', *The Times*, 27 February, 8.
Anon. (1893), 'Editorial', *The Times*, 8 March, 9.
Anon. (1908), 'Maps and Map-Reading for Motorists. I', *The Times*, 1 September, 11.
Anon. (1915), 'The Map Sense', *The Times*, 6 April, 9.
Anon. (1919), 'Map-making', *The Times*, 26 September, 11.
Anon. (1931), 'The Map-Reader', *The Times*, 10 December, 15.
Anon. (1932), 'The Ordnance Survey', *The Times*, 3 August, 11.
Anon. (1941), 'Looking at the Map', *The Times*, 16 April, 5.
Anon. (1960), 'Off the Map', *The Times*, 13 April, 11.
Anon. (1963), 'According to the Map', *The Times*, 10 May, 15.

Anon. (1965), 'The Map Age', *The Times*, 9 March, 13.

Anon. (1973), 'Putting IT on the Map', *The Times*, 3 January, 13.

Anon. (2007a), Ordnance Survey Invites You to Explore [Online], (Updated 14 September 2007), http://explore.ordnancesurvey.co.uk/public/document/about_explore [accessed 22 September 2007].

Anon. (2007b), Get Lost. Artists Map Downtown New York [Online], www.newmuseum.org/getlost/index.html [accessed 24 September 2007].

Bendelow, G. and Williams, S. (1998), 'Introduction: emotions in social life' in G. Bendelow and S. Williams (eds).

Bendelow, G. and Williams, S. (eds) (1998), *Emotions in Social Life: Critical Themes and Contemporary Issues* (London: Routledge).

Burke, T. (1932), *City of Encounters: A London Divertissement* (London: Constable).

Cantor, D. (1977), *The Psychology of Place* (London: Architectural Press).

Chesterton, G. K. (1901), 'Walking Tours', *Daily News*, 23 September, 55.

Davidson, J., Bondi, L. and Smith, M. (2005), 'Introduction' in J. Davidson, L. Bondi and M. Smith (eds).

Davidson, J., Bondi, L. and Smith, M. (eds) (2005), *Emotional Geographies* (Aldershot: Ashgate).

de Certeau, M. (1984), trans. S. Rendall, *The Practice of Everyday Life* (Berkeley: University of California Press).

Gilbert, P. (2004), *Mapping the Victorian Social Body* (Albany: State University of New York Press).

Golledge, R. (1999), 'Human Wayfinding and Cognitive Maps' in R. Golledge (ed.).

Golledge, R. (ed.) (1999), *Wayfinding Behavior: Cognitive Mapping and Other Spatial Processes* (Baltimore: Johns Hopkins University Press).

Harley, J.B. (Edited posthumously by Laxton, P.) (2001), *The New Nature of Maps: Essays in the History of Cartography* (Baltimore: Johns Hopkins University Press).

Hochschild, A.R. (1998), 'The Sociology of Emotion as a Way of Seeing' in G. Bendelow and S. Williams (eds).

Humpherys, A. (2002), 'Knowing the Victorian City: writing and representation', *Victorian Literature and Culture*, 30, 2, 601–612.

Massey, D. (2005), *For Space* (London: Sage).

Monmonier, M. (1996), *How to Lie with Maps, Second Edition* (Chicago: University of Chicago Press).

Nead, L. (2000), *Victorian Babylon: People, Streets and Images in Nineteenth-Century London* (New Haven: Yale University Press).

Nold, C. (2006), Christian Nold Interviewed by Anna Bentkowska-Kafel [Online] (Updated 3 August 2006), www.biomapping.net/interview.htm [accessed 9 September 2007].

Nold, C. (2007), Greenwich Emotion Map [Online], www.emotionmap.net/GreenwichEmotionMap.pdf [accessed 9 September 2007].

Oatley, K. (2004), *Emotions. A Brief History* (Oxford: Blackwell).

'Oracle' (2006), New BBC Weather Maps. [Online] (Updated 3 September 2007), www.weeklygripe.co.uk/a275.asp [accessed 24 September 2007].

Ramesh, R. (2007), 'War of words as highest battlefield prepares for first tourist invasion', *The Guardian*, 18 September, 31.

Rodaway, P. (1994), *Sensuous Geographies. Body, Sense and Place* (London: Routledge).

Wood, D. (1993), *The Power of Maps* (London: Routledge).

Wormley, N. (1977), 'The Fascination of Maps', *The Map Collector*, 1, 2–3.

Section 2

Introduction: Moving Off – Autobiographical Perspectives

Gayle Letherby and Gillian Reynolds

Writing Auto/biographically

Our own interest in auto/biography is reflected in one of our earliest publications: a multi-authored book chapter focusing on experiences of the postgraduate process (Holliday et al. 1993). Thus, and as we have argued before (Letherby and Reynolds 2005), we would agree with Charles Wright Mills (1959, 204) that: 'The social scientist is not some autonomous being standing outside society, the question is where he [sic] stands within it.' Not surprisingly then we are impressed by his advice regarding the use of personal life experience in intellectual work and his view that we are personally involved in the intellectual work that we do (Mills 1959). The use of 'I' in our research accounts and other writing has a particular value, as the 'autobiographical I' is 'inquiring and analytical' (Stanley 1993, 49–50). Writing in the first person helps to make clear the author's role in constructing rather than discovering the story/knowledge (Letherby 2000; Bertram 1998; Mykhalovskiy 1996; Stanley 1993). Yet, historically, the writing of *sociological* autobiography that overtly draws on the life experiences of the author has been less common:

> Academic discourse in general isn't very good at acknowledging the materiality of its own production, the resources and labour that enable its existence … Only the acknowledgements page – split off from the main body of the text … as euphemized recognition of hierarchized 'debts'; intellectual over personal or domestic – gives any clue as to the text's material origins (Potts and Price 1995, 102–3).

This situation has since improved, not least because of the work of the British Sociological Association Auto/Biography Study Group and reflection on the differences between biography, autobiography and auto/biography in sociology (and the social sciences more generally). Autobiography and biography focus on the importance of one, several or many lives, recognizing the need to re-socialize the individual, to liberate the individual from individualism – to demonstrate how individuals are social selves – important because a focus on the individual can contribute to the understanding of the general (Evans 1997; Mills 1959). Self-conscious auto/biography recognizes the relationship between the self and other within the research process (e.g. Letherby 2003; Okely 1992). We, like some others, would argue that research is always auto/biographical in that, when reflecting on and writing from our own autobiographies, we reflect on our relationship with the biographies of others: similarly, when researching, interpreting and writing the biographies or narratives of others, we inevitably refer to and reflect on our own autobiographies. Acknowledging such connections increases the academic rigour of our work.

Background Issues to Moving Off

In 1999, Liz Stanley described herself as a 'child of her time', suggesting that intellectual/academic socialization affects our interests and approaches. We too would describe ourselves as 'children of our time', influenced by (amongst other things) an auto/biographical revival within sociology in the 1990s. Of course, thinking of the more traditional use of the term socialization, we have also been influenced by parents, peers and early life experiences, some of which are evident in our first book together, *Train Tracks: Work, Play and Politics on the Railways* – which specifically addressed train travel, space and place (Letherby and Reynolds 2005). Below are extracts from brief autobiographical statements in the Introduction of *Train Tracks*:

> [Gillian] I continue to use trains for both work and leisure – I have been known to go to a station and purchase a ticket for the next departing train without even knowing beforehand where the train will be going ... Researching for this book was an opportunity to explore not only the train per se, but also my own love affair with it.
>
> [Gayle] The train is an important place for me – a space where I work and play. 'I'm on the train' is a phrase that I could use more than anyone I know. Sometimes I reflect on the number of days that I've spent on the track. But it's not time that's been wasted, it's been productive and enjoyable (Letherby and Reynolds 2005, 14).

In his argument for the use of mobile methods to study mobility/ies, John Urry (2007) suggests that social researchers' own time-space (travel) diaries prompt reflexivity. We would suggest that auto/biographical reflexivity is limited neither to diary keeping, nor to sociologists. In this book, for example, it is present in various ways. Our Acknowledgements, for example (see reference to this by Price and Potts (1995) above), give you some insight into our particular 'debts'. For personal detail – including some indication of how contributors' past experiences and passions are relevant to current concerns with travel and transport – look at Notes on Contributors. The other three main sections of this book are more 'traditional', focusing as they do on theoretical background issues, travellers' and transport workers' experiences. Yet, even here, there is clearly some connection to the auto/biographical: some contributors draw on empirical work and therefore are concerned with the biographies of others; some highlight the significance of their identity as sociologist, historian and so on; some draw on their own autobiographical interests and experiences and some do combinations of these. Issues of autobiography are more explicit, however, in this section, in that contributors draw on personal experiences in order to outline some of their own engagement with gender, emotion and travel.

Moving Off

Having argued the case for the seriousness of auto/biographical practice within academic work, it is important to note that the chapters in this section of the book are not academic pieces in the traditional sense. Rather, we asked academic colleagues to 'step out' of their academic interests and disciplines and to write about issues and experiences that affected them personally, and we asked non-academic friends and acquaintances to similarly reflect on their emotional relationship to gender and travel. This meant that most of the authors here were working outside their usual practices, outside their comfort zones, and thus the stories told reflect the 'raw' emotions of the teller, rather than a sanitized research account. Auto/biography is sometimes criticized for its self-indulgence but, like Judith Okely (1992), we would suggest that 'self' awareness and a critical scrutiny of the self is quite different from self-adoration and self-indulgence. As Michel de Certeau (1984, 70) argues:

> ... 'stories' provide the decorative container of a *narrativity* for everyday practices. To be sure, they describe only fragments of these practices. They are no more than its metaphors. But ... they represent a new variant in the continuous series of narrative documents, which ... set forth ways of operating in the form of *tales* ... A similar continuity suggests a certain *theoretical* relevance of narrativity so far as everyday practices are concerned.

Beyond a connection with the auto/biographical and the central themes of this book, there are other links to be made across and between the 15 short chapters in this section. Other editors, and indeed other readers, will find different connections and links and we do not present the following as the only ways to read what follows, merely as some suggestions for consideration. Deciding how to order the chapters in this section was not easy and in the end we opted for an approach that reflects popular sociological concepts: the research process, public and personal identity, paid employment, place/space/time and the body. Again, others might have organized the section differently.

With reference to the research process, it is not as unusual as it once was for the researcher to locate her/himself within the research process and produce 'first person' accounts. This involves an explicit recognition that, as researchers, our research activities tell us things about ourselves as well as about those we are researching (Steier 1991). Further, social scientists acknowledge that we need to consider how the researcher as author is positioned in relation to the research process: how the process affects the product in relation to the choice and design of the research fieldwork and analysis, editorship and presentation (Letherby 2003; Sparkes 1998; Iles 1992). Several of the chapters that follow represent stories of research and/or stories from research. In Chapter 4, 'The Railwaywoman's Journey', Helena Wojtczak overtly relates some of the gendered and emotional frustrations involved in researching the history of railwaywomen in the UK, where railway interest is still largely perceived as an exclusively masculine pursuit. This focus on the female researcher in a 'man's world' is continued by Zannagh Hatton in Chapter 5, 'In Search of the Tarmac Cowboys'. Here, the gendered positioning of the researcher is more oblique: family relationships, a gender-subversive childhood, questions of dress code and the gendered perception of risk-taking. Hatton's research focus was on a specific section – local young men – of the community, and, as artist Rachel Grant (Chapter 6) reflects on her art project within a geographical community in ' "Inside Out": Walking a Community Art Journey', she also explores both her own emotions and those of a marginalized group of young people. These three chapters are all examples of women tackling issues that are politically controversial and largely excluded from traditional gendered perceptions of research and researchers: evidence that, as women engage with community-building and new forms of political and affective attachments, 'they may be inventing new kinds of gendered mobilities' (Sheller 2008, 262).

Grant is not the only author in this section to highlight the connections between art, travel and emotion. In 'Rural Life on Ynys Môn: Journeys Made and Unmade' (Chapter 7), Ruth Waterhouse travels mentally into a picture that generates for her a significant set of childhood reminiscences. Combining auto/ biographical commentary, personal reflection, and rigorous sociological research, she interweaves the image before her and the images in her memory to explore ways in which her private identity connects with, gets tangled in, or diverges from, historical, public (social) identities embedded in the social history of North Wales.

The concepts of public and private identity lead us to a group of contributions concerning paid employment, the world of work – and, incidentally – to jobs that are all historically associated with being 'in a man's world'. In 'Double Clutchin', Bucket Tippin', Juggernaut Driving, Truckin' Time: A Trucker's Tale' (Chapter 8*)*, Stephen Handsley explores how the trucking industry has been perceived as the 'last bastion' of 'real men'. Using the examples of language, humour, dress codes and sexuality, Handsley shows how this perception is constructed and maintained, often by both men and women. In 'From Embryo to Dinosaur? A Railwayman's Journey' (Chapter 9), Bob Hart illustrates what might, at first glance, also seem a classically masculine account of a masculine career. But such accounts have tended to distance themselves from the existence of any emotion other than excitement. As well as that excitement, Hart here acknowledges the emotions of anger and frustration involved in his passion for driving trains, a career sought after by 'all' boys of previous generations (Golding 1918).

In Chapters 10 and 11, the theme of paid employment is continued, but Debra Langan and Karen Overton both illustrate different kinds of challenge to the masculinist perception of working in/with transport. In 'Roll On Down the Highway' (Chapter 10), Langan describes her experiences of driving taxis in Canada, indeed following in her own mother's footsteps. Emphasizing the advantages of operating against the prevailing gendered norms, she also, like Hart, acknowledges a wide mixture of emotions. Karen Overton, on the other hand, reflects on her time of heading up a youth project in New York, which teaches the building, re-building, maintenance and use of bicycles. In her account, 'Of Life and Bicycle Hubs' (Chapter 11), she recalls the difficulties, and sometimes hilarity, involved in operating amidst the gender-bias among the young men and women she worked with, and cared for, in the project.

Paid employment, of course, is not the only place where gendered identities are constructed and enacted. Home and family are also influential in such constructions. Jonathan Kington and Jen Marchbank both reflect on their experiences of grief and how travelling affected, and was affected by, this emotion. In 'Living on Wheels' (Chapter 12), Kington describes living with a large dog in a small camper-van, then a caravan, following the death of his wife. In Chapter 13, 'Travelling Through Veils of Tears', Marchbank writes about being in the public spaces/places of aeroplanes and airports, and the private space of a car, following the deaths of her grandmother and father. Both writers illuminate the gendered aspects of expressed grief and perceptions of its legitimacy, within the context of personal and social identity. Their contributions make it clear that women, and indeed men, may experience the mobilities associated with migration as 'simultaneously liberative and coercive, enabling new projects of the self, yet constraining them into certain gendered/racialised performances' (Sheller 2008, 260), which itself depends to a large degree on where they are at the time of the 'performance'.

Space/place/time is a concept widely featured in the final group of contributions. As Kay Milton (2007, 71) notes, '[a] study of people's cultural understandings of nature ... begins with an analysis of how they, *as individuals*, engage with the nonhuman things in their environment, and of the emotional content of that engagement.' In this vein, the remaining contributions to this section relate to emotional, gendered and utilitarian negotiation with material vehicles (Chapters 14, 15 and 16); and also with the natural nonhuman world we often encounter whilst travelling (Chapters 17 and 18). The former group represent a different approach to emotion and gender, in that it is the vehicle itself rather than external issues that generates the feelings. In 'Road Rage' (Chapter 14), for example, Keith Sharp reflects upon the largely extreme and gendered emotions that come from driving on congested roads. Andy Reynolds ('Learning to Fly', Chapter 15), conversely, reports the need to set aside all emotion until after landing the plane, and in 'Born to be Wild?' (Chapter 16), Mike Barnsley explores his own ambivalent feelings about his masculinist passion for a certain kind of motorbike.

The final group of contributions to this section are much concerned with our (gendered) bodies and their engagement with the natural world. Women are often defined as lacking a 'mobile subjectivity', being rooted in place and home, while narratives of masculine becoming often hinge on travel and freedom from home (Sheller 2008, 258). Carole Sutton's account (Chapter 17, 'Moving Bodies in Running') both supports and challenges such gendered norms, as she analyzes her own 'running' diaries. Sheller (2008) goes on to argue that the male body is culturally performed as a more mobile body, while the female body becomes more restricted and spatially circumscribed. Again, John Shiels' contribution (Chapter 18, 'No Ticket to Ride') both challenges and supports these norms. Describing hitchhiking as an escape from the confines of home and a proscribed social identity, he explores his increasingly 'fatalistic acceptance' of powerlessness where the 'only certainty was uncertainty' – an emotion more easily stereotyped as feminine.

In a variety of ways, then, all the contributions to this section explore aspects of gender and emotion. These, in turn, both affect, and are affected by, the experience of travel.

References

Bertram V. (1998), 'Theorising the Personal: Using Autobiography in Academic Writing' in S. Jackson and G. Jones (eds).

de Certeau, M. (1984) (trans. Stephen Rendall), *The Practice of Everyday Life* (Berkeley: University of California Press).

Evans, M. (1997), *Introducing Contemporary Feminist Thought* (Cambridge: Polity Press).

Golding, H. (ed.) (1918), *The Wonder Book of Railways for Boys and Girls* (London: Ward Lock).

Holliday, R., Letherby, G., Mann, L., Ramsay, K. and Reynolds, G. (1993), 'Room of Our Own: an alternative to academic isolation' in M. Kennedy, C. Lubelska and V. Walsh (eds).

Iles, T. (1992), *All Sides of the Subject: Women and Biography* (New York: Teacher's College).

Jackson, S. and Jones, G. (eds) (1998), *Contemporary Feminist Theories* (Edinburgh: Edinburgh University).

Kennedy, M., Lubelska, C. and Walsh, V. (eds) (1993), *Making Connections: Women's Studies, Women's Movements, Women's Lives* (London: Falmer Press, Taylor and Francis).

Lee-Treweek, G. and Linkogle, S. (eds) (2000), *Danger in the Field: Risk and Ethics in Social Research* (London: Routledge).

Letherby, G. (2003), *Feminist Research in Theory and Practice* (Buckingham: Open University).

Letherby, G. (2000), 'Dangerous Liaisons: Auto/biography in Research and Research Writing' in G. Lee-Treweek and S. Linkogle (eds).

Letherby, G. and Reynolds, G. (2005), *Train Tracks: Work, Play and Politics on the Railways* (Oxford: Berg).

Mills, C.W. (1959), *The Sociological Imagination* (London: Penguin).

Milton, K. (2007 [2005]), 'Emotion (or Life, The Universe, Everything)' in H. Wulff (ed.).

Morley, L. and Walsh, V. (eds) (1995), *Feminist Academics: Creative Agents for Change* (London: Taylor and Francis).

Mykhalovskiy, E. (1996), 'Reconsidering Table Talk: critical thoughts on the relationship between sociology, autobiography and self-indulgence', *Qualitative Sociology* 19, 1, 131–51.

Okely, J. (1992), 'Anthropology and Autobiography: Participatory Experience and Embodied Knowledge' in J. Okely and H. Callaway (eds).

Okely, J. and Callaway, H. (eds) (1992), *Anthropology and Autobiography* (London: Routledge).

Potts, T. and Price, J. (1995), 'Out of the blood and spirit of our lives: the place of the body in academic feminism' in L. Morley and V. Walsh (eds).

Shaklock, G. and Smyth, J. (eds) (1998), *Being Reflexive in Critical Educational and Social Research* (London: Falmer).

Sparkes, A. (1998), 'Reciprocity in Critical Research? Some unsettling thoughts' in G. Shaklock and J. Smyth (eds).

Stanley, L. (1999), 'Children of Our Time: politics, ethics and feminist research processes'. Paper presented at Feminism and Educational Research Methodologies Conference, Institute of Education, Manchester Metropolitan University.

Stanley, L. (1993), 'On Auto/Biography in Sociology', *Sociology* 27, 1, 41–52.

Sheller, M. (2008), 'Gendered Mobilities: Epilogue' in T.P. Uteng and T. Cresswell (eds).

Steier, F. (1991), *Research and Reflexivity* (London: Sage).

Urry, J. (2007), *Mobilities* (Cambridge: Polity).

Uteng, T.P. and Cresswell, T. (eds) (2008), *Gendered Mobilities* (Aldershot: Ashgate).

Wulff, H (ed.) (2007), *The Emotions: A Cultural Reader* (Oxford: Berg).

Chapter 4

The Railwaywoman's Journey

Helena Wojtczak

Feminist writer Dale Spender (1990) made many interesting observations about men's attitude to women's history research. Her argument that women's history is as rich as men's, and that our lack of knowledge of it is part of our oppression, strikes a particular chord with my experience. The reason this seems so pertinent is that, while researching and writing the history of women working on the railways, I have met with ridicule and discouragement and have even met people who think that, to be interested in women's history, a woman must be either a man-hater or a lesbian, which they use as labels of insult.

I began my journey not as a student or academic but as a teenager from a working-class family, employed as a train guard for British Rail. Few women worked on the railway and most were carriage cleaners or canteen assistants. It was frequently remarked that women had never worked on the operational side of the industry and that I had been the first female guard when recruited in 1977. All my colleagues were men and I spent many hours in their company. We would read during breaks between trains and, spotting my books on suffragette history, they poked fun at me, treatment noticeably absent when male colleagues read, say, military or transport history.

I developed an awareness of the historic side of the railway and was particularly keen to study the history of my predecessors, the railway workers who had run the industry since the 1830s. Fortunately, there were a number of published books on the subject. Some made no reference to women; others mentioned that they replaced men during the 1939–45 war. Such scanty coverage gave the impression that even the war workers were not numerous and so I was astonished when, within a 700-page history of a railway trade union (that, incidentally, contained only three references to women), I read that 100,000 were employed in 1944. I decided to research them, hoping to garner sufficient material for a short article.

During the early years of my research, the ridicule, pessimism and derision I received sometimes made me reticent to mention my project. My male colleagues made fun of me; some suggested I interview the many 'old women' amongst us ('old woman' in this context being an insulting term for a man). Visiting archives, record offices and museums, I met railway enthusiasts, some of whom suggested that I was wasting my time because railwaywomen had no history 'unless you count cleaners'. Some laughed; others expressed bewilderment: 'wasn't women's railway history the same as men's?'

While researching the Second World War workers, ostensibly the pioneers, I discovered that their mothers' generation had performed identical work during the First World War. Delving further, I unearthed a cornucopia of hidden history: women had been employed since the dawn of the railway industry in the 1830s and in hundreds of different jobs. After fifteen years of research I had amassed nearly two hundred photographs spanning one-and-a-half centuries and a plethora of documents that emphatically disproved the myths I had been told. My narrative amounted to a hefty 300,000 words – a far cry from the brief article I'd envisaged. Being armed with so much data about railwaywomen's contribution to the industry gave me the confidence to speak knowledgeably and assertively to those who dared to deride my research subject.

Spender (1990) observed that men's superior position in society enables them to decide what is valued and what is real. This theory was soon put to the test. When an amateur railway historian stated that no women had worked in the industry until quite recently, I informed him that they had been crossing keepers for 150 years. However, he deemed them insignificant because of their low numbers. Luckily, I was able to counter that objection with an impressive statistic: 13,000 women were employed before the war in 1914. He asserted that these women were of no importance; they were only cleaners, caterers and clerks, not 'real' railway workers. Nobody would dispute that track-workers, guards and signalmen are real, and in wartime women performed all three jobs. But no, he retorted, they didn't count either. They were temporary. I reminded him that many railwaymen's service was also five years or less. But, he argued, in wartime women didn't take their work seriously; after all, post-war, they returned to the home. No straw was too flimsy for him to clutch in his determination to prove that women can never be 'real' railway workers. Men, not women, are the 'real' workforce and only men's definition of 'real' is valid.

On Internet railway history discussion groups I was almost always the sole female member and was tolerated until I related an anecdote or statistic referring to female staff. This would always provoke reactions that were wholly absent when male staff were discussed. After mentioning a wartime signalwoman, for example, I was told they did not exist. Providing a newspaper cutting as proof, I was told newspapers were 'unreliable'. Supplying a photograph was futile: it was deemed 'wartime propaganda'; a personal memoir from a former signalwoman was 'a pack of lies'. Hearing that a railwaywoman was awarded a medal for bravery provoked comments that she probably didn't deserve it. Because my references to women always inflamed antagonistic comments, one website administrator asked me to leave and start a separate group to discuss railwaywomen. Initially, I refused to collude with rendering women invisible by placing them in a ghetto where they could be ignored and forgotten. But it was so infuriating to hear women's achievements belittled, so exasperating to have every piece of primary source evidence disallowed, and so exhausting to wage an incessant sex-war single-handedly, that I left, allowing the members to revert to their pretence that women have never worked on the railways.

The staff of one railway union ignored my several requests for information so I complained to the general secretary. He said he doubted if anyone would read my book, withheld the information and told his staff to ignore me. Since publication, all attempts to get my book reviewed or featured in that union's journal have been ignored. I have received criticism for mentioning the institutionalized discrimination against women within the railway industry, because all other industries acted the same way. Of course, if every historian of every industry omitted this information, all sex discrimination would be absent from written history and deemed not to exist.

My motivation for researching women was assumed to be different from the motivation to research men. I have frequently been challenged to justify why I am so interested in women's past. Men's history is the norm; no man ever had to give a reason for studying it. My reason for researching women is often misconstrued as antagonism towards men rather than a desire to tell women's story. (It is curious how often the focus of attention is placed on men by others, even though they are not the subject of my research.)

As I have noted before (Wojtczak 2002), Deidre Beddoe, Britain's first Professor of Women's History, points out that, in excluding women, conventional history only tells half the story. Women's experience of railway work is entirely different to that of men because, for the first 150 years of their employment, they were governed by a set of rules and regulations, customs and practices that applied only to females. The fact that my manuscript amounted to 300,000 words proved conclusively that railwaywomen have their own, unique, untold story, one that has been omitted from the many published histories of railwaymen that are mistakenly thought of as histories of railway workers.

It cannot be doubted that earlier writers of railway labour history found documents referring to women while examining primary sources: it would be impossible to bypass them. There is, in particular, an enormous and easily accessible collection of First World War photographs of women in formerly male-only, uniformed positions. It is clear that my predecessors made a conscious decision to omit women, helping to exacerbate the myth that the history of railwaymen is the definitive history of all railway workers. Moreover, by failing to mention this omission, they concealed the fact that railwaywomen even possessed a history of their own, thus helping to keep them shrouded in mystery and ensuring the invisibility of a possible future research subject. One is reminded of another of Spender's (1990, 4) assertions: 'a patriarchal society depends in large measure on the experience and values of males being perceived as the only valid frame of reference for society, and that it is therefore in patriarchal interest to prevent women from establishing their equally real, valid and different frame of reference.'

Although my research was completed in 2005, my troubles were far from over. Obstacles have been placed in my way that would not have existed had the book been about men. As my book was the first to be published on the subject of railwaywomen, nobody had any previous experience of how the subject might be received, and yet Britain's largest railway publisher rejected the book; a railway-specialist bookshop refused to stock it because 'we cannot waste shelf-space on a book that won't sell', and an online specialist railway bookseller declined even to advertise it on his website because 'our customers are all male chauvinists.' The editor of a leading railway magazine declined to review the book, sight unseen, stating that none of his ten thousand readers worldwide would be interested in the subject. They were wrong: almost all my trackable sales (i.e. website and mail order) are to men.

There is no such thing as an homogenous 'male attitude' to my research. When my investigations began, my daily life was populated with blue-collar railwaymen, many of whom poked fun at my research and made lewd or belittling comments. As I moved forward on my journey and began to mix with railway enthusiasts and amateur historians, such remarks were fewer and were diluted by many favourable comments. As my research brought me into contact with professional people such as librarians, archivists, curators, academics and historians, my subject was treated as any other piece of serious research. These days my railway journey runs through a different terrain: my research is highly regarded and the book has been praised in 35 published reviews and dozens of private compliments from readers.

In one (otherwise flattering) review, however, I was accused of having a predetermined agenda before I wrote the book. This bias was, apparently, an 'anti-male' one. My book is certainly critical of men's oppression of women, but this is based purely on facts unearthed during a 16-year journey of discovery. The book was compiled from material collected from railway companies', trades unions' and government documents, from newspapers and other publications, and from the first-hand testimony of dozens of women who worked on the railways between 1930 and 2005. This material, which is meticulously cited and referenced, reveals an unbroken flow of 175 years of attitudes, words and deeds that are transparently and consistently anti-female. The only way to avoid being labelled 'anti-male' would be to deliberately conceal railwaymen's poor treatment of their female colleagues, or to become an apologist on their behalf by continually justifying their misogynistic behaviour in a desperate attempt to excuse it. Is it part of women's oppression that we are expected to collude with it by suppressing information that reveals misogyny? Interestingly, the reviewer who made this accusation was female, while none of my 25 male reviewers thought the book anti-male; indeed, some have cringed to read how members of their sex treated women.

Having ceased to work on the railway, I am no longer subjected to colleagues' disparaging remarks, though I do encounter pockets of hostility among railway enthusiasts. I still meet with bewilderment; sometimes while marketing the book I am asked: 'Railwaywomen? What on earth are railwaywomen?'

References

Spender, D. (1990), *Women of Ideas and What Men Have Done to Them* (London: Pandora).
Wojtczak, H. (2005), *Railwaywomen: Exploitation, Betrayal and Triumph in the Workplace* (Hastings: Hastings Press).
Wojtczak, H. (2002), *Women of Victorian Hastings* (Hastings: Hastings Press).

Chapter 5

In Search of the Tarmac Cowboys

Zannagh Hatton

Researching and writing *The Tarmac Cowboys: An Ethnographic Study of the Cultural World of Boy Racers* (2007) as a doctoral student might have seemed an unusual activity for a forty-something-year-old woman, but for me, raised in a climate of cars, motorbikes and motor sport, it did not present an onerous task. My father, an entrepreneurial type of person, a builder by trade, and collector of cars and motorbikes in his spare time, harboured a passion for motor sport. For him the glitz and the glamour of the world of Formula One Racing with its millions of pounds investment and sponsorship deals, the clean cut lines of the cars and the sinuous expanse of a Le Mans race circuit held little appeal. His passion was found in the dirt and grime of scrap dealers' yards where he regularly negotiated a route around snarling and snapping dogs of indeterminate breeds in his quest for a vehicle which he could rebuild and thus create his own 'racing machine'.

On such visits there was seldom a 'Eureka' moment and he would emerge somewhat dishevelled, not only with a car body shell but with a variety of other pieces of car including engines and gear boxes. Having taken safe delivery of his purchases he would disappear into his garage for prolonged periods. Occasionally he would surface for food and brief conversations, the subjects of which never extended much beyond spark plugs and manifolds. My mother despaired. When he thought my hands were big enough to pass him a series of spanners and wrenches I was recruited as his assistant. His garage was an exciting place, an Aladdin's cave where a variety of objects adorned the walls, floors and workbench and bits of cars lay all over the place. It was a Health and Safety Officer's nightmare yet my father's toolbox was immaculate, with tools clean and shining, organized like those of a surgeon.

We lived in a rural area where public transport was nonexistent so having access to a vehicle was essential. We had a 'normal' family car but this spent most of its life in an open fronted implement shed as the garage was usually fully occupied by the latest in a long line of projects. Unfortunately, my father would seek to change the family car with unerring frequency. It reached the stage whereby my mother refused to drive any more due to having constantly to adapt her minimal driving skills and nervous disposition to meet the requirements of a variety of vehicles, including a small tipper lorry, a motorcycle and sidecar, a Morris Minor, a Morgan sports car and a Ford Capri. At one stage my father became the proud owner of a vintage steamroller. It was evident to me that he derived a deep sense of personal satisfaction from spending his time and disposable income on cars and car related practices. It was an interest not shared by my mother and her resentment towards the time (and money) he devoted to these interests was instrumental in bringing about an acrimonious divorce a few years later.

Having acquired a vehicle, my father would spend ages subverting its original specification, removing things like external badges and insignia, and increasing its engine capacity. His justification for such practices was not just for aesthetic purposes: he could take the reworked vehicle and race it on a grass or cinder track, demonstrating not only his consummate driving skills but also his engineering abilities. His work provided a talking point for onlookers as they tried to determine what make and model of vehicle stood before them, especially when the modifications were often so extreme. In brief, my father was an early exponent in the art of 'moddin', modifying a car's appearance and performance.

At the age of 16 I 'hung out' with the local lads who were car fanatics and regulars on the Autocross or Banger Racing circuits. My mother was thoroughly disapproving and blamed my father, but undeterred, almost every weekend I would travel the country with what she determined were 'undesirable influences' in their cars, in order to compete on various circuits. Unlike many of my peers, preparing for 'a date' didn't present me with agonies about what to wear, how to do my hair or make-up because I knew that such efforts would be wasted once my prospective date set eyes upon my mode of transportation. This was particularly evident when at 17 my father produced for me a heavily modified Austin A30 saloon. It was unrecognizable as such because he had lowered the suspension, chopped the roof, extended the bodywork, uprated the engine and covered its unfortunate lime green bodywork in graphics. It was a truly awesome machine, and I experienced a rush of enormous satisfaction and glee at traffic lights or at a road junction when something that had cost three times as much pulled up alongside. I knew that I could out-accelerate it and would inevitably do so, shrieking, 'Eat my dust', leaving my fellow road users choking in my wake and staring in disapproval (or was it disbelief) as this apparition roared away.

Fast forward my life 20 years, several different vehicles later and a number of penalties for various traffic violations, usually speeding; inevitably, perhaps, I became attracted to the car-based cultural practices of a group of young men who lived close to my home. Many of them appeared to have been labelled as dangerous or as accidents waiting to happen, and some media had attributed to them an umbrella term which was simply 'Boy Racers'. This appeared to be used as an all-embracing description of any young man, usually under the age of 25, who drove a particular make and model of car 'with attitude' and who accompanied such outings with loud music with a predominately bass beat. It seemed to me that this music was their trademark or anthem, and the sound of the bass was the quintessential signature of Boy Racers, signifying a certain insubordination, the very sound of undisciplined youth. You heard them; even felt the vibration of the music before you saw them as they drove through the towns with their stereos playing at full decibels and their windows open as they used their music to set the mood or tone for their planned night of activities ahead. The way they invaded these public domains, reclaiming and redefining them as their own, their performative displays of driving skills and daring, their occasional challenges to authority and the camaraderie they displayed, was setting them apart from other young male car drivers. In some ways these young men had come to represent the cowboys of the twenty-first century who rode into town, not on American bred 'Quarter Horses', but in highly modified cars which challenged the senses and stirred the emotions. So, for me, these 'Boy Racers' were, and always will be, the 'Tarmac Cowboys'.

To find out more about the lives of these young men, their beliefs and the motivational factors which drove them to modify their cars and engage in such risky exhibitionism, I undertook a lengthy ethnographical research assignment. My fieldwork began with four young men, mechanics from a local garage, who felt that it was important I should visually fit in with them, for appearance was paramount. Accompanying them had all the hallmarks and formality of being invited to a prestigious event where certain protocols had to be followed, even to dress code and behaviour. Yet there was never any agonizing decision about what to wear: it was a simple uniform such as they all wore, comprising T-shirt or sweatshirt and jeans, baseball cap and trainers. Undoubtedly, some of the richest encoded masculine fantasies surround elements of speed, control, risk and daring, and in my chosen role of researcher, I was faced with the dilemma that unless I was to take an active part in their world, I would be unable to 'live' or experience these fantasies: simply reporting second-hand experiences would lose some of the 'raw' vibe. At first, jumping into a proffered car, the thought used to cross my mind that in less than a few minutes we could be encased in metal and wrapped around a tree or a lamp post. Yet this was my chance to experience first hand the thrills (and spills) as the young men engaged in the sort of performative, risky practices and speed with which the description 'Boy Racer' was becoming synonymous. Initially, I was content just to be a passenger, observing, listening and soaking up the atmosphere; more often than not consigned to the back seat, surrounded by what they termed my 'gear' consisting of note book, a supply of pens, tape recorder, spare batteries and tapes, films and camera, loose change, chewing gum and extra sweatshirt (the latter items hardly ever for my own use).

A gathering of boy racers, or, to use their parlance, a 'meet', often occurred in an 'out of town' retail park or a multi-story car park. Many of the car parks' owners had attempted to restrict access after a certain time at night by installing barriers across the car park entrances. In implementing such measures they were effectively reducing the boy racers' repertoire of 'playgrounds'. However, they underestimated the excitement and challenge such installations brought. Far from presenting a minor inconvenience, these barriers, which had been imposed to curtail undesirable nocturnal activities, provided a challenge: they were obstacles to be overcome, signifying the liberation of a venue where atmosphere could be created and where anything could happen. A place where there was an existential freeing of the self to an uncertainty which for the boy racers seemed to be 'new' or 'different' every time. Accessing these prohibited areas opened the way to adventure where possibility constituted a kind of grounded aesthetics of risk and risk-taking, where risk was esteemed, yet the adventures which followed might be trivial: a bet or wager against whose car was quickest between two fixed points, or who had the best music system in 'sound off' competitions. The events created a *frisson*, a heightened atmosphere of possibility where they or their peers could be stopped by the police or local authorities. It was almost as if some of the young men wanted to invent through their car-related activities, their own trials by performance in uncertain situations. The nature of the risks they took, the way they structured these risks, the way they dealt with them, indicated components of young masculinity which were perhaps denied to them in other dimensions of their daily lives. Unfortunately, some of them did not live to see my work completed, having become the victims of their own, or others', driving misadventures or having committed suicide.

Once completed, my research revealed a great deal about the Tarmac Cowboys and their cultural world, many aspects of which have been ignored by other strains of social enquiry and media. These young men who gave so much of themselves, their time and their emotional commitment to the research were largely working class, often unskilled, often inarticulate, and often unemployed (and in some cases unemployable). Yet through their cars and car-related practices, many had determined the power of disposal over their lives, over the resources they deemed necessary to define it, and to live the lives they wished to lead.

References

Hatton, Z. (2007), *The Tarmac Cowboys: An Ethnographic Study of the Cultural World of Boy Racers*, unpublished PhD Thesis, University of Plymouth.

Chapter 6

'Inside Out': Walking a Community Art Journey

Rachel Grant

I am a textile and mixed media artist and my current work has been created in response to my experience of living in an Area of Major Intervention during regeneration in Stoke-On-Trent. I began exploring this subject in 2004, when large sections of the terraced rows with which I was so familiar began to be removed, marking the beginning of a very slow demolition process that is still ongoing today. The sporadic nature of the demolition has meant that, for some time during the process, internal walls have been exposed to form external walls. Often, patterned wallpaper hangs rotting in the rain and whole walls of bathroom tiles stand intact. Personal touches like mirrors still hang precariously on what was once a bedroom wall. The scene offers little respect for the lives and memories of its previous occupants.

From here I began my journey of research and visual response to my changing views, in terms of both landscape and my opinions. Again, the process remains ongoing. When I study the walls of the semi-demolished terraces I like to peel back the layers of wallpaper that have been added to over the years. It makes me wonder how many times that home has been passed on to someone else. It feeds my fascination with the transient nature of our existence and the way that our lives run along a continuing path where, essentially, our own experiences repeat and mirror those of previous generations.

Initially I approached this fascination in a very personal way as I found that my role as both resident and observing artist became interwoven in a conflicting mix of emotional connection and professional detachment. I began working in layers on canvas, building the surface in the same way as the layers of wallpaper I had torn through on the semi-demolished homes I was studying. Household emulsion lent itself well to the re-creation of the domestic scenes I was photographing, whilst discarded shreds of redundant paper and fabric torn and re-worked created a surface that, when stitched to enhance form, had an ethereal quality that suited the subject matter well.

In 2006 I began to feel that I wanted to explore this subject in a more public way and particularly to hear the voices of the community. I carried out two community projects, one being within a reminiscence group and the other being a year of action research. I began the research with a view to creating a body of evidence to document real people's experiences of living within a clearance area and the subsequent effect of this on their lives.

I worked in two clearance sites: one was already cleared and the majority of homes demolished; the other had just been declared for clearance and the process of negotiation was at an early stage. I interviewed and collected images, documents and narratives from residents. I located the residents in a variety of ways. Some I searched for and located from electoral rolls, some I met through community centres and churches, and others were chance meetings at the school gate or the oatcake shop. With their random memories, coupled with additional research I carried out in the local archives with maps and records, I began to build a community timeline that ran from the beginning of the twentieth century with the industrial boom and continued through to today, as I documented residents' feelings about demolition.

I was particularly interested in the movement of the community around these traditional terraced homes and the way in which they were passed on from one generation to another, either within the same family or within the existing residents. Nellie, for example, had inherited her house, where she had lived for 80 years, from her parents; Gwen, on the other hand, had actually swapped a house at one end of the street for her in-laws' home at the other end because it was a bigger family house! I was also keen to explore the emotional attachment that we have with our homes. As the research progressed, however, the relationships within the community actually overtook this as I found that the primary concern of residents facing clearance appeared to be the loss of their neighbours:

> It's like our neighbours – we aren't relatives, we're closer than relatives, we've lived together for 36 years – and that's what we're losing, they can't get that back ... and so many memories (Carol).

My aim in the visual work I created in response to this research was to create something beautiful that would express the depth of heritage buried in these clearance streets. I wanted to encourage people to engage with it and understand the relevance of its place in history. But in 2007, having exhibited in numerous gallery settings, I was becoming aware that the people who inspired this project were not necessarily having the opportunity to see it and engage with it in any meaningful way.

This was when I heard about a number of commissions that had become available through the 'Place Space & Identity' programme, a unique collaboration led by Arts Council England West Midlands and co-funded by Renew North Staffordshire. It is a new programme of temporary arts projects providing opportunities for artists and the general public to respond to the social, economic and environmental changes taking place in North Staffordshire and is designed to give people the chance to reflect on the upheaval they are experiencing. I was commissioned to produce the exhibition 'Inside Out' which was created with the idea of bringing outside something precious and vulnerable as an analogy that refers to the experiences of the community being exposed in the same way. In planning the exhibition of artwork, I wanted to create more of an experience than a traditional viewing of the art itself. I wanted to use the work to create a reason to come and see the area for the last time, to encourage people to travel around it, to consider its history, its future, and to challenge their previous perceptions of it.

The project involved creating 15 stitched and mixed media panels which I then exhibited for two weeks on the exterior walls of homes awaiting demolition in a Stoke-on-Trent clearance area, creating a walk, often termed 'art trail', that could be followed using a printed map showing the locations of the art work. At various points the map indicated to look at a certain 'view'. To reinforce this, I had painted circular 'viewing points' on the pavements around the streets. The walk itself was equally as important to the exhibition as the artwork and I planned the route carefully so that the site was explored in the most thorough way. My aim was for visitors to leave with a much deeper understanding of the place, past and present.

The site itself, like most clearance areas, is one that has changed little in physical appearance over the years, yet in terms of its culture and community dynamics it is probably unrecognizable to those who knew it 30 or 40 years ago. The traditional terraced homes were originally built to house the workers on the thriving industrial area adjacent to the estate. It is clear from the electoral roll in the 1940s that these were very much family homes, often housing a number of generations at a time. The community was close-knit and there was a culture of codependency and support. As time went on, the local industry experienced a gradual death and social demographics began to change. Increasingly, the value of the properties began to drop and, through the wider programme of Housing Market Renewal in the area, the site was declared for clearance in preparation for new builds.

Both the artwork and the walk itself referred strongly to the historical aspects of the area but there were also elements that were very relevant to the future. By using the map to guide people around this space I was able to pose questions at different points. A number of the viewing points, for example, take in distant views of wide open spaces, presently obstructed in places by the factories and terraces. I posed the question 'will our views be enhanced by the impending demolition?'

At the opening event I had the opportunity to physically guide visitors around the site. I was able to express, as we walked, the journey of discovery that I had been on in order to create the work, and my motivations behind each piece. We followed the trail of artwork snaking in and out of streets and back alleys – it was very rewarding to see the audience really looking at the homes, not just the art. They were looking up at the roofs, in the back alleys and the open gates, peering through windows, discussing with one another the plans for the future and expressing their own feelings and opinions about the site. This real engagement would never have occurred to the same extent within the four walls of a gallery space. It was the physical walk that set the paintings into the actual context in which they were created.

The final piece of work in the trail was titled 'Visitor Book'. As with a regular gallery exhibition, I wanted people to give their comments on the work and the concepts behind it. In this case I wanted the reflections to be a more public expression and so I created a canvas panel with a waterproof pen attached for anyone visiting the site to write their response to it. This was added to both on the opening day and throughout the life of the exhibition. It signified the end of the walk – the final stop.

My intention through using the walk alongside the artwork was that residents, visitors and children would be able to explore the site and discover perhaps new perspectives on an old view, giving the dilapidated streets a *reason* to be walked. The success of this aim was particularly evident during a visit by some young people from a local Pupil Referral Unit. The students attending the unit had a range of differing reasons why they were unable to attend a mainstream school and, although their behaviour may be a little challenging in the classroom, their exploration of this site was truly inspirational to watch.

Although the declared purpose of the visit was perhaps to see the artwork, their reaction to the site and the things that they saw on our walk around it will, I believe, be the predominant memory they'll keep with them. They left no stone unturned and their inquisitiveness led to a more thorough investigation than any other visitor. They were fascinated by what people left behind in their homes and yards, the alleyways, the demolition debris, the door plaques, the roofs, the eccentricities of each brick along with the loose wires and the yard gates. This was interspersed with questions about the wider issues: why were the homes being demolished? Who lived here before? Where do they live now? The most rewarding moment for me was when, *en route*, I took the group to see a semi-demolished terrace, the scene that had inspired the very core of my current practice. Just like me at that time, they had never seen anything like it before; one young girl in particular was noticeably moved and expressed her shock: '... that was actually the inside of someone's house ... right there? No!'

This indicated to me that the physical journey and the intergenerational exchange of historical understanding around the site were complete. Also complete was the journey that I had taken to express this path of heritage that weaves itself in and out of the labyrinth of streets and back alleys while they, and the communities that inhabited them, live out their final days.

Chapter 7

Rural Life on Ynys Môn:[1] Journeys Made and Unmade

Ruth Waterhouse

I am moving through the landscape without leaving my room. Always the journey begins in the same way. I follow the line between light and shade to the centre of the watercolour print where the farmhouse stands, its outbuildings arranged on all sides like fortifications against time and weathering. Behind the slate roofs the mountains rise into skies dominated by summer blues and greys. I am drawn into the cleft formed by the Nant Ffrancon Pass. There is a division between the patterns formed by agriculture, the purple and green fronds of the root crops and the mighty Cambrian and Ordovician rock which is where the industries once thrived. Here for millions of years, mud mixed with water, air and heat waiting for wind and ice to expose the slate. Sericite mica, quartz, chlorite and haematite slowly shaping itself into materials for gravestones, mantelpieces and billiard tables. This may be the Land of My Fathers[2] but all the scars, the shards, the fragments are female: according to size and colour the slates were known as Empresses (blue/grey); Duchesses (red); Countesses (blue) and Wide Ladies.

I tread a delicate balance between the neatly ordered arable fields and the silent chaos of petrified rains and snowfall. Near the farmhouse there is a barn full of hay and a red cart, which is not going anywhere today or any day. There are no people in this picture but their history is everywhere recorded in the imprint of hands on brick, on soil, on crops, on the quarries in the far distance. It is a gendered history, as is mine.

I am looking through the shadowed windows of the farmhouse but I can't see who lives there. The title of the print is 'Swedes and Mangolds 1949'.[3] The artist, Charles Tunnicliffe, is concerned with patterns and a calm orderliness of form. There is stillness in his line of vision which is not spoilt by a line of washing flapping in the prevailing winds or the cry of a child grazing her knee on the bicycle fender. He lived on Ynys Môn from 1947 until his death in 1979. He observed the

---

1 Island of Anglesey, North Wales.

2 'Land of My Fathers' is the English translation of the title of the Welsh National Anthem which is 'Mae hen wlad fy nhadau'.

3 'Swedes and Mangolds 1949' Watercolour with body colour. Artist: Charles F. Tunnicliffe R.A. Illustration for Rogerson, S. (1949) *Both Sides of the Road: A Book About Farming* (London: Collins). Facing Page 1981.

island's birds and animals, recording what he saw. Cormorants, falcons, guillemots and shell-ducks were documented in his sketchbooks and paintings: their weight and shape, colours and textures, habits and demeanours partnering his life.

He was walking this landscape in a different way to the way my family walked it in the early 1950s when we came to spend our summer holidays near Church Bay. We came with city shoes and no eye as yet for the detailed fold of feather against bone. It was a foreign land a few hours by steam train from Liverpool. As children we knew Tunnicliffe's work already. He illustrated the Brooke Bond tea cards[4] we avidly collected and Williamson's (1948) 'Tarka the Otter'. During our expeditions his illustrations kept us busy as we studied our Ladybird books. They were a safeguard against boredom as the train sped us westwards towards our destination.

We're holidaymakers, not tourists: we have to work hard at playing, we're urban, and we're spending time in the country in a land famous for its saints and bonesetters. The farmer's daughter is called Rhiannon (a Celtic Goddess) and the fields are full of rabbits dying with mixamatosis. They don't look like my Beatrix Potter rabbits, they don't wear aprons or jackets, just a sick look, giddy with disease. We're city folk with city folk sentiments about animals. We don't know slate, we don't know rock. We know words and we're learning them from the TV now, my brother and me. The *Omo* and *Daz* washing powder signs along the Dock Road and the 'Esso Sign Meanz Happy Motoring' sung by a Chinese cartoon character on a screen the size of a postage stamp. We are the 'baby boomers' awash with free milk and orange juice thick as treacle in bottles capped with a forget-me-knot blue metal top.

We are walking along a footpath. We're still walking it. All my family are here. My grandfather teaches young men how to pole vault and understand poetry. He survived the trenches so he understands mud and bone. My father is a clergyman who walked through the jungles of Burma and returned home weighing seven stone, with £10 in his pocket and a brand new overcoat. A forgotten man from a forgotten army. My grandmother was a milliner and knows silks and stitches and how to save buttons. My mother was promoted to Assistant Librarian in the absence of the men and knows about books and why people need to have literature. So we have plenty of wordsmiths amongst us, but monolingual: we are ignorant of the local language.

We walk up the path across the cattle grids, picking our way between fallen rabbits and the spoors of foxes. It is my grandmother, made bold by her time in a Birmingham store selling hats to idle ladies, who protests about the dog whose paw is caught in the trap. It is my mother's empathic indignation that causes his master's voice to falter. But the farmer merely nods silently and then walks away in the weak sunshine, muttering 'later, later'. In the farmhouse there is a smell

---

4 Brooke Bond Tea gave away an educational postcard inside every packet of tea. From 1954 the company ran a series of cards on British Birds. Tunnicliffe contributed to the series.

of Calor gas and mice. They live behind the skirting boards. I am told by a farm worker that I am 'bold for a girl' because I'm not afraid of mice. But we have mice in the city. They live in the manse and tap dance inside our dreams. My brother and I are becoming what we must be, middle class children privileged by welfare and faith in our abilities to jump through the hoops of a liberal education. Even girls can succeed.

This land is layered by class and gender, by language and nationality, each status petrified like the rocks beneath our feet: the very geology of social strata but as shifting and unstable as spoil-heaps. There are incomers and exiles, the Irish and the English amidst the Welsh and the Proper Welsh. As Tunnicliffe traverses his island, we fill our little sabbatical buckets with seaweed and sand. Each granule an echo; a memory of journeys taken with reluctance and trepidation by peoples regarded as the Walha – the outsiders, the strangers. But known to themselves as Cymry, compatriots. Here, gender is fused and shaped by industry and capitalism, assimilation and attrition. Perhaps most of all by the emotions of resistance.

There is the journey made by the Roman centurion, a communion of sand, mud and sea. The waters closing over his head as he imagines a sun filled courtyard where sleek cats sleep. Centuries later there is the forced exodus from Beaumaris to Newburgh, the women bearing the community with them, recreating it on the far side of the island. To the North at Amlwch a journey is scuppered, enraged by the price of bread, protesters maroon a ship leaving the harbour full of grain. There are the pathways beaten bare by the boots of the women as they walked to the copper sheds, their voices volleying upwards like gunfire and their legs heavy with protest against the burden of industrial time and sour wages. Heads bowed, wearing their 'Jim Crow' hats, their skin taut against the knuckles like a drum. Resentment and resignation in their eyes, knowing that they earn less then the men, knowing that this cannot be changed, they sing out loud above the sound of metal on stone. Then it is the weekly journey of the quarry men across the Straits to the Anglesey Barracks at the Dinorwic quarry (now a ghost village for a new generation of industrial tourists). The workers commuted between island life, silicosis and septicaemia; the slate being slippery in the wet and the resulting cuts being deep and fine and lethal. Tunnicliffe knows this history; a rural life dominated by Penrhyn castle built out of slavery and the quarry workers' strife. It shadows his landscape made small at last by perspective and cloud. From here, hungry women tossed shameful charity aside in a refusal to take 'Lady Janet's Cabbage'. Ynys Môn was also known as Mam Cymru, the Mother and Breadbasket of Wales but not for these women and children of Bethesda; not for these workers locked out in bitter dispute over pay and conditions in 1896–1897 and again in 1900–1903. The others, the ones who answered the clamorous calls of the body by taking the scraps they were sanctimoniously given, were shunned and stigmatized as 'blacklegs'. The walls of their communities bearing the vitriol of the politically righteous: '*bradwyr!*': 'Traitors! Traitors! Traitors!' There was no vacation from want and desperate need (for further detail see Perrin 1997).

But here we come again in our holiday clothes. The men talking politics. The boys 'all of a go' and can't sit still for five minutes: they seem to have legs made of elastic. Developing our emotional antennae we girls sit closer to our mothers. We are watching the men in their tweed coats, their hair dark with *Brylcreem*, talking of expeditions which never get off the ground. Their skin is grey, the colour of gas masks and there is a hopeless restlessness in their 'Civvie Street' shoes. But it is the women who make an impression, keeping us 'all of a piece' by tying double bows in our laces and petitioning for more heat in the bedrooms and more milk for our cocoa. It is the women who keep the journey up, making it time and again. It is the women who trail us down to the beach, carrying thermos flasks of Bovril and cream cracker sandwiches. Each journey changes us. We do not return the same.

I am walking this landscape again with the artist, his exacting eye making a relentless reckoning against the declining light. Each time I return to this sequestered land there is a familiar banishment, a slitting of the memory like shards of slate across a bone. There is flatness in Tunnicliffe's vision: an erasure of effect; an obliteration of affect. His careful tones are a muted re-assurance against the trauma of history. It is a way of forgetting. In this place of order and composure we bury deep the girls and boys who could not escape into storybooks. Those who departed on different trains and were freighted ever eastwards on some dark journey. This is peacetime: reconstruction, family time. Children of the 1950s, we glued Tunnicliffe's beautiful tea cards into our scrapbooks. Everything in its place now. No messiness here, all emotion tied up against time and loss. In sandalled feet ('Start-rite') we traversed unknowingly the fugitive colours of the past. We entered the mythical land of 'Never had it so Good',[5] our plastic water bottles full of 'Corona' and our only displacement a wakes week away by the Irish Sea. But residual images resurfaced like fossils set free from stone. Even then the planet was heating up; the birds less numerous; the Snowdon Lily dying back for lack of frost; gridlocked feelings an empty ache behind the eye. The footsteps still. The sketchbook closed.

References

Williamson, H. (1948), *Tarka the Otter* with illustrations by Charles F. Tunnicliffe R.A. (London: Putman Press London).

Perrin, J. (1997), *Visions of Snowdonia: Landscape and Legend* (London: BBC Worldwide Publishing).

---

5 In celebrating the success of the post-war British economy in 1957, the then Conservative Prime Minister, Harold Macmillan declared to the public that: 'You've never had it so good.'

Chapter 8

Double Clutchin', Bucket Tippin', Juggernaut Driving, Truckin' Time: A Trucker's Tale

Stephen Handsley

Before returning to academia in 1995, much of my professional working life was spent operating and driving trucks, of all descriptions, mainly around the United Kingdom and the Irish Republic, both as an employee and on a self-employed basis. I still vividly remember nights spent away from home, sitting in a public bar or truck stop, swapping stories and 'truckers' tales' with fellow drivers, most of whom were men. Indeed, there was often little else to do when faced with the delights of a lonely bunk – located in the truck's cab – and the cold comfort of a TV screen.

From driving trucks to co-directing and managing a small transport and distribution company, I spent almost 25 years in an industry which saw me engaged in the transportation of a disparate range of items including fresh produce, soft drinks, pottery and ceramics, clothing, engineering tools and machinery, before a mixture of ill-health and disillusionment brought this period in my life to a close. During my time as a 'trucker' I experienced a wide range of feelings and emotions and encountered phenomena that, ultimately, helped shape my view of the world. In fact, I believe these adventures and experiences prepared me for my present role as a sociologist, given its quest to understand the structure and dynamics of society and their intricate connections to patterns of human behaviour and individual life changes. This then is my story.

As many people are probably aware, trucks and truck drivers are a constant presence on UK roads and motorways and even the shortest drive by members of the public is likely to encounter a truck or two transporting a variety of goods. Indeed, in the UK, almost 95 per cent of goods are now transported using this method. However, despite the current effort to break down notions of stereotyped employment by attracting women to non-traditional industries, this area (at least) of the transport industry has largely been male-dominated and in my time as a truck driver it was extremely rare to see women truckers. If my memory serves me correctly, in all my years within the industry, I encountered only two women truckers, one of whom appeared to be 'sacrificing her femininity' for the sake of equality by dressing in the proverbial trucker's garb of oversized overalls, baseball cap and rigger boots. For years, the sex-role, stereotypical image of a truck driver, whilst obviously being male, was of food-busting bellies, greasy T-shirts, hairy armfuls of tattoos accompanied by the proverbial cigarette hanging from the corner of the mouths whilst listening to such delightful Country and Western sounds as 'Diesel Smoke And Dangerous Curves' by Bobby Sykes; a description which, thankfully, did not apply to me.

The romantic image of a truck driver has long captured the imagination and, for some, part of the masculine and machismo fantasy is the almost cowboy-like existence in which the adventurous vigilante hero eventually 'delivers the load', metaphorically speaking. Such double entendres, in which patriarchal patterns of behaviour were, I recall, often used as a way of reinforcing representations of men and male identities, served as a common characteristic of the truck driver's vocabulary. The way in which the concepts of masculinity and femininity are re-created through such coworker interactions has, in the trucking industry, historically seen the portrayal of truck drivers as 'real men'. Indeed, the common perception within the truck driving fraternity was, and always had been, that women are simply not capable of handling such enormous vehicles and that such a task is 'best left to men'. Historically, therefore, the truck has, first and foremost, been constructed as a masculine attribute or, put another way, a giant phallus on wheels.

Such occupational sex-role stereotypes were, and still are, largely a reality both within and outside of the trucking community. Truck driving can be a demanding job and is probably the last bastion of machismo in which around one per cent are women. Some self-employed long-distance truck drivers, many of whom independently own and operate their own trucks – commonly referred to as owner-drivers – spend most of their lives away from home. For them, the 'cab' provides a number of creature comforts including bunks; TV; radio/CD/DVD; fridges; microwaves; in short, a rolling residence. Given the mobile and transient nature of the truck drivers' world, the traditional role of women as homemakers and childminders, is considered by many to be anathema in such an environment.

During my time within the industry, such ephemeral working practices certainly fostered a transient type of social network in which the only means of contact was often via the CB radio (Citizens Band). Here, truckers would often use CB slang to communicate with each other. Whilst CB radios were meant to be used, primarily, as a way of communicating directions, traffic problems, and other things relevant to the task of truck driving, they also became a useful medium for exchanging much more general information. Similar to the Internet chat rooms a quarter century later, the CB allowed people to get to know one another in a quasi-anonymous manner.

Whilst many of these verbal exchanges contained general chitchat, often light-hearted in nature, some conveyed a much more serious message. For instance, whilst some simply spoke of the aesthetic and technological qualities of certain trucks, others conveyed vivid details of sexual conquests. For example, when referring to a 'heavenly body', this was more than likely in terms of the sensual lines of the latest Scania or Volvo truck, rather than the scantily clad and seductive shape of a woman's body. In contrast, I distinctly recollect the airwaves being filled with earthy expletives recalling sexual conquests, often using licentious language which would, no doubt, cause uproar and distaste amongst those who prefer the use of a more gender-sensitive approach. For example, in the course of these verbal exchanges, I would often hear women described in such pejorative terms, as beaver (female), with the caller on beaver patrol (the hunt for women). Conversations of shared experiences often included graphic tales of sex and debauchery in which women were inevitably constructed as second-class citizens. I remember hearing two male truckers exchanging opinions on the size and shape of their respective partners' breasts. Others were more than happy to publicize their own sexual encounters and fantasies, often making over-inflated claims regarding their manhood and the ways in which they belittled women. Such perceptions of women as inferior sex objects were pretty much taken for granted amongst the trucking fraternity and, therefore, constituted the embodiment of maleness and masculinity.

Such public performances of testosterone-filled narratives, whilst apparently enhancing feelings of masculinity, did, nevertheless, strike me as slightly bizarre given that possibly hundreds, if not thousands of truckers, were listening into these emotionally charged outpourings. However, one quickly got the distinct impression that many of these truckers' tales were probably embellished and exaggerated. Indeed, in an ironic twist, these online discussions almost became a type of counselling service in which manly and masculine truckers revealed their indepth and innermost emotions.

These dichotomous performances of gender became commonplace in the mainly masculine world of the trucker. One particular performance that springs to mind is the time I was returning from a delivery in convoy with four other truckers. At around 3.00am, whilst heading north up the M1 motorway, a call came over the CB from one of my associates: 'J...s, I can't believe what I just saw', he called out. 'She's hasn't got any f...ing clothes on', he quickly added. Struggling to catch his breath, he added, 'She's coming up alongside you in the middle lane and she's stark bollock naked.' Checking my rear view mirror, sure enough a small car, carrying a lone female, came cruising up alongside my vehicle. Gazing down from the heady heights of my cab, I could just about make out the naked silhouette of a woman's body seated in the driver's seat.

What then took place, even now probably sounds unbelievable. Having overtaken our convoy, the female driver of the car eased her vehicle into the nearside lane, dropping her speed as she did so. Each of us subsequently overtook her, once more returning our trucks to the nearside lane. Having completed this manoeuvre, she once again positioned her own vehicle alongside us, slowing down to such an extent that we were invited afresh to feast our eyes on her naked body. This catalogue of exhibitionism was repeated a further five or six times before she eventually left the motorway and we continued our journey homewards, contemplating the night's events. Whilst trying to make sense of what we had witnessed, drawing on our shared experiences, we came to the conclusion that she was either simply a pleasure-seeker who got her kicks from soliciting truck drivers, or one the ever-present 'ladies of the night' who regularly scoured the motorways looking for business. Indeed, it was quite commonplace, when parked overnight at a truck stop, to see prostitutes leaving the cabs of fellow drivers in the dead of night having 'done the business'. Many of these same women, I recall, owned CB radios and, broadcasting from their home bases, often kept truckers entertained with sexy chat whilst arranging clandestine meetings in lay-bys or truck stops.

A number of these same truck stops often featured male entertainment such as striptease artists or comedy acts featuring an explicit and risqué repertoire of sexual innuendo. That is not to say that all truck drivers were engaged in sexual shenanigans. Rather, much of the time, the trucker's life contained nothing more exciting than gazing at the rear of the truck in front, or time spent whiling away the hours at the numerous 24-hour distribution centres; many of which are now an integral part of truckers' lives given the just-in-time culture of twenty-first century business and industry. For example, I remember suffering constant bouts of boredom whilst waiting to 'tip' (a colloquialism used by drivers meaning to discharge their load) or feeling absolutely appalled at the thought of another early start (by early, I mean one or two a.m. since most drivers rise early to avoid the dreaded rush hour). On the other hand, truck driving can, for many, be source of great joy, satisfaction and fascination given the relative freedom and autonomy one experiences when 'heading down the highway'.

As for me, my truck driving days remain something of a distant memory. Nonetheless, during my time within the industry, I guess I learned much, both about my self and my fellow truckers. Not least, my constant discomfort and angst when required to perform the proverbial specific gender roles associated with maleness and machismo. Nevertheless, despite the shifting paradigms of conventional male identity which began to infiltrate the illiberal world of the trucker during this era, in order that I might be accepted as one of the crowd, I was often required to perform roles which reinforced the traditional gender ideology, so as to gain the respect and everyday support, contact and camaraderie of my fellow truckers. A balancing act that, ultimately, gave way to my transformation into the enlightened individual I am today!

Chapter 9

From Embryo to Dinosaur?
A Railwayman's Journey

Robert Hart

I started work as an 'embryo' on the railways at the age of 15, in 1962. I began as a cleaner because in those days you worked your way up to being a driver. It took me 17 years from being a pass fireman to being a registered driver – it was a case of 'waiting for dead men's shoes'. Now I am sometimes called a 'dinosaur'. I'm not quite the senior dinosaur yet – I'm almost at the top but there are still two drivers senior to me at my depot. I know that as someone who can still regularly drive steam locomotives, I am like a super-hero – people often approach me and say 'you don't know how lucky you are', but I *do* really appreciate how lucky I am, that I am doing something I love doing and get paid for it as well. When I climb on a steam locomotive, all arthritic pain disappears. I can fire five tons of coal and it doesn't bother me because the adrenalin takes over.

The shift work involved in driving trains is unpopular with many people but I have adapted my entire life to the shifts. When my family and I moved house, neighbours thought I was unemployed. I was doing early evening shifts because I was working mainly on Royal Mail trains that ran through the night. Now I work freight trains. I don't like the long shifts of eleven hours, but there are compensations – every five weeks I get a week off. In the days before privatization, I could get a fast turn-around train, but now I can spend several hours waiting for my return train to come in – I tend to eat my butties very slowly to pass the time! I will also watch the TV in the mess-room and talk to drivers who have come in from other areas. But the camaraderie that used to exist has disappeared since privatization. In the days of steam we would know all the shunters and signalmen by name; they would ask us for coal, and they would give us hot water for a brew of tea. Now people can become drivers within 12 months of starting – they are given nice smart uniforms, and they don't really mix with the drivers from the days of the nationalized railways. Even when I am taking youngsters on a route-learning train, they don't offer much respect for my experience.

The freight trains that I work can be quite lonely. I am entirely on my own, no guard or anyone for company. Freight trains have a higher failure rate than passenger trains and we get a lot of brake problems on them. If you've got a train half a mile long, and there's only the driver – and inevitably the problems will be near the back of the train – then any difficulties are not going to be sorted out within two or three minutes. It will take at least half an hour. If I have to do maintenance on the side where there's another track, then I must communicate with the signalman and get all the trains stopped on that track too. And if my train is carrying dangerous goods, then the fire fighters have to be informed as well, because of the risk of fire from dragging or overheated brakes.

Sometimes I work the Royal Train – the Queen was once presented to me when we were using a special steam locomotive for the first time in nearly 40 years. We all had to wash our hands and put on clean overalls beforehand. As a young fireman I thought I would never get the chance – senior firemen always did the Royal Train. I never know in advance where that train will be going, because of the risk to security. The train is a very secure environment for royalty. One of my great ambitions was always to bring the Royal Train from London to Crewe. I did that last year.

Also, I still do main line runs with steam – I will even come back early from my holidays to do a run! Unlike the diesels, which are a bit like cars – you have the power and you just put your foot down, change the gear and go – if you don't drive the steam engine correctly, you exhaust all the steam too early. If you put your hand on the boiler you can feel that the steam engine is alive. There is a real technique to it and every locomotive requires a different technique, so there is also a great sense of achievement in both driving and firing one. At the end of the run from Carlisle to Crewe, for example, you know that *you* have achieved it: as a fireman you have shovelled six tons of coal and used something like 15,000 gallons of water – it is *your* achievement. There is also a sense of satisfaction in the attention we draw. I wouldn't say we have film star status but when we are bowling along next to a road we see people in cars craning their necks to have a look at us, and we wonder that there isn't an accident. Shap Fell is the mountain to climb on the West Coast main line; all steam railwaymen boasted about going over Shap. When steam went, I thought there would never be an opportunity for me to do that. But since steam returned to the main lines I have done it. I have fired a steam engine over Shap. That is quite an achievement with a 13-coach train. If the driver is to drive the train properly, you as the fireman have to *make* the power, maintain the boiler and keep the steam going.

Even in the diesels, though, you get a buzz. You go through Milton Keynes station at 100 miles per hour, you blow the horn, and you see the people on the platform put their hands over their ears as you go through. There's a feeling of power to it. I don't know if others think that way – but it helps to keep me interested in the job. I think probably one of my best trips ever was a steam run down the East Coast main line non-stop through Doncaster. It was with an A4-class locomotive, either Nigel Gresley or Union of South Africa. These locomotives have a specific whistle called a double chime. It is absolutely beautiful, like an American whistle. We blew the whistle as we were approaching Doncaster station. It still made the hairs on the back of my neck stand up, just as it did when I was a boy standing on that very platform with my trainspotting friends, probably in our short trousers. So the passion is still there for my job.

When I was young, all boys wanted to be engine drivers. These days we have all kinds of drivers on the railways. I am a bit old-fashioned; the railway I grew up on was very male-dominated. I was with a woman driver recently who had lovely long fingernails. Now, when you start a diesel you press a button, so I said, 'I bet you have to be careful you don't break your fingernails.' But she used a pencil instead of her finger to start it. I get quite bemused. I still feel there are parts of the job that maybe they cannot do. Modern trains, for example, are fitted with what we call 'buck-eye couplers' which weigh in excess of a hundredweight. I struggle to lift them myself – but if the women are doing that job then I guess they have to show that they can lift them too.

One aspect of driving a train is that it gives you a lot of time to think. That is sometimes a positive thing, but not always. Accidents happen, people do make mistakes, and sometimes those mistakes do have serious consequences. If I thought about that too much I simply wouldn't be able to drive trains any more. We get people throwing stones at us – I actually caught some of them years ago when I was younger. I remember taking one lad home to his father, who gave him a 'clip round the ear'.

The most distressing part of the job is when we have people on the track. I accompanied one driver who told me that his nickname was 'killer'. I thought this meant he was an aggressive driver. But he was called 'killer' because he had had seven suicides on the line to deal with. Although he claimed that it hadn't bothered him, he was still able to explain every one of those suicides in graphic detail. They had evidently left a long-lasting impression. I have had two suicides to date. The first one was lying down on the track, probably a quarter of a mile ahead of me. Even though I'd never had a suicide, I knew instantly that it wasn't just a pile of rubbish lying there. I put my hand on the horn, put the brake into emergency, and turned my back on the whole scene. That was because I had been told by other drivers that people tend to look up at you at the last few seconds so the very final thing you see is their face. I hit this person but I didn't even feel the bump.

The second suicide was more horrendous because it happened in a split second. I was angry because I had a trainee driver with me, just starting out on his career, and it meant he had an extra stress to deal with. We were rattling along at about 75 miles an hour, with a 1,600-ton freight train behind us. About a hundred feet in front of us a man just scrambled up on to the track and stood there. All we heard was the thud in front of the locomotive. We put the emergency brake on and then rang through to Network Rail. They dispatched the emergency services and stopped all other trains in the area. I never go back to check on the mutilated body; I am quite a resilient person but I think if I did, I would never drive a train again. After the police had checked we were okay in the cab and taken a basic statement from us, I agreed to work the train into the next station. Then one of my employers' managers took me home in his car. Afterwards, it was report, report, report. I had to attend both inquests. I have tried to keep my distance: the more involved you get, the more emotional it all becomes. What angers me is why they want to involve a third person. They wanted to kill themselves, but I didn't want to kill them. Suicide is such a selfish act because the people who are left behind have so many unanswered questions.

I never travel by train any more, even though I – and my wife – get free passes. The last time I travelled by train it was such a terrible journey – trains running late, missing the connections. I missed the last official train, but I knew that later ones would stop at Crewe to change drivers, even though it wasn't announced for the benefit of the passengers. There is little encouragement to travel by train, despite what governments say about wanting traffic off the roads. In reality, the railways cannot cope with increases in custom. Despite all this, I am happy with my lot as an engine driver. There was once a guy called Richard Hardy who wrote a book called *Steam in the Blood* (1971), and I think that's basically what it is – it gets into your system. All I ever wanted to be was an engine driver. I have achieved all my ambitions. I don't want to do anything else.

References

Hardy, R. (1971), *Steam in the Blood* (London: Ian Allan).

Chapter 10
Roll On Down the Highway[1]

Debra Langan

As upset as my parents were when, in my third year of university, I told them that I was going to start driving a cab, they could not escape the fact that my mother had also been a taxi driver, in 1926, at age 16! In our home town of Leamington, Ontario, Canada, Mom would go to pick up fares when they had called my grandfather's hotel, which doubled as the local taxi service. As the story goes, this was a safe arrangement. My grandfather reportedly knew everyone in the town, and where my mother would be going. 'Fifty years later, in the big city, the job is not the same,' my parents would warn. Never dissuaded, I referred to my mother's indisputable history as a 'taxi driver' whenever they tried to keep me from following in her footsteps. 'It must run in the family!' I would argue.

Now, when I look back, I shudder at the chances that I took in that job, but I felt invincible. It all began over a few beers, in the university pub in Ottawa with my friend Susan. With great enthusiasm, she described her summer as a taxi driver, the only woman and the only university student, in an all-male company. I was immediately drawn to what sounded like a great adventure, and Susan suggested that I join her, as a part-time driver. It turned out that the owner of the company liked Susan, as did the broker from whom she rented her taxi, and riding on her coat tails, I began renting a cab on days when I didn't have classes. The majority of our fellow cabbies were full-time drivers, older than us, with limited formal education. They treated us with brotherly or fatherly affection, a paternalistic relationship that Susan and I enjoyed, for although we were quite independent we also liked the fact that these men wanted to take care of us. Our broker took great pride in his fleet of luxury cars – Cadillacs, Buick Electras and Delta 88s. Our clientele ranged from government officials to residents of subsidized housing projects in Ottawa, Canada's national capital.

Much to our parents' horror, Susan and I both ended up taking the next year off from university, securing full-time cabs for eight months and then back-packing around Europe for four months. That was thirty years ago now, but I still love to pull out my taxi drivin' identity whenever I can. This disclosure tends to enliven most conversations, as people stare in wonder, and express disbelief that I, a 'girl', who is now a sociologist working in higher education, a wife, a mother, middle-class and middle-aged, could ever have done such a thing. When I was driving a

---

1 'Roll on down the highway' is a lyric taken from the song, 'Roll On Down The Highway' by C.F. Turner and Randy Bachman of Bachman Turner Overdrive (1974).

cab, the reactions from passengers were similar, and the implicit, if not explicit question always was, 'What's a nice girl like you doing in a job like this?' People's responses, then and now, speak to the disjuncture between my features of identity and stereotypic expectations about *who* should be driving a cab. In Canada, cab-driving remains a male-dominated industry. I challenged the status quo, not only because of my identity as a woman, but also because it was apparent that I was a *young, white, educated* woman (read 'economically privileged'). It is only through writing this autobiographical reflection that I have come to see how I took my privileged social locations for granted. The combination of these features of identity allowed me to shrug off any sexist remarks or treatment that I experienced on the job. I implicitly knew that, regardless of what others thought of me as a woman, I had a host of opportunities waiting for me once I left taxi driving because I was young, white, educated, able-bodied and heterosexual. These features positioned me in a way that profoundly influenced how I experienced being a cabbie.

If a passenger was particularly patronizing because I was a woman, I had to endure only a limited encounter with that person. This enabled me to play with my identity, to construct a presentation of self in any given encounter. For example, I could 'come out' as university educated, or not, and my choices in this regard depended on what I perceived to be the social class of the passengers, their demeanour toward me, and whether I wanted to adjust my social status up or down. Of all the things that happened during those thousands of rides with various passengers, most poignant in my memory is how much pleasure I got out of showing them (and in a sense, 'the world') that I was defying gender stereotypes about women's place in society. Including taxi driver as a dimension of who I am contributes to an identity as adventurous, risk-taking, street-wise, and perhaps sexy,[2] arguably more exciting attributes than those attached to the roles of academic, wife and mother.

I recall few details about my interactions with specific passengers. Rather, I have flashes of scenes that are connected to the emotional dimensions of the work, and when I recall, publicly or privately, my taxi days, I re-experience the emotions evoked by these various aspects. I feel the anticipation that accompanied not knowing how my day would unfold or who I would pick up next; the frustration and boredom over long waits in mall parking lots for my next fare; the exhilaration when my day unfolded like clockwork, when I picked up, dropped off and picked up fares in an orchestrated sequence that kept the metre ticking and my senses keen; the high of rollin' down the Queensway with the stereo blaring, the white lines rhythmically clicking by mile upon mile. I recall the embarrassment of realizing that I had no idea how to get a passenger to the requested destination, and having to admit this to them and/or the dispatcher; the satisfaction of talking

---

2 I was asked a few years ago at an interview for a tenure track position: 'Why haven't you written on taxi driving? It would be so nice to know about all that's going on in the cab!' The other substantive areas that I had concentrated on in my teaching and research just couldn't compare with the 'sexiness' of taxi driving.

with passengers about their problems in a candid way that is only possible between strangers, and the sense of celebration at the end of a long day, when I would meet with other cabbies for ribs and beers at one of our favourite haunts. I re-live my triumph at making it out of bed at 4:00 a.m. to catch the government workers' rush to the airport that would pay for the day's overhead costs, and then some, by 8:00 a.m.; the flashiness of always having a roll of cash in my pocket and the sense that I could spend this freely, because I could replace it with only a few more fares.

But sharing these kinds of recollections with others is less than exciting for them, and I usually respond with a more sensational story, often the one that involved an attempted attack by a male passenger. I had been on the job for only a few months, when a fellow cabbie was robbed and stabbed to death. Weeks later, while in the same residential neighbourhood, I was flagged down by a woman who motioned wildly for me to stop. She jumped into the back seat on the passenger side, and at the same time a man jumped into the back seat behind me. I realized then that she had been trying to get away from him, as he was hitting her and trying to force her out of the cab. I yelled at him to 'Get out!' at which point he took a swing at me. Without thinking, I turned off the ignition, and ran from the cab to a nearby corner store where I telephoned the dispatcher to send help. As luck would have it, I had left the cab just metres from a bus stop, and as I ran back toward the cab, men who had been waiting at the bus stop pulled the man out of the cab and pinned him down. I got back into the cab and left with the woman, who was crying hysterically. As we drove downtown, she regained her composure while telling me the story of her abusive relationship. At her request, I dropped her off at the strip club where she was late for work. Only then did I realize that in all the commotion, my radio had been turned off. I contacted the dispatcher who was frantic, along with other cabbies who had arrived at the scene. By the time they had got there, all involved had disappeared and they were left not knowing what had happened to me.

I wish I could recall more than the sensational events on the job. Had I known then what I know now about methodological possibilities, I would have collected rich data. A stranger to qualitative methods, I never knew enough to keep fieldnotes, even though I was in a superb 'insider' role as the cabbie. I often feel that I missed a wonderful opportunity. After returning from Europe, I tried to incorporate my interest in women as taxi drivers by doing my honours thesis on the sex role identities of female cab drivers. Sandra Bem's (1977) sex role inventory informed my survey research, and revealed that female cabbies had more androgynous sex role types than did female waitresses, waitressing being the more traditional occupational choice for women. The research didn't come close to capturing the nuanced elements of the work, nor the dynamic, emotional experiences that the job involved for me as a woman.

Now, as a sociologist, I am able to interpret this experience in a way that illuminates the gendered, racialized, classed, and aged dimensions of cabbie/passenger interactions. I also see how my emotional experiences on the job were not generic, but closely tied to my social locations. Many of the 'highs' on the job were because I was a woman who was challenging social expectations, and this allowed me to construct an identity that I saw as exciting. As a single woman, I had limited responsibilities, a university education behind me, and a family who could always step in if need be. As a white woman, I would not have to face the barriers to employment like other cabbies, who were of racial minorities. The taxi driving work was indeed a choice for me, not an occupation to which I had been relegated. Although technically doing the same work, I did so in a privileged capacity, for I could move on.

While sociology has made me re-think taxi driving, so too has taxi driving informed my worldview as a sociologist.[3] The exposure to a diverse range of people and their differing life circumstances has helped to ground me in the lived realities of everyday lives beyond the ivory towers of academe. The work taught me how to communicate, both superficially and earnestly, with groups of people whom I would not otherwise have encountered. The transitory, day by day existence that characterized taxi driving has served as a metaphor for my view of life more generally; plans can change at any given moment, there will always be another 'fare,' new people to meet, new journeys to embark on. Being a cabbie provided me with more than a desired facet of identity; it taught me a street sense that has served me well. I often muse aloud about taxi driving as an option if I ever lose my limited contract position within the university, and this possibility is one that instils a sense of security for I know that I can always drive a taxi, come what may. The trick is to keep my eyes on the road and my hands upon the wheel.[4]

References

Bem, S. (1977), 'On the utility of alternative procedures for assessing psychological androgyny', *Journal of Consulting and Clinical Psychology*, 45, 2, 196–205.

---

3 My thanks to Deborah Davidson, for reminding me of this and for feedback on earlier drafts.

4 'Keep your eyes on the road and your hands upon the wheel' is a lyric from 'Roadhouse Blues' by The Doors (1970).

Chapter 11

Of Life and Bicycle Hubs

Karen Overton

Recycle-A-Bicycle (RAB) is a non-profit organization dedicated to environmental education and job training for New York City youth. It began in 1994 as a project of Transportation Alternatives, one of the first professional bike and pedestrian advocacy groups in the United States, and it spun off to become an independent organization in 1998. RAB first partnered with Children's Aid Society, a highly respected youth organization, and Intermediate School 218 (located in a low-income neighbourhood) to offer daytime, after-school and Saturday programming. This serves as a national model in which classes teach young people how to maintain and repair bikes, ride safely in the city, and to be good environmental stewards via cycling and recycling. Participants may opt to do the earn-a-bike program that allows them to 'cash in' volunteer hours in exchange for a bike that s/he built and to join the ride club. Students are also encouraged to do community service projects, as a way to give back to the community in expression of gratitude for all the material donations (primarily bikes) that RAB receives. Since the project's inception, RAB has expanded to four NYC boroughs, worked with over 6,000 young people, recycled over 15,000 bicycles, and published two manuals on how to start a youth program and how to run a youth ride club. Additionally, it operates two retail stores, which generate over 80 per cent of earned income for the organization. For more information, visit www.recycleabicycle. org. I am the founder and former Executive Director.

'A properly overhauled hub will spin smoothly and perpetually', said the bike mechanic. He held the axle at both ends and spun the wheel to demonstrate his point. Like the middle-school kids in the class, I too was learning how to fix a bike. At this moment I thought, 'Recycle-A-Bicycle needs to be designed so that it will operate in just the same way.' That moment was 13 years ago. I have just passed on the torch as Executive Director. What I failed to realize then, is that with constant use the hub requires regular overhauls. I was destined to get greasy on a regular basis.

One of my first tasks was learning the art of bike repair. Obtaining the necessary level of skill was not nearly as difficult as earning the respect of our students, who were predominantly Dominican and male. The truth is, one rarely encounters a female mechanic in any NYC bike shop and this reinforces the notion that it is an unladylike activity. Combine this stereotype with machismo, and that spells c-h-a-l-l-e-n-g-e. One particular group of after-school participants was concerned for my welfare. Leandro, the spokesman, approached me with, 'We think you should marry the mechanic. He says he can cook and we know he can really fix bikes.' The group was chagrined to learn that the mechanic was engaged. I took heart in the fact that they didn't relegate me to the kitchen.

I realized that these young people were reflecting values in society at large. As the lone volunteer mechanic at the Bronx rest station for Transportation Alternative's fundraising bike event, I spent the first three hours idle. Since it was one of the last stations, I assumed those with mechanical failures had had them repaired or had quit the ride. At some point, a desperate man decided to take a risk and ask me to adjust his Derailleur – the part that allows you to shift gears. I put the bike on the repair stand, pulled out a screwdriver from my tool box, gave it a few twists while spinning the wheel to check my work, and then announced it was ready to go. A long line of people queued behind this man. My original theory was blown and I had to ask for help in dealing with so many people at once.

At some indeterminate time, my ability as a female mechanic was no longer questioned. Perhaps it came with the grey hair. More likely, it came from the fact that I could spout bike terminology at ease and exuded a certain level of confidence. I was lucky in that many people shared their tricks of the trade with me, knowing that I would do my best to pass the information along. However, I also acted on sage advice: hire excellent mechanics to teach new skills and handle the difficult repairs in time of need.

Recycle-A-Bicycle has always struggled with how to obtain a gender balance in staffing and youth participation. From the beginning, volunteer nights were organized to teach adults bike repair skills and to tap into their other talents. 'Ladies' Night' was born from this initiative as it became apparent that women often preferred an environment dedicated to their learning efforts. At first, this new initiative aroused quite a bit of curiosity. On the designated evening, male customers would show up at closing time and linger around until I kicked them out. It was fascinating to think that empowering women through teaching them how to use tools and fix bikes was so transfixing! The ladies and I speculated that perhaps they envisioned us getting naked and rubbing grease all over ourselves. In reality, we remained clothed at all times and Ladies' Night has successfully served as RAB's informal training program and hiring source for female instructors. On a more personal level, it was the only two hours of the week I could count on for, and luxuriate in, sisterhood.

To this day, RAB has never achieved an equal participation rate for girls. We get equal numbers when we specifically request our school partners to consider this in enrolment. However, in the after-school and weekend programs where kids sign up voluntarily, this does not happen. Over the years I have asked girls why they come. The most common responses include: 'My friend (or boyfriend) signed up, so I joined', 'I want to earn a bike', 'The teacher is cute', and 'It's cool to do something that isn't associated with being a girl.' There is also a correlation between age and participation: the rate drops the older the girls get. I have ascertained that the girls who show up tend to have the self-confidence that allows them to go against the accepted norm of behaviour or perceive a social benefit. Participation is usually not about the bike.

I often asked staff and youth how to attract more girls. We came up with some effective strategies:

- try to ensure that there are two staff per project and recruit one female for the team;
- group girls together when doing repair tasks in class (boys tend to dominate the tools in group assignments);
- immediately address any issues of sexual harassment in the class;
- create a girls-only time in the shop;
- speak with parents to address their issues or stereotypes;
- spend extra leadership development resources on girls expressing interest and dedication;
- be proactive in identifying, training and employing teenage girls.

Despite our best efforts, RAB consistently achieves between a 30–40 per cent female participation rate.

I have not included 'trickery' in the strategy list. In a recent case, however, I felt the means justified the ends. Children's Aid Society designed a project entitled Smart Girls. Ten girls were asked to spend afternoons at the RAB shop as a way to meet the science component of the conditions of funding. We assigned a senior and teen staff member to the project, both of whom were female. After the girls' second day in class, they rebelled against the 'dirtiness and grease'. The staff and I decided to approach the group with a proposition. We asked them to consider deconstructing bikes to mine for small parts and refashion them into jewellery. They accepted the new class parameters and came up with the business name, Cycle Craft. The girls produced jewellery for themselves and for sale as a way to buy beads and other necessary supplies. In the end, three girls participated in earn-a-bike and each took home a bike they had built.

Running a fledgling non-profit organization requires a wide variety of skills. Raising money was one of the more daunting tasks. Recycle-A-Bicycle had lots of youth with energy and enthusiasm, and lots of second-hand bikes. We decided to capitalize on our assets. It started with an annual bike auction, graduated to monthly bike sale days, and then progressed to running a retail operation.

If there were a 'School of Street Smarts' I might have earned a degree in business. Our first 'store' was located in a community centre that had been taken over by former gang members who had rejected violence in exchange for political action and the celebration of Hispanic art and culture in the Lower East Side of Manhattan. The Recycle-A-Bicycle project was on the third floor of this building with no elevator. People really needed to love our project, because hauling a bicycle that many flights 'ain't easy'. Whether attracted by love or low prices, our customers were artists, students, local residents, and environmentalists. In the first full year of operation, we made enough to pay rent and stock basic accessories. In the second year, we could afford to pay one wage. By our fourth year, we opened a storefront. A year later, we opened a second retail store. By 2001, Recycle-A-Bicycle was recognized as a successful model of social entrepreneurship and became one foundation's model of success.

I tried to create the image of 'Fearless Leader'. Sometimes I succeeded. Sometimes I fell a little short. Once, while leading a summer youth bike ride, I underestimated an obstacle being warned against. I proceeded to ride into wet cement, and then somersaulted onto dry pavement while my 10-speed Atala got mired in the muck. The most amazing aspect of this incident was that not one single teenage boy – all donning their best ghetto look – laughed. That moment was two blocks away from Brighton Beach on a hot August morning. I hosed myself and the bike down at an open fire hydrant and then led the group to the Atlantic Ocean. Upon arrival, the lifeguard informed us that there was no swimming due to a possible shark attack. We hadn't cycled 13 miles to be denied a dip in the ocean, so we waited two hours until the lifeguard let us in. No one spotted a fin during our entire tenure on the beach.

There are moments that can break a person. Mine almost came after I signed a lease to a raw space that required staff, youth and volunteers to fashion a 1,500 square foot room into a bike store and youth training centre. I bought into the vision that this industrial wasteland, known as DUMBO (not an elephant, but rather Down Under the Manhattan Bridge Overpass), would turn into a vibrant waterfront neighbourhood – bike paths in the planning and all. Feeling confident that I had mastered bike repair, I assumed I could tackle a construction project. However, a month into the lease, the raw space remained unchanged: an empty room recently subdivided by cylinder blocks – no bathroom, no electricity, nothing. My moment of despair had arrived.

Seemingly simple tasks were daunting. Take, for example, a trip to Home Depot, a big chain hardware store. Choosing to go at night to avoid the crowds and find people to answer our rooky questions, my crew selected materials to last us a month. This included such large items as a shower, toilet, planks of wood, plywood and so on. At the checkout, when I state that we are going to pay for the delivery service, we are told to put everything back on the shelf and fill out a form so that items can be delivered in a week's time. Right: five hours wasted! The following week, dumpster diving (scavenging in skips left in the roadway) became an adopted practice. Why pay when you can claim perfectly salvageable material out of metal containers that hold construction debris, *and* avoid Home Depot?

The summer construction team developed into quite a crew. To begin with there was me as Superintendent: unqualified but nevertheless the 'Fearless Leader'. I was often found prowling in the local hardware stores or the dumpsters, wearing my favourite overalls (lots of pockets for bike parts or nails and always a tape measure). Then there was the foreman: a retired gentleman who had worked in the Army Corp of Engineers during the Korean War. Bob was the brains and spirit of the whole project. There was Boy Racer – a really fast guy on a fancy bike, who just graduated from college with aspirations of going professional. Pat signed on as Bike Repair Instructor and instead became Head Carpenter. A few weeks into construction, we hired Ray as Bike Shop Manager a.k.a. Plumber. Finally, and most importantly, there were six Summer Youth Employment teens under the Henry Street Settlement partnership program with RAB. They, too, thought they were going to be fixing bikes. Instead, they laid flooring, built workbenches and tool boards, painted walls, and pounded lots of nails out of used planks of wood. In the end, it was their shop, it was our shop, and most importantly, it was not my shop.

Each new season brought new challenges. As RAB matured and expanded, my challenges became more administrative in nature. I learned and then oversaw the bookkeeping, negotiated leases and partnership arrangements, made personnel decisions, wrote funding applications, guided the management of two retail stores, authored start-up manuals, and represented the organization at public events. In this process I, too, matured and grew. Somewhere along the way, I stopped having fun. I missed working on the bikes, and I missed working directly with youth.

Recycle-A-Bicycle embodies so many of the things I believe in: youth empowerment, environmental stewardship, mobility, health and fitness, fun and adventure. It is a hub that will continue to spin with proper maintenance. It will be there to welcome me as a volunteer: teaching, wrenching and cycling.

Chapter 12
Living on Wheels

Jonathan Kington

For many years I had harboured a dream, a romantic idyll if you like, one where I could be constantly on the move – a modern nomadic way of life. Then in October of 2002 my wife Wendy passed away, leaving me with a dog and a campervan. Because the lease on our flat ended with her death, I decided that Jake (the dog) and I should use the camper as a temporary home. At first it was very difficult for both of us, coping with bereavement and a new way of life, which included a totally new job.

One major issue that had to be addressed was the lack of space; by campervan standards ours was quite small, just two single berths and a very small amount of floor space. With Jake being a rather large collie-cross, this did not leave much room for anything else. I had to go from being materialist to minimalist in a very short time: if I didn't use it, I didn't need it, a very strange attitude for me to take.

The first half of that winter was spent working at a garden centre in Surrey, and parking on a campsite in Sussex at night. Although before finding a campsite that was open during the winter months, a lot of nights were spent at a service area on the south side of the M25. This was not as bad as it sounds: if you buy an HGV parking ticket you get a free meal, use of the washing facilities (including a shower) and the security is excellent. This knowledge has stood me in good stead many times over the past four years.

My strongest memory of the closing months of 2002 is the rain; it seemed to be constant, the campsite was always flooding. This meant that we were rarely in the same pitch for two nights running; always having to pester the warden to find out where to park. The rain caused another problem – noise. We had to get used to the almost constant hammering on the roof, although I think I got used to it more quickly than Jake did. With the rain came further problems, a permanently damp dog and wet waterproofs. Overcoming the waterproofs dilemma was quite easy, a hook next to the door used as an entrance. The damp dog was more of a challenge as, even if he was dried, where was I to put his towel? Eventually I just gave up and we put up with being damp all the time. Although I didn't know it at the time, the trials and tribulations were only just starting.

January 2003 saw us moving from the South to the North: I had been offered a job working at a brewery on the Isle of Skye. Having spent time saying goodbye to my sister and my elderly mother, feeling that I might never see her again, we set off with a very strong feeling of trepidation on my part. Our first major problem arose on waking to a very hard frost after spending the night on Tebay Service

Station beside the M6 in Cumbria. Trying to light the gas heating and discovering that it had frozen, my first reaction was to burst into tears. After the tears I very nearly gave up: 'this is a stupid idea, you've just lost your wife, your best friend, you have only got a small campervan *and* a large dog *and* it's the middle of winter.' But I couldn't give up now – that's what I had always done in the past and, after all, I was starting a new life; I had something to prove, if only to myself.

Having been brought up in the north-west of Scotland, I had always considered it as 'home'. So I had jumped at the chance of returning to the sea and mountains of my formative years: in my mind I would be able to relax and enjoy life. Contrary to the popular belief of family members I didn't feel I was 'running away' – oh, how wrong could I have been!

We quickly found a campsite that was open all the year round and parked up: our new life had started. Arriving at the brewery I found that my main job would be doing deliveries around the south of Scotland, including Glasgow, Edinburgh and Stirling. This meant being away for at least two days, but what could I do with Jake? The only answer was to take him with me, much to the annoyance of the transport manager. We had to sleep in the front of the van on service station car parks, which was not good for either of us. But at least I was squeezing three days' work into two, the brewery owner allowed me three days off a week and having these days off meant that we could 'disappear' with the campervan.

The usual destination was a place called Glenbrittle, just a beach, a campsite and a few houses with an amazing mountain backdrop. Because it was winter the campsite was closed but the local farmer would let me park in a sheltered corner near the river. This was somewhere to unwind and regain my sanity. This was what my dream was about; working for a few days and then finding places to park.

Eventually I could take no more of the transport manager's attitude, and I left the job. Because of my mobility it meant that this was easy. I did not have to give notice to any landlord: just 'up sticks' and go. From here we went to Kinloch Hourn, a place that I had always promised myself we would visit one day, having heard that there was an unofficial campsite there. Located on the west coast of Scotland and very remote, there is only one road and that is 22 miles long. After about 15 miles there are huge signs that say 'No Caravans Beyond This Point'. I hesitated briefly and then decided that we did not have a caravan, but a campervan. We managed to scrape (almost literally) down a very narrow road to a small community that seemed to consist of just a shooting lodge and a few houses.

Now this was the life that I had always dreamed of, I had no job and no money – but that didn't matter. I had the freedom of the open road. We spent a week exploring in isolated bliss, long walks, no phone signal and just the occasional sighting of people. But all good things have to come to an end eventually, and we had to return to civilization and reality. It was a bitter pill to swallow, but perhaps my family were right and I really was running away: maybe it *was* too soon. Although I was not ready to give up the dream entirely, Jake and I returned to England.

After spending a few nights on my sister's drive in Staffordshire, I started to look for somewhere to park up, and look for a local job. The new season had not yet started, and the few campsites that were open only allowed a maximum stay of 28 days, but a chance telephone call led me to a nice campsite that would allow me to stay longer. Still living in the campervan, I managed to get a job working at a local Zoological Park.

A couple of months later I made a successful application to a nearby university and enrolled on an Honours Degree course in Ecology as a (very) mature student. This meant that the campervan was going to be too small. Just at that time a caravan came on the market; it had never been moved off the campsite (nor even moved pitch) for about 11 years. It seemed an ideal option and, with financial assistance from my mother, Jake and I moved into (slightly) larger accommodation; so we still lived on wheels, using the caravan to live in and the campervan for holidays. I was still working part-time at the Zoological Park to provide me with a small income to help eke out the student loan; the rent was (compared with a flat or house) very reasonable, and included electricity, water and washing facilities.

Eventually I gained my degree and started work full-time at the Zoological Park. At about the same time the owners of the campsite retired and sold up. The new owners allowed me to stay on the same terms as before, but I was uneasy. Did I want to remain or was it time to move on? Recently, after three and a half years, we moved to another campsite. There is a 28-day limit, but with a further site just across the road that will take us for a further 28 days, I can keep swapping. When all else fails, I am able to use my sister's facilities on a temporary basis. I also use her home as my legitimate postal address.

Making this move has caused me to re-evaluate my present lifestyle. I am registered with local social landlords and waiting to be housed, although this takes time (mostly because I have a dog). But do I really want to settle down? A part of me says 'yes': but then there is an even bigger part that says 'no, not yet'; I am 49, not content in my job, wanting to see new places and meet new people. Although I still miss my wife, I feel that after four years it is time to stop mourning and get on with my life. Maybe it is time to look for temporary or seasonal jobs elsewhere and move on: after all, I take my home with me and therefore I do not have the hassle of looking for accommodation when I get there (wherever 'there' is). The ideal solution may be a larger campervan and do away with the caravan, but financial constraints prevent this at the moment.

Although very popular in America, a lifestyle such as this still seems to be in its infancy in the United Kingdom. It remains the domain of the wealthy and/or retired. Younger people, especially those with caravans, are labelled as Gypsies and/or Travellers. Although seen as a stigmatizing label, I feel this is simply something that has to be endured. There does not appear to be a manual available for living on wheels, so maybe it is time for me to write one. But first I have to live the life.

Chapter 13
Travelling through Veils of Tears

Jen Marchbank

My journey is a reflection on the experience of grief. My relationship to grief and travel has included several transatlantic journeys anticipating loss, including my relocation to Canada. These journeys were very public, taken by aircraft and other public forms of transportation. In such environments, expressions of grief have to be managed, to be minimal, and not to interfere with the actual process of travelling and aim of arriving. My other experience of grief and travelling was private. A regular daily commute, which provided a private space in which to gently acknowledge my loss. The private journeys involve my daily travel whilst working in England following the death of my father. The public journeys relate to the time my grandmother was dying. She was in Scotland whilst I lived in, firstly, the USA and then Canada.

Relevant to all of these journeys are my gendered, and other, identities. My biological and social identities match, I am both female and feminine. My femininity appears to have become enhanced by my motherhood, that is, motherhood seemed to unlock the door to the 'adult women's club' populated by other mothers. In addition, both my feminine appearance and my motherhood operate to mask my lesbian identity. This is not something I seek, but my ability to 'pass' as heterosexual reduces the anxiety felt by family members that my identity might not be accepted in our small Scottish community. As such, every time I make the return to my 'home' I enter into an environment where I am expected to behave, react and respond from behind a mask. Even whilst grieving.

My father died in 2000. It was not a gentle death, surprising many, including close relatives. It did not surprise my mother, my siblings or me. My father kept his ill health a secret but we knew, although it was not really discussed. I approached my Departmental Head, told him I was off to Scotland and asked, if I needed it, for permission for leave. I needed it. Within hours of reaching Scotland, my father was admitted to Emergency, then Intensive Care. He died soon after. This is not about his death; it is about how I found space to grieve for him.

The day before my father died, I discovered that the pregnancy I had long awaited was finally a reality. What should have been a most joyful moment was overshadowed by my father's suffering. This most joyful moment was completely without joy for me. I could not celebrate a potential new life at the crux of my father's fight for life. He died, we buried him, and we settled his affairs. I went back to work.

After my father's death, I was focused on a combination of grief, familial support and anticipation of motherhood. The latter I kept from my family for six months for I believed they needed time to grieve before learning of a potential new member borne by a lesbian mother. Nine months after my father's death my child was born – a great joy. He filled my life, yet I still needed to grieve for my father. I found that space, not at home, but in my car on the daily return commute between work and my child's day care.

Cars are viewed as private: as private property and as private spaces. For those of us who drive, a car can be our mobile bubble in a world of sensory information. They are a sanctuary, only shared by those invited in. As the sole traveller and driver in a car, we can determine not only where and how we drive, but also what we listen to and how we react.

What I relate here was not deliberate. It just happened. It was a long and slow process rather than a moment of catharsis. A year or so after my father's death I began to cry. I only cried in my car, and only between leaving work and collecting my child. This was, on reflection, the only private time I had in my day and the privacy of that drive afforded me space to grieve.

By contrast, my transatlantic journeys were very public and exposed. I made these journeys to and from the USA and Canada in 2005, the first in March to be with my grandmother for what we believed to be her final days. She survived that time, and I had to return to the USA to complete my contract. My next journey was when I left the USA permanently. This coincided with another crisis in Granny's health, so again I travelled fearing that I would not win this second race against time. My final journey related to Granny was my move to Canada. This journey I took alone, so also felt bereft at leaving my child, who had to remain for some time in Scotland. Each of these was a highly public journey, involving the negotiation of many instances of scrutiny, of complications and of emotion.

Different forms of travel expose us to varying degrees of scrutiny. We are particularly under observation when crossing international borders and before boarding aircraft. This inspection is personal; it involves our legal identity and our personhood, sex and gender become conflated during such scrutiny, especially when it involves an invasion of our personal space. My femaleness is obvious and never questioned by officials, which is not the case for transgendered people who often face demands to 'prove' their biological rather than social identity. There have been, though, occasions when my parenting relationship to my accompanying child has been checked (I do not object to this for I assume it to occur to protect against child abduction).

Although my femaleness has never been an issue, aspects relating to my gender identity always arise during such public travel as on aircraft. As gender is socially constructed, it involves not just biological sex but other social identities. I am often misread. As my physical appearance accords with what society accepts as feminine, as my passport states 'sex, female' and as I am travelling with my biological child, certain assumptions are made: for example, asking my child if he is looking forward to meeting up with 'daddy' or assuming we are always travelling for pleasure. Yet it was a single, lesbian mother who took these transatlantic journeys. I was returning to my place of birth, to say goodbye to a very close relative and to grieve my loss. Later, my return from Scotland to the USA would not be for family reunion, nor for vacation; it would be to return to my academic post.

The gender element of this experience began long before the actual journeys, arising from the nature of my relationship with my grandmother and other family members. I shared a strong emotional bond with my grandmother, one based in our shared femaleness but also strengthened from periods living together. There was also a time in my childhood when my mother was absent fulfilling her duty of care as a daughter, to her dying father. During this time, my paternal grandmother was the main female presence on a daily basis. Observing my mother diligently and lovingly assume responsibility for nursing my beloved maternal grandfather instilled another understanding in me. I understood that the duty of care, that the greatest expression of love, involved being present during the process of dying and death. Further, although the men in my close and extended family do assume care duties of loved ones, the message received was that it was most expected of women. This social learning and these relationships influenced my decisions and desires to be present when I felt my grandmother needed me most.

The first 'race against time' began a couple of weeks before my son and I flew to the UK. We were in the USA and I was receiving daily reports from my mother regarding Granny's health. My family are well aware that Granny and I were very close and there was an unspoken expectation that I should be there and an acknowledgement that I wanted and needed to be with her. Although my grandmother never pressurized me to come, she was aware I was in the USA for a limited period, and frequently asked my mother how long it was until I would be back. The actual journey involved two flights, one train, one bus, one taxi, one drive and a walk. My son was only five and I did not want him to witness the situation, nor me, operating through grief. I arranged for him to stay with my ex-partner, once we reached the UK. The final legs of this journey I took alone.

The matrix of emotions experienced on this journey included stress and anxiety, concern about leaving my son, trust in my ex-partner for his care, and fear that I would not be in time. All of these were experienced within the dispassionate and sterile space that is an international airport. We flew out of Washington, DC. We flew post 9/11. We flew on British passports, mine indicating that I am an academic. As always happens when I fly from/within the USA, I was pulled from the line at security, body-checked and asked questions. Whilst I am usually immune to this, this time I was anxious. Anxious that some security scare would delay me. One cannot display such emotions in these circumstances. Security officials are prompted to respond to passengers showing anxiety, nervousness or stress. I could not afford to show my emotions for fear that I might be subject to further questioning, potentially causing delay. I feared not only delay but also, if I were to be held, where would my son be and what would he experience? As such, numbness was the safest emotional display.

Over a day after the beginning of my journey, I got to my 'home' village. I had already assumed the persona required of me in this situation. I dropped my bag at my mother's house and she and I immediately headed for the nursing home a few streets away. I found my grandmother frail and tired, not surprising at 100 years of age. Although I had expected this, I was still shocked. I spent each day with her, talking to her and attending her last communion. Although she drifted in and out of consciousness each day, she lived through my whole visit. I travelled back to the USA by the reverse route, collecting my son at the first airport. I returned to the States: I had left Granny still alive, without closure, yet not expecting to see her again.

In the end, Granny survived my second 'race against time' as well. I was leaving the USA at the end of my visa. This trip had been planned, but it was thwarted by bad weather, which resulted in delays, diversions and lost luggage. Yet she was still there when I returned to Scotland, and again I thought I only had time to collect my mother and immediately go to her nursing home. I remained in Scotland for four months awaiting my visa for Canada, each day taking several trips to her bedside. I wished for closure before I moved to Canada, to be with her at her last moment. I suspect she wanted to have every visit she could have. Our last visit was just hours before I flew out. I arrived in Canada, wrote to her, and she died hours after having my letter read to her. I suspect she knew that this time she could not outlast my absence. The excitement of my relocation to Canada was tempered both by having to leave my child behind and by my inability to return to bury my grandmother. I faced grieving alone, in a foreign land. This is an extremely lonely experience.

One of the main aspects of this whole experience for me is the fact that it took place in the public domain, with each journey taken under the scrutiny of anti-terrorist activity. In addition, each period in Scotland required that I assume the role of 'appropriate' womanhood, which excludes my lesbianism. At least in Canada, although I was alone and no one knew of my loss, I could be open and true about myself.

These two experiences hold commonalities and differences. Grief, loss, love exist in both. Fear and anxiety also shaped the second. One set of experiences was extremely public, the other very private. The rawness of the emotions I felt has returned in this journey of revisitation.

Chapter 14

Road Rage

Keith Sharp

Generally speaking I do not go around wanting to kill people. Or even to hurt them. I am usually pretty tolerant of people's mistakes (well, at least as tolerant as the next man) and even when someone has been especially mendacious or stupid I am more inclined to try to analyze their motives, or errors, than be moved to violent remonstration. Why, then, is it that a silly mistake, or act of petty selfishness, which ordinarily would be overlooked, laughed off or in more serious cases, subjected to some sort of pseudo-Freudian psychoanalysis, can become the source of irrationally violent and near homicidal rage when carried out by the driver of a car in the presence of drivers of other cars?

Do not misunderstand me: I am not saying I am any more prone to episodes of 'road rage' than most other people. Actually, given that last year I covered some 30,000 miles, mostly either very early in the morning, or at the end of a gruelling day, I think I am fairly even tempered in the car. But I cannot deny that there have been moments behind the wheel of my car when, as a result of what at the time seemed like extreme and unbearable provocation (but what in the cold light of day was, in reality, an act of petty incivility), I have simply wanted to kill someone.

All drivers are, I suppose, different. In general I am much more sanguine about the honest mistake than the act of loutish selfishness. A driver who carelessly pulls out in front of me without looking, but then quickly gestures an apology, is far less likely to incur my wrath than one who deliberately undertakes (even though I might be sitting mindlessly at 60 mph in the outside lane of a motorway). I have regularly experienced that sudden surge of emotion, the precursor to genuine rage, as a result of some minor transgression by another motorist, only to find it subside as quickly when they hold up their hand or, better still, mouth an apology. I have even been known to feel a twinge of guilt on such occasions, not at anything I have done, but at what I *might* have done had the apology not been forthcoming.

The thing I nearly always find impossible to tolerate, however, is any suggestion by another motorist that I am in the wrong. Whether or not I am actually in the wrong is completely irrelevant to how I feel and react – indeed, I have often wondered whether perhaps I find it even more intolerable when I *am* in the wrong. Probably the most minor, but frequently experienced, example of this is when a traffic light changes, I do not notice and the car behind me sounds its horn. For some reason this fills me with rage. Sometimes I am able to maintain the façade that it simply has not happened and move off in the normal way. Too often, however, I will react by uttering – or shouting – an obscenity (far more extreme and disgusting than anything I would ordinarily say *outside* the car, whatever the provocation) or worse still, engaging in some act of absurd defiance. I have, for example, simply sat there through a whole further cycle of the lights in the hope that this will teach the horning offender a lesson in manners. Once I sat through two complete cycles and sped off just as the light turned red, thus leaving my by now confused and angry victim sitting at a red light for the third time in succession. The initial satisfaction this sort of thing gives me is sublime; as the emotional surge subsides, however, joy soon gives way to shame and the hope that no one I know has seen me perform this act of ridiculous childishness.

Another example, where usually I feel my over-reaction is much more justified, is when another motorist shakes their head at something I do. I imagine them 'tut-tutting' too, and this makes me worse. On these occasions I want to drag the offending driver from their car and perform medieval acts of torture on them. I want to see them so chastened, so full of remorse, that they hand over their keys, cut up their licence and decide never to infect our roads with their foul presence again. In reality, of course, none of these things actually happen. But I have, on occasion, braked sharply in front of an offending head-shaker and then driven some distance at a preposterously slow speed in road conditions where overtaking is impossible. Again, rage quickly subsides into joy and an absurdly inappropriate sense of moral self-righteousness, as I look in the mirror and see my anger transferred into the face of the 'offender'.

I have followed people too. Not far, admittedly, but with lights on full beam and at a frankly unsafe distance. Nearly always they have turned off the route I am taking minutes or even seconds after the precipitating incident and I have judged, by this time, that it is simply not worth my while going out of my way for them and I just continue on my way. But this is a far cry from my initial furious resolve to follow them to the end of the earth and disembowel them with a pitchfork.

Why do people – and me in particular – get so angry in the car? In one sense there are good reasons to be angry with people who endanger our lives and those of our passengers by stupid, thoughtless or wilfully dangerous acts. But I don't think this is really the reason for most cases of 'road rage'. For one thing, most of the provoking actions – in my case at least – are fairly trivial and have not even involved a threat to my car, let alone its occupants. Also, again in my experience, when I have felt my life has genuinely been threatened by the actions of another motorist, I have felt completely different. Shaken, frightened and deeply grateful that I have survived a near miss, rather than the surge of infantile fury associated with road rage.

Part of the answer might lie in the curious blurring of public and private which car travel involves. In one sense driving a car is obviously a public act – by definition it is a public act in that it takes place on public roads in the presence of other members of the public, both fellow motorists and pedestrians. In another, it is a very private act. The interior of one's car, for example, is an extension of one's home: people keep all sorts of 'private' things in their cars, from items of clothing to personal papers, and one's car can be 'messy' and not on public display in just the same way as one's home. Cars are similarly extensions of private, or even intimate, social spaces. Conversations with other occupants of the car are private and even when travelling in a car alone, one is in a private space, alone with one's music, mobile telephone conversations or even one's own private thoughts. We have, I suspect, all seen the lone driver of a car singing lustily along with his or her favourite tracks, or aggressively picking his or her nose as they might in the privacy of their own home but never would whilst sitting in a café or walking down a busy high street.

Road rage, then, might be seen in part as a consequence of the sudden incursion of hostile strangers into one's private domain. We perhaps feel almost as we would were a complete stranger to wander into our home and start sneering at our taste in furniture, or the pile of unwashed dishes in the kitchen. They do not pose a physical threat as such, but they certainly do pose a threat in other ways, perhaps threatening the very essence of our ability to manage our public identities and thus to be who we want to be. And so we lash out in a state of misplaced moral indignation – just as we would at the sneering stranger in our kitchen.

What of gender? In writing this piece I have deliberately refrained from searching any psychological or criminological literature on the subject of gender difference in driver behaviour or patterns of conviction for motoring offences and the like. My impression – and that is all it is – is that whilst women are far from immune from road rage, it is more commonly a phenomenon found in men. In that sense, it would not be unlike other categories of violent or aggressive behaviour. In my experience, however, gender does play into it in some quite specific ways.

First of all, my impression is that when women become seized with road rage, it tends to be less extreme than when men do. I have noticed that they tend to confine themselves to a single gesture, or mouthed expletive, rather than the more reckless manifestations of aggressive and dangerous driving sometimes displayed by men. That is not to say, however, that relative to women's 'normal' behavioural range, female road rage cannot be quite extreme. The first occasion I ever heard my mother use really foul language was when someone pulled out in front of her in a car – and 30 or so years later this remains one of the very few such occasions, at least of which I am aware.

There are also, I believe, differences when the perpetrator of an outburst of road rage is a woman. I am certainly much less inclined to exhibit the sort of behaviour described above when I am the 'victim' of some thoughtless act by a female driver. I have even found myself gesturing apologies to female drivers whom I mistakenly believed initially to be men and reacted to their thoughtlessness accordingly. And although I do find criticism of my driving as hard to tolerate from a woman as from a man, I am far less prone to extreme overreaction in the former cases. Before now I have never really considered why all of this should be so. Simplistically and with self-justification I might say it is because I am a 'gentleman' and, as such, find aggressive behaviour towards women unattractive and unacceptable. But even I am not going to let myself get away with this. However superficially appealing I might find it, I have spent enough of my life in the company of formidably intelligent feminists to realize that 'chivalry' is rooted in assumptions of female inferiority and that those who invoke it are inescapably asserting the intellectual, physical and moral superiority of men – albeit in the nicest possible way.

I suppose, in the end (and, to be honest, I really hate coming to this conclusion), that it probably has a lot to do with the way men are conditioned to 'perform' their masculinity in our society. Cars are, however we may qualify this, phallic symbols. They symbolize masculinity (and I heave a heavy sigh as I write this) in a culture in which physical power (for that you can read speed) and competitive aggression are the valued indices of true masculinity. Threats to one's car and, more specifically, threats to the position of one's car in the competitive hierarchy of the roads on which masculinity is played out, cannot be tolerated any more than physical emasculation itself. An assault on one's competence as a driver is an assault on one's competence as a man, and everything that entails.

Chapter 15

Learning to Fly

Andy Reynolds

My employer had despatched me to a three-year stint in the USA, a land where aviation is a part of the fabric, yet had left me less than taxed in the workplace. I'm an engineer and I need constant mental stimulation, preferably of a technical nature. I can't say that I had always yearned to fly, boyhood daydreaming apart, but I was in need of a new personal challenge. My research suggested that becoming a private pilot could not only provide the technical challenge of learning how aeroplanes work, but also might be suitably demanding in spatial terms with the need to navigate in three dimensions and visualize airspace. As I was to discover, the third and greatest reward would lie in the successful coordination of eyes and limbs.

I signed up with a local flying school and started to take lessons. It was a small school that had once thrived, but following the terrorist attacks of 2001 its proximity to the now heavily protected Washington DC airspace made operations very difficult. I had to be cleared by the US Secret Service to fly to and from the airfield, and navigation errors would quickly have resulted in interception by US Air Force fighters, or worse. The runway was paved, but only 40 feet wide and not very long. It was surrounded by tall trees, overhead power cables, flocks of resident vultures and Andrews Air Force Base. The school's two Cessna aircraft were aged but airworthy. I imagine their undercarriage had withstood some abuse, given the peculiar currents of squirrelly air that made every landing an adventure back at base.

I flew my first 30-odd hours with this outfit, learning the basics with an instructor who was not yet old enough to rent a car. He was paid about $10 for each hour the aeroplane's engine ran, but the main benefit to him was the accrual of logbook hours on his long path to becoming a professional pilot. After my first 20 hours or so – about three months – the poor lad had to make a big decision: was I sufficiently skilled to start flying solo? He braced himself and sent me aloft to fly some circuits (taking off, circling and landing) around the airfield. I was at once terrified and thrilled when the aircraft leapt into the air, free of the burden of a second occupant. The first landing went well, but I chose to abort the next two because I was unable to stabilize the final approach. I was very relieved when my fourth attempt proved successful, and was then able to fly five more without incident. Back in the shack, the wizened old airfield manager confided that his first solo had been very similar; he had gone on to fly for the airlines for decades, and the warmth of his encouragement was my first introduction to the legendary camaraderie that binds together pilots of all ages, genders, abilities and logbook contents.

I would like to have met more student pilots, to compare notes, but only the aeroplane gets to do that. With few exceptions, students work full time to earn the money to pay for the lessons, so they seldom have time to hang around airfields chatting. But I do remember one student who was largely resident at the field: a diminutive 50-something woman, friendly yet determined, who had flown several hundred hours as a student but was yet to qualify. I would often see her carry her booster seat out to the aircraft and set off on ferry flights to a nearby maintenance base. Although this relationship was symbiotic in that she gained logbook hours while the school benefited from free ferry piloting, I couldn't help wondering what more the school might have done to get her through her remaining hurdles.

The second big milestone for a student pilot is the first solo cross-country flight. When the weather is right, and the navigation plan is approved, the intrepid student is authorized to proceed alone to a distant airport. He or she must handle all the navigation and communications, and is officially the pilot-in-command of the aircraft. For all the racking of nerves and technical concentration, it was a tremendous feeling of freedom to be crossing a hundred miles of rural Virginia at 6,000 feet.

The school ran through a bad patch after that first cross-country. Aircraft frequently became defective, instructors became unavailable, and the manager became elusive. I moved to another school, more expensive but much more professional. Although a longer drive to get there, the runway was huge and the airspace a little less demanding. My new instructor was a friendly young fellow who made a large dent in the aircraft's weight-and-balance calculations. He is now flying regional jets across the USA. Once I had gained his confidence, I flew further cross-country solos, and did some night flying and simulated instrument flying, ticking off the experience requirements of the Private Pilot syllabus. I also passed the knowledge test, a computer-based theory examination of several hours' duration.

The final hurdle is the practical examination. Few fail their 'final checkride', not because it is easy (it is not) but because Schools prepare their students well. They do this because the exam is conducted by an external examiner designated by the Federal Aviation Administration, and the student's performance contributes to the reputation of the school at the FAA. The Chief Instructor accompanied me on a 'stage check' flight, giving me demanding navigation and manoeuvring tasks including a very tense short-field landing among tall trees on a downhill runway. The aeroplane must have known that I was to be pressured, because its engine began to run very roughly as we entered a ground reference manoeuvre only 800 feet above the earth. There was limited power, but luckily we were only a few miles from a large regional airport with multiple runways. We limped in – in fact I landed rather well under the circumstances – and phoned the school's office for a lift home while the engine was repaired. Few students are lucky enough to experience a partial engine failure with the Chief Instructor on board: his steel was exemplary and my memory of the occasion might just make some future emergency a little bit easier to handle.

I had imagined that, by the time I flew for the practical examination, after 65 hours' flying experience in a year of training, I would be quite confident in the air. Not so: I was very anxious. On the day, it was 100 degrees Fahrenheit and the air was thick with haze. After several hours of oral examination on the ground, we were away. The visibility was marginal, concealing the horizon to make flying by visual references quite challenging. I thought I had slipped outside the tolerances on many of the manoeuvres, but after a gruelling two hours in the air, whilst taxiing back to the parking area, I learned to my surprise that I had passed the test. I was too exhausted to be elated; too relieved to be proud. My wife drove me home.

Piloting my wife aloft features highly among my reasons for flying. Soon after qualifying, I took her on a short sightseeing flight through the Shenandoah Valley and over historic Harper's Ferry, bringing her back safely and feeling very pleased with myself. She no longer sees flying as an end in itself, which I suppose is a vote of confidence akin to a car passenger feeling able to fall asleep. Sometimes it's humbling to be trusted; I felt the same way when a friend asked me to take his teenage son out for a pleasure flight.

Before leaving the USA, I flew my wife from Washington to Niagara Falls and back, crossing five states, for an afternoon's sightseeing. It was a very rewarding five-hour round trip for a two-hour stroll and an ice cream. My 'co-pilot' proved to be a capable navigator, matching the features below with those on the chart to keep us on track and maintaining a keen lookout for other aircraft.

I suppose I have a disappointingly prosaic view of flying. Not for me the 'dance on laughter-silvered wings' of John Gillespie Magee's[1] famous wartime poem; rather, I'm afraid, the deep satisfaction of a skilfully executed crosswind landing with its crossed-control final approach extracting every ounce of coordination to smooth first the windward main wheel, then the leeward, and finally the nose wheel gently onto the tarmac. In flight, apart from a brief *frisson* when the setting sun puts a glint in my wife's eyes, I try to allow myself no emotional departure from the minute-by-minute business of managing risk: my eyes continually shift between engine and fuel gauges, instruments and sky; my ears scour the airwaves for potentially conflicting traffic; hands and feet constantly feel the aeroplane's health through the flying controls. It's a serious business for me, and I save the Zen moments until I'm back on earth. As the old-timers say, 'Rule one: fly the aeroplane.'

---

1 John Gillespie Magee (1942) 'High Flight', Faith and Freedom, an exhibition of poems held at the Library of Congress in February 1942.

Chapter 16
Born to be Wild?

Mike Barnsley

I have always been somewhat infatuated with bikes. As a teenager I used to read bike magazines with great enthusiasm. I liked the idea of riding long distances, exploring, covering miles. One article I remember clearly was a comparison of touring bikes including a Harley-Davidson Electra Glide, a Honda Goldwing and a big BMW. The test ride was a coast-to-coast trip across the States from New York to LA. Wonderful. Around this time I bought and built a model of the Harley Electra Glide. I was fascinated by its massive engine, footboards and three lights at the front. Even the model seemed huge.

I lived in a rural area and had been getting about by cycling for several years. At 16, the opportunity to buy a moped for £10 changed my life. I could travel further, faster (just about), more comfortably and later at night. (I guess you could cycle late at night, but it wasn't much fun!) Life was great. I had real freedom for the first time.

A succession of European and Japanese bikes followed. I covered many thousands of miles, for work and pleasure. The longest trip undertaken was a touring holiday of Spain and Portugal. Then changes in life meant leisure riding all but disappeared. The BMW I then owned was too much bike just for commuting and it was sold. I can remember it being driven off by its proud new owner. I stood and watched until he went out of sight. A strange feeling. I had decided to sell the bike. I got a good price. I even knew it was going to a 'good home' and would be well looked after. But I knew I had lost something important. One or two smaller bikes after this were no substitute and didn't last long. I then spent ten years without a bike at all. Then my job took me to America.

I decided to try and get a Harley like the model I had made so many years before. But things were not that easy. Most dealers had no bikes in stock. New bikes were ordered a year or so in advance and were picked up as soon as they were delivered. Because of this the price of used bikes was ridiculously high, often more than new models. The local dealer had decided to sell all the next year's allocation on one day. I queued overnight to be sure of getting the only model I could nearly afford. Nine months later, in the middle of a severe Nebraska winter, it arrived!

I owned a Harley! It was in the garage. I spent most of the day in the garage. Looking at the bike. Starting it up and listening to it. The garage was huge, big enough for three cars. I cleared the garage and rode the bike around. It was wonderful. I gave the kids rides from one side of the garage to the other. They thought it was wonderful too. I called friends in the UK so they could listen to the bike. Oddly enough, they didn't seem quite as excited as I was, but there you go.

This level of insanity continued for several weeks until we had some relatively good weather. ('Relatively' because it was still around freezing point, but it had been dry for a while and the road surface seemed good.) I wrap up like the 'Michelin Man' and set off. Soon I'm out of town. I open the bike up to somewhere between 50 and 60, (I'm running in a brand new engine). I felt great. I loved the experience. I was freezing to death. I headed back. I'd covered about 20 miles. I visited a friend on the way back. 'Hey look, I'm out on my Harley. Cool, or what?' He was impressed and took some photos. I got the bike back to the house and took some more. I was a happy man.

Some time later I got the bike out again. I decided to fill up with petrol as the dealer hadn't put too much in. The weather was still cold enough to keep most sane bikers off the roads, so I attracted some attention. The attendant looked at the bike and asked, 'Is that a Harley?' Poker-faced, I grunted back, 'Yeah.' I hoped to convey, 'Of course it is – do I look like someone who would ride anything other than a Harley?' I had covered 50 miles on a Harley and about 100,000 on a variety of other bikes. But that was in a different life. I was a changed man. A Harley convert.

As explained in the free video that came with the bike, I had become part of the Harley-Davidson family. No going back. I soon got the chance to buy my longed-after, dreamed about, Electra Glide: in black. The roads were calling my name. I answered. I attended the famous Sturgis rally three times, Daytona Beach Bike Week and a run down the Florida keys, various charity runs in Nebraska and Iowa, Harley Owners Group State and National Rallies, and a whole variety of dinner runs, ice cream runs, days out, and weekends away. I visited the Harley plants at Milwaukee, Tomahawk, York and Kansas City. I loved every minute of it, every mile on the roads, every farm passed, every small town driven through, every roadside restaurant eaten at, every encounter with other riders. The Harley is built to meander across America's vast landscape and it does so admirably, soaking up the endless miles of roads across the prairies in the Mid West.

I soon discovered a significant difference between biking in the UK and the US. People in the States like bikes, particularly Harleys. When filling up with petrol, people of any age will come and ask where you're heading, discuss the bike, compare it to one they used to own or would like to own or is owned by a friend or relation. I've had conversations with admiring children and wistful pensioners. People wave at me not just from other bikes, but also from their cars, pick-ups, eighteen-wheel trucks. This is even more the case on the way to or from a rally when there are a lot of bikes on the road. People seem to appreciate the freedom that a bike represents and they respect those who are out there enjoying that freedom, especially those on Harleys. In and around Sturgis, Daytona Beach or any other popular destination, the message 'Bikers Welcome' is displayed on huge signs. And they mean it. Bikers are no longer the Wild Ones, but respectable, interesting people with serious potential as good customers to be courted. Businesses, and the police, arrange bikes-only parking areas at the major events, and they are in the best locations – not two miles out of town. The police generally take a relaxed view at biker events, ignoring many discrepancies between enthusiastic customization and the letter of the law. Bike events at Daytona Beach are the most popular held in the area: there is less trouble, better business, and better tips, than with any other visiting group. The small town of Sturgis thrives on the image of their rally and the 500,000-plus visitors that are attracted each year. A significant part of this attitude is, I believe, due to the incredibly positive image created by my Harley-Davidson 'family' who have not only changed the attitude of the nation to their brand of bike, but to the whole image of motorcycling. I am, and will remain, extremely grateful to them. Americans' appreciation of, and affection for, Harley-Davidson as representing all that is positive in their history and heritage, is quite phenomenal.

The aura of the Harley and its association with freedom and individuality is important. Owning a Harley makes a stronger statement than owning any other brand of bike. Owning a customized, rather than an off-the-shelf, Harley makes that statement even more powerfully. Over the years I have spent more on making changes to my bike than I originally spent on the bike. I have changed the engine, gearbox, tank, screen, seat, pannier bags, front fender, forks, handlebars, levers, grips and switches as well as adding lights and a variety of rails and trims. Many of the changes were designed to refer back to the 1965 Electra Glide that I had been obsessed with for years, others to improve functionality in some way, others still simply to improve looks. It is no longer obvious what year or exact model my bike is. I like that. I think it makes it interesting. Even though, in all probability, nobody else would really understand what I have done or why.

Spending some time analyzing my own adventures, it struck me that although I was attending huge events or going on rides with hundreds of other enthusiasts, my biking activities were effectively undertaken alone. As time went on, and particularly after I returned to the UK, this became more true. I typically ride to events, rallies or meetings on my own. I observe rather than participate in what goes on. I enjoy the atmosphere and the camaraderie, but I am really an outsider. I don't really have a problem with this. I guess I've always enjoyed the solitude of riding and the 'events' give me a destination to ride to.

Over the years I have come to enjoy the detachment of riding more than anything else. It gives me the opportunity to completely disconnect and truly get away from it all. I set myself targets of places to go, journeys to undertake, miles to complete, really just for the sake of doing it. I rode coast-to-coast and border-to-border across the States. 8,000 miles, one trip, two weeks. I have ridden over 1,000 miles in a day in the UK. I have ridden from John O'Groats to Land's End. I recently undertook a sponsored ride around all the Harley-Davidson dealers in the UK and Ireland. It was great. I rode 2,500 miles in just over a week, but had to visit all the dealers during opening hours to pick up stickers as proof of the visit. The day after I finished I set off for a rally in Southern Austria, about 1,000 miles away. All undertaken on my own. I got tired, lonely, stiff, wet, hot, cold. Life was good. I rode, ate, slept. Looked at my map occasionally. Not necessarily as often as I should.

I spend what little free time I have during the winter planning my trips, targets and goals for the next riding season. Sometimes I think the way I spend my time on the bike is very sad. Most of the time I think it's wonderful. I still love my bike. I have owned it over ten years now, and we have got to know each other. We are comfortable together. I can't really see myself buying a different Harley. I certainly can't see myself ever buying another brand of bike. I can't really envisage any situation in which I would ride any distance with anyone else. I still attend large events, but make my own arrangements and ride on my own. I would like to get to the point where I am not driven by some goal or target, and just be able to go out for a ride. I think this is possible. But maybe not for a year or two yet. I am not quite sure why. I think maybe I am trying to prove something to myself or others about being a 'real' biker. But I'm not even sure what that is. Maybe it's actually something to do with not having to prove yourself to anyone. I certainly don't feel a need to prove myself in terms of speed. I guess for me a real biker covers lots of miles, in all kinds of weather. But for what purpose? My job precludes me from using my bike for work any more, so any riding is for pleasure only. If the only purpose for riding is to prove something about how much I ride, isn't it self-defeating and aren't all my efforts in vain? I can't cope with thinking about this much more. I think I'll go out for a ride.

Chapter 17
Moving Bodies in Running

Carole Sutton

When I reflect on how I have progressed from being a nonrunner in my early 30s to a marathon endurance runner in my late 30s, I have no positive recollections of participating in athletics or sport as a girl/young woman. In fact I can remember with dread the summer term at school where the sports day was an opportunity for all to join together in house games involving track and field events. I would always opt for a throwing event such as shot-put, as it involved lots of sitting around chatting to classmates. In the winter I distinctly remember the breathlessness caused by cold winter cross country runs and the feeling of salty sweat on my face, frozen limbs being rapidly warmed as I scurried back into the classroom for the next lesson. Back then, I felt there was nothing enjoyable or pleasant about such experiences.

As an adult, my own route into running has been a journey that started with a charity 5km race before progressing to ever longer distances and eventually a marathon. My experience mirrors the global popularity of mass participation running events such as the London marathon. Running is now part of my life and it is only when I meet up with friends and family who have not seen me for a few years who comment on my newfound 'sportiness' that I am starkly reminded of how this contrasts with my early years.

Running is an embodied activity that alters according to the environment, time and social setting. I am constantly aware of this as I run alone or with others; run in the morning or the evening; at different speeds; in urban or rural locations; in cold and warm weather conditions, and as I undertake the more general management of fitting running into other everyday activities. Here, I focus on the different ways in which I 'run', by contrasting two environments that form part of my regular training. These are the track-based interval training and endurance-based longer runs. My reflections are based on personal training diaries kept during a period of marathon training in winter 2005 and spring 2006.

On a cold, windswept Tuesday evening I am with my friends in the car driving to the local running track. We are laughing and half-heartedly moaning about the cold weather conditions – it's about 2°C. We arrive at the running track and as usual we warm-up before completing a track session. This session has been planned by the club coach and is based on our preparation for a marathon. We are to run 400m at our predicted marathon pace followed by 400m at a faster

5km pace. This is to be repeated for a total of 20 laps. My marathon lap will be 2 mins and 5 seconds and my 5km lap will be 1 min 50 seconds.

We are endurance runners and share the track venue with faster track athletes from the local athletic club. In recent weeks there has been an increasing tension between the different users of the track space and there is now a debate about who should run in which of the six available lanes. We, 'the endurance runners', have been told to use the inside two lanes, however some of the faster endurance runners within our group now want to subdivide further by relative speed. They argue that having to overtake slower runners impedes their training performance as they have to run out from lane one into lane two to overtake, while others argue that this has positive effects by improving racing and overtaking skills. The majority of the faster runners are men, although there are a couple of faster women in this group. It is only a few of the men who complain.

I keep quiet and stay out of this debate. I feel uncomfortable about it all and pretty angry. It's not like we are high performers! In my small group we exchange knowing glances of discontentment with the situation. It could easily start to feel that we are not welcome at this track, perhaps we are just a nuisance for being slow? And maybe because we are women?

We decide to concentrate on our own running and in our small group we all run at a similar speed. I run in lycra tights and a close fitting thermal top. I am slightly self-conscious that I am still a 'relatively heavy and slow runner' compared to others here, but the clothes are practical and appropriate for the conditions. I have my lightweight track shoes on and my multiple lap watch. I am repeatedly lapped by the 'faster' runners but I feel unperturbed as I am actually enjoying myself – heart beating fast, exhausted, breathless, hot and sweaty. As we get to lap 10, limbs starting to ache. Now breathing a little harder, by lap 15 I can feel individual muscles starting to protest that they are tired and as the lactic starts to build it is a case of literally willing my body to complete the last five laps. I ignore the voice in my head that says 'you could just stop short and not finish the last few laps' but I know this would leave me disappointed and angry that I did not push myself just that little bit further. I am determined to finish the session and at the end I lay on the cold wet grass, gasping for air. As I feel my heart rate slowly decline to a normal pulse a steam of sweat rises from my head. All the endurance runners are now standing together congratulating each other for finishing the session. The earlier debate on who runs in what lane discarded to one side but I have not forgotten what was said. My exhaustion overrides my anger. After a few minutes I remember how cold it is and rush to put on a sweater: it has a lovely soft warm feel against my damp skin (November 2005).

It's a Sunday morning and time for my long endurance run. Normally I would run with one or two other women but today they are unable to meet up. I enjoy running with others but the solitude of running alone is also enjoyable – time to think and reflect. It does not involve negotiating aspects like routes, the time to meet, who leads the group, setting the run pace and when to take drinks breaks. Today I need to run 22 miles and it will be my longest training run in preparation for the marathon. I decide to run the cycle path that starts in the city centre before it follows along an old disused railway line up on to the moor. 11 miles out and 11 miles back. I start out at 08:00 hrs; it's a warm sunny morning with a slight breeze.

At first the path follows along a main road and there is little traffic on the road at this time in the morning. This is a slow run so I can take in my surroundings. As the path then joins the old railway line volunteers are repairing the fencing for the steam train that operates over a short stretch. As I pass them we say 'good morning'. In the shade of the trees I look up into the canopy and spot the odd bird and squirrel. I think about home and work, and make vague plans for completing various tasks. My legs feel good and strong as a result of the previous month's training. There are a few people using the path, mainly other runners and people walking their dogs, we exchange polite greetings such as 'hi', 'good morning' and 'nice weather'. With few users it is easy for me to choose the exact route I take. I can run on either side of the path; the choice is mine though I tend to stay on the left side. After 110 mins of running I reach the halfway point and it is time to turn around. I have a five-minute break to drink some water and a high carbohydrate nutritional supplement for energy. I am still feeling good, the weather is a little warmer now and the sun is starting to warm my slightly sweating face.

As I follow my route back, the path is now busier with much more traffic to negotiate. There are more dogs and some owners let their dogs run up to me which I hate as I fear the dogs barking. Cyclists appear from nowhere and like runners they travel at different speeds swerving in and around people. Casual walkers weave across the path ahead of me and I am unsure as to whether I should change my running line. This is now not such a relaxing run and I start to feel anxious that I will be tripped or bitten. A few users speak and acknowledge my 'hello' while many others do not. After a while I stop greeting people as I start to feel a bit stupid saying 'hello' to strangers who look blankly back at me. I wonder what they are thinking. The path is now not so tranquil and I have to concentrate on the route ahead, anticipating others' actions. It is much harder to follow the left hand side back to home.

My legs start to ache at 16 miles. With six miles to go tiredness starts to set in but I am now only one hour from a warm bath and lunch. It is starting to get quite warm now and I need to drink more water to replenish my thirst. For the last two miles I leave the shade of the trees and return to the urban city. I notice the heat from the concrete path and how hard the path is compared to the gravel of the cycle trail. The road is now busy and I feel the fuel fumes on the back of my throat as I breathe. Finally, I arrive home safely. Happy but exhausted. I bend down to unlace my running shoes and walk into the kitchen. I switch the kettle on and make a cup of lovely warm tea to go with my marmite on toast (March 2006).

Both accounts illustrate how the moving body has different social, political and emotional meaning depending on the environment. The circular loop of a running track resulted in the visibility of individual speed and performance, based on club, age and gender, where effort is taken as an indicator of commitment to self-improvement. Bodily sweat, heavy breathing and strained faces gasping for air signified a 'hard worker' pushing at the boundaries of their physical capabilities. While disputes over rights to the inside lane existed, there was a common understanding over the laws of the track in recognition that an enclosed physical space raised the risk of personal injury. Gender divisions were reinforced through differences in individual physical strength and stamina. Despite the competitive element at the end of a track session there was a sense of camaraderie and friendship with a mutual understanding that interval training is hard work no matter how slow or fast you can run. In comparison, early morning longer individual runs along the path are taken at a comfortable pace, typically peaceful and relaxing, allowing for personal reflection and enjoyment of the rurality of the natural environment. Users are predominantly there for leisure but, unlike the sporting arena of a running track, there are not explicit or mutually understood rules.

I successfully completed my Spring marathon and continue to run several times a week. In Spring 2008 I achieved a bronze medal in the local ten-mile county championships and over the past 12 months I have gradually introduced swimming and cycling into my training in preparation for my first triathlon later in 2008. Engaging in these new sports has introduced me to new emotional and physical challenges, developing and learning to discipline my body in different ways as well as learning the rules and expectations of participation.

Chapter 18

No Ticket to Ride

John Shiels

It might be a good idea to begin by distinguishing what I experienced and still think of, as two distinct types of hitchhiking. They have convenience in common (it is easier to have someone take you somewhere than to walk) but they differ in terms of distances involved, age, motives and time constraints (e.g. 'be in by x o'clock or else...'). For me, Type A was purely instrumental, usually occurring within walking distance of my home near Bolton in Lancashire; it started around the age of 13 or so. Type A hitchhiking introduced me to the practice and showed its feasibility. It might be seen as a preamble (no pun intended) to Type B hitching: a useful way of getting to more distant places and people and of doing things which would often have been financially beyond me and in fact probably wouldn't have occurred to me otherwise.

Born in Bolton in 1948, I left school at 16 with good enough qualifications to get what my parents' generation of manual working-class people considered a 'good' (i.e. white collar) job: 'trainee manager' in a London and Manchester-based manufacturing company. Even as an accomplished fantasist and victim of chronic naivety, I saw the future as limited and the humdrum present as an inexorable part of a tedious plod into the ranks of the middle-aged brain dead. Escape attempts involved things like drinking and going to football matches and Manchester nightclubs with friends. At places like the Heaven and Hell Club and The Twisted Wheel I learned new meanings for 'uppers' and 'downers' and that reds and blues were not just the colours of local, rival football clubs. 'Good shit' had other than arcane intestinal or farmyard connotations and 'good' or 'bad' trips did not necessarily involve holidays in Scotland rather than Blackpool – though, increasingly, there could be a travelling allusion. These were all escapes from the tedium of work and, unconsciously, part of a life which increasingly straddled different generational and social class styles and subcultures. Hitchhiking became another alternative and a more varied escape.

Retrospectively, it is tempting to paint all these experiences with a romantic gloss. The minute-by-minute reality of hitching, though, was not always great fun and much depended on one's companion. For various reasons, by their choice, I very rarely hitchhiked with girls and then only ever for Type A purposes. Their reasons were no doubt influenced by socialization, considerations of (dis)comfort, doubts about my motives and intentions and the like, but the result was that my experience of hitching was strongly gendered.

My first and most frequent hitchhiking buddy was my older brother, Martin. The eldest, Mike, was six years older than me and in childhood that gap had been unbridgeable, but Martin and I had always been close. He suggested that we should hitch up to the Lake District one weekend and camp out in a newly acquired 'two-man' tent. With nothing better planned, my response was an unenthusiastic 'why not?' I certainly did not foresee how relatively frequent the pastime would become, how much I'd get from it or how I'd talk other friends into trying it.

On that first trip the first thing we learned was the importance of forward planning. In retrospect, our lack of thought about possible eventualities was laughable. It really is pretty stupid to carry a spare towel but not enough socks to allow for bad weather. The word 'carry' is significant, too. It is important to think of necessities in the knowledge that they have to be toted. With thought, some things are obvious but some subjective judgements can only be made with experience – I really regretted carrying a transistor radio for five miles in the hilly dark but loved it when I heard the first air-play of 'Hey Jude' in the starry open air in a field near Luxembourg 24 hours later. The practicalities of bare necessities were fairly quickly picked up, along with the need to re-define 'necessities' and 'luxuries', sometimes in quite unexpected ways.

The unexpected, as things worked out over time, came to be accepted as commonplace. One major reason for this is a result of some unique features of hitchhiking: for example, the extent to which, in some ways, one is totally dependent on others while, in other ways, one is freer and more autonomous than in 'normal' forms of transport. This may seem too obvious a point to be worth mentioning but it can bear on the emotional, experiential aspects of this mode of travel, positively or negatively, more forcefully and elementally than an inexperienced person might think.

We are hitching up to Edinburgh for the Festival. The journey across the moors into Yorkshire is fine. We choose to walk, in lovely weather, through Bronte country. Calm, peaceful, pleasant talk, with the birds for company. Then a good lift from outside Harrogate to near Consett. It would have been nice to get a bit closer to the A1 highway but we should be ok. The mood of happy confidence continues through a couple of beers and the walk towards Gateshead/Newcastle as night approaches. So does the rain, for a couple of very wet hours. No one seems interested in forwarding the passage of two increasingly saturated, cold and miserable travellers. Quite a few cars pass: groups of young people singing along to car radios and making witty remarks about our condition (we assume), individuals studiously keeping their eyes on the road and the occasional wagon driver, not bothering to avoid eye contact but not bothering to stop either. We'll have to catch a bus. There isn't another bus. As it gets quite late more groups pass, coming back having revelled and competing over who can make the most inventive and vigorous gesture to keep us entertained. Happy revellers. We are feeling increasingly ravelled and inspired to occasional bursts of inventive blasphemous obscenity, also with gestures, which at least briefly warm us up. We have just invented road rage: two sodden, gesticulating, hopping scarecrows bellowing foul insults after happy, oblivious passers-by. We look for a barn or any sort of shelter without success and are prompted to another spasm of filth at a sign risibly pointing to a place called Sunniside. Even the road signs are mocking us.

These rather self-pitying tales are recalled with odd affection as examples of fairly common experiences whilst hitching and, though memorably bad, are by no means the worst. When, after what felt like an eternity, a lorry would actually stop for us, my main feeling was relief rather than happiness. I always travelled in the expectation of a lift, however long it might take. The mix of emotions involved was fairly standard to all my hitchhiking experiences. Underlying all, and becoming more pronounced the longer I waited for someone to stop, was a fatalistic acceptance of one's powerlessness: lack of control over time, dependence on the good will, sympathy or whim of strangers, and helplessness over weather conditions. With experience, of course, I learned to carry and consult maps and to ask to be dropped at a promising-looking spot even if it meant sacrificing a few miles of travel. The 'lift' invariably asked where I was bound and one sometimes got a result by innocently and 'subtly' asking advice on the best spot to be dropped, hitch on from or whatever. It was not altogether unusual for a good-hearted lift to go a couple of miles out of their way to drop me in a convenient or busy spot. In this respect there was a definite difference between wagon drivers and other private motorists. Wagon drivers tended to be more instrumental but also more likely to stop at night.

Generally, though, most drivers' motives for offering a lift were coloured by self-interest. It was very much more common to be picked up by a single driver than by a couple or a family. I am sure that a generally heightened fear of crime, constant publicity and periodic moral panics about violence and the threat of violence have had an impact on hitchhikers' success rates, people's willingness to hitch and the likelihood of drivers to perceive their situation as vulnerable and be correspondingly hesitant. At the least, it must enter their heads that young male strangers seeking a lift in some remote or unpopulated place may be looking for something more than a cheap way of getting from A to B. I think it is inevitable that an even more pronounced outcome *vis-à-vis* women's willingness to hitch may have occurred but I have no firsthand knowledge of this. Factors such as fear of strangers, vulnerability, the enduring power of discourses of perceived gender-appropriate behaviour, demeanour and 'presence' and so on are undoubtedly compelling influences on hitchhikers and potential lift-givers.

In this regard, gender has of course always been very pertinent. It was very rare to be offered a lift by a single woman. Imagine this from the motorist's point of view: a couple of young men looking to be picked up at night in a lonely spot. From our viewpoint, on the other hand, I don't think the idea of risk or danger ever entered our minds. At the time, I was probably much more conscious of considerations other than gender. One's presentation of self had to be considered: dress comfortably but not scruffily, maintain a good humoured, philosophical airiness despite being cold, waterlogged, bone-tired, miserable, hungry and generally knackered, and in the presence of some mind-achingly stupid 'lift' who wants to talk about his father-in-law (this happened). In passing, as it were, it might be worth mentioning that whether or not the hitchers are carrying backpacks can affect the driver's attitude. There seemed, for example, a clear split between the 'head-shake brigade', looking at the packs rather than at us, and those who seemed reassured as to our genuineness. It could be hard to choose between backpack display or backpack hiding as lift-getting tactics.

As a summary view, a main feeling is of having a destination in mind when starting out, hopes but no certainty about the time it would take, the transport we would find, the sort of people we'd meet or the attitudes or treatment we would meet with. Quite how wet or cold we would get and the route we might be taken on were all unpredictable. The *leitmotif* might be 'sod it, we'll get there', but the only real certainty was uncertainty. And this could be part of the appeal once one had come to accept it. Even the getting there could be 'iffy'. One time, Martin and I were picked up by a young(ish) guy, the manager of a quarry near Settle, when we were hitching to a folk concert in York. We spent the next three days in his lovely old stone cottage, walking, talking, drinking and generally having a good time and never got to York.

Looking back, there was a sort of deliberate indeterminacy about it all which seems typical of our ages, generation, indeterminate class, status, work or future positions – a kind of dislocation in social structures which lent itself to hitchhiking as an aspect of lifestyle and leisure. So much for my starting point here: the idea of a destination in mind without the means to make it in comfort. Are there other sub-cultural outlets for this sort of sloppy, drifting, marginalized stance? The fact is that the experience, status and hazard of being a hitchhiker were fulfilling enough for me to continue it for some years. Even when I didn't need to, I needed to.

Section 3
Introduction: Working on the Move

Gayle Letherby and Gillian Reynolds

Background Issues

Workers' constructions of their organizational workspace encompass issues of control and resistance as well as other experiences, memories and identities (Halford 2004). Following other researchers (e.g. Whitehead 2001; McDowell 1999; Marshall 1984), Susan Halford and Pauline Leonard (2006) analyze ways in which men and women position themselves in terms of masculinity and femininity at work. Their focus is on negotiated relationships between nurses, doctors and patients. Similarly, for those whose work involves travel and interaction with the travelling customer, the experiences of practices at work are also affected by the (gendered) identity and embodiment of self and other (including fellow workers and passengers): they must manage their own emotions, the emotions of other workers and those of passengers.

In *The Managed Heart* Arlie Hochschild (2003[1983]) explored the relationship between the (predominantly) female flight attendant and her passengers, and made a distinction between 'emotional work' and 'emotional labour'. Unpaid emotion(al) work takes place anywhere where there are people; emotion(al) labour, on the other hand, occurs in the context of paid employment, where such management of emotion is considered to be part of someone's job (Hochschild 2003[1983] and see Frith and Kitzinger 1998). Key to Hochschild's (1983) argument is that emotion labour is the direct result of the 'commercialization' of emotions and is part of the package that companies are selling to their customers and control over emotions is no longer voluntary. For Hochschild, this suppression of authentic feelings has a personal cost to the worker, with a spectrum of negative outcomes. More recently Stephen Fineman (2005, 6) has argued that emotion labour 'leaves some workers depleted and distressed, but others challenged and feeling good.'

Because emotion labour is 'hot, exploitable capital' in the currency of the service economy and its focus on 'customer-service' (Fineman 2005, 5), the *display* of negative emotions is much more likely now than it was a quarter of a century ago when Hochschild was researching and writing. This is partly because consumers are used by successive governments as the means to drive up the performance of public services, including transport. As we have previously pointed out (Letherby and Reynolds 2005, 179), 'customers are encouraged to develop expectations in order to drive up the standards of a public service and this can legitimate the anger or rage that many people feel.'

Hochschild (2003[1983]) argues that emotion labour is gendered in that it is more likely to be an aspect of a female-dominated occupation rather than a male one. Many researchers and theorists have explored this aspect (e.g. Whitelegg 2007; Wolkowitz 2006; Letherby and Reynolds 2003; Hunter 2001; Duncombe and Marsden 1998; Rattue and Cornelius 2002; and other articles in special editions of the journal, *Soundings* 2002 and 1999 which focus on emotion/al labour[1]). Some suggest that Hochschild's analysis is limited in that she focuses attention on only a small number of female workers employed by large commercial organizations. Hochschild herself notes, however, that the job of flight attendant is not the *same job* for a woman as it is for a man: 'Male flight attendants tended to react to passengers *as if they had more authority* than they really did ... Female flight attendants, on the other hand ... used more tactful and deferential means of handling abuse' (1983, 178) (original emphases).

Working on the Move

In this part of the book Jo Stanley, Drew Whitelegg, and Gillian Reynolds and Jackie Rose consider themes and issues relating to those who work, or worked, on different forms of transport. All the contributors to this section have analyzed and interpreted primary and/or secondary data. Each chapter confirms the growing acceptance that the vehicle – the mode of transport – is a space/place where social life is *organized*: it is an organizational place for those who work on it, and emotions are 'intimately tied into' a sense of place (Urry 2007, 77). In addition all authors here acknowledge that emotion work is complex and likely to include both positive and negative emotions (Fineman 2005; Wouters 1989; Stenross and Kleinman 1989; Tolich 1993). To ignore the presence of emotion is to be content with a very incomplete analysis of travel and the organizational space in which it takes place.

The authors consider the emotional tension created in the public-yet-privatized spaces and places of ships, planes and buses (it is important to note that these represent exemplars of transport; it is not an exhaustive list). Such emotional tensions are influenced by, and impact upon conflicts and negotiations between travellers, workers and the provision of a transport service (Letherby and Reynolds 2005; Wolmar 2005).

Stanley, Whitelegg and Reynolds and Rose all identify situations in which the labourers feel, at the very least, ambivalent about their emotion labour. In Stanley's historical work (Chapter 19 "Caring for the Poor Souls': Inter-war Seafaring Women and their Pity for Passengers'), women seafarers reflected that they had gained a sense of positive identity from their position of caring for female passengers on sea-going liners. Whitelegg's interviewee air cabin crew

---

1 *Soundings*: A journal of politics and culture (special editions Summer 2002 and Spring 1999), published by Lawrence and Wishart, London.

acknowledged the positive aspects (as well as negative ones) from what they called 'jump-seat therapy' on planes (Chapter 20 'When Being at Work isn't Work: Airline Cabin Crew, Emotional Labour and Travel'). In similar vein, in Chapter 21 'Ambivalent Journeys? Some Emotional 'Ups' and 'Downs' of Service Bus Drivers in England', Reynolds and Rose report from local service bus drivers the positive emotional satisfaction they gain from helping passengers, and meeting new faces, as well as the causes of the negative emotions they feel.

Whilst Stanley's chapter is concerned specifically with female workers, some of the occupations considered in this section are ones in which men as well as women find themselves undertaking the emotion labour of managing the emotions of the clients/customers/travellers. Clearly bus drivers (like airline cabin staff) – who, in the UK, at least, are mainly men – are on the 'front line' of the battle for a satisfactory bus service and are the ones who as part of their labour have to 'manage' the consequences of a perceived unsatisfactory service.

References

Bauman, Z. (1997), *Postmodernity and its Discontents* (Cambridge/Oxford: Polity/Blackwell).

Bendelow, G. and Williams, S. J. (eds) (1998), *Emotions in Social Life: Critical Themes and Contemporary Issues* (London: Routledge).

Davidson, J., Smith, M. and Bondi, L. (eds) (2007), *Emotional Geographies* (Aldershot: Ashgate).

Duncombe, J. and Marsden, D. (1998), '"Stepford Wives" and "Hollow Men": doing emotion work, doing gender and "authenticity" in intimate heterosexual relationships', in G. Bendelow and S.J. Williams (eds).

Fineman, S. (2005), 'Appreciating Emotion at Work: paradigm tensions', *International Journal of Work, Organisation and Emotion*, 1, 1, 4–19.

Frith, H. and Kitzinger, C. (1998), 'Emotion Work as a Participant Resource: a feminist analysis of young women's talk-in-interaction', *Sociology*, 32, 2, 299–320.

Halford, S. and Leonard, P. (2006), *Negotiating Gendered Identities at Work: Place, Space and Time* (Basingstoke: Palgrave Macmillan).

Halford, S. (2004), 'Towards a Sociology of Organizational Space', *Sociological Research Online*, 9, 1, www.socresonline.org.uk/9/1/halford.html.

Hochschild, A.R. (2003[1983]), *The Managed Heart: Commercialization of Human Feeling* (Berkeley: University of California Press).

Hunter, B. (2001), 'Emotion Work in Midwifery: a review of current knowledge', *Journal of Advanced Nursing*, 34, 4, 436–44.

Letherby, G. and Reynolds, G. (2003), 'Making Connections: The Relationship between Train Travel and the Processes of Work and Leisure', *Sociological Research Online*, 8, 3, www.socresonline.org.uk/8/3/letherby.

Letherby, G. and Reynolds, G. (2005), *Train Tracks: Work, Play and Politics on the Railways* (Oxford: Berg).

Marshall, J. (1984), *Women Managers: Travellers in a Male World* (Chichester: Wiley).

McDowell, L. (1999), *Gender, Identity and Place: Understanding Feminist Geographies* (Minneapolis: University of Minneapolis Press).

Peters, P.F. (2005), *Time, Innovation and Mobilities: Travels in Technological Cultures* (London: Routledge).

Rattue, R. and Cornelius, N. (2002), 'The Emotional Labour of Police Work', *Soundings: A Journal of Politics and Culture*, 20, Summer, 190–201.

Stenross, B. and Kleinman, S. (1989), 'The Highs and Lows of Emotional Labour: detectives' encounters with criminals and victims', *Journal of Contemporary Ethnography*, 17, 435–52.

Tolich, M. (1993), 'Alienating and Liberating Emotions at Work', *Journal of Contemporary Ethnography*, 22, 361–81.

Whitehead, S. (2001), 'Woman as Manager: a seductive ontology', *Gender, Work and Organization*, 8, 1, 84–107.

Williams, S. and Bendelow, G. (1998), 'Introduction: emotions in social life: mapping the sociological terrain', in G. Bendelow and S.J. Williams (eds).

Urry, J. (2007), 'The Place of Emotions within Place', in J. Davidson, M. Smith and L. Bondi (eds).

Wolkowitz, C. (2006), *Bodies at Work* (London: Sage).

Wolmar, C. (2005), *On The Wrong Line: How Ideology and Incompetence Wrecked Britain's Railways* (London: Aurum Press).

Wouters, C. (1989), 'The Sociology of Emotions and Flight Attendants: Hochschild's 'Managed Heart'', *Theory, Culture and Society*, 6, 95–123.

Chapter 19

'Caring for the Poor Souls': Inter-war Seafaring Women and their Pity for Passengers

Jo Stanley

Ms Motility watches, listens, pities as,
with egalitarian ferocity, the ship heaves
Mary O'Leary, maid-to-be, in her Steerage bunk
And Lady Stella Glitz, vomiting on her First Class divan.

Miss Motility and her team
can't flee the job,
but only ride out the storms
and soothe the suffering We-Would-Travel Sisters.

(Jo Stanley, unpublished)

Introduction

Women voyaging across the world's oceans in a floating palace heading towards new lives in the New World during the Roaring Twenties sound rather admirable. We might expect that the female transport workers travelling uniformed and in harness – mainly as stewardesses – would envy the women that they served. But oral testimony and written autobiography from inter-war British ships' stewardesses, matrons and conductresses (who might all be likened to longer-haul air cabin crew) show, surprisingly, that pity was one of the central emotions felt by working seawomen charged with the care of female passengers.

In this chapter I discuss the main reasons for the pity and how the pity was expressed, particularly through the word 'poor' (as in 'poor things', 'poor souls', and 'my poor passengers'). I also look at how pity was acted upon. To feel sympathy, empathy or sorrow for the plight of others, particularly one's social superiors, requires a sense of agency and relative privilege that is unusual for abjected carers. So the central questions in dealing with this subject include:

- what relational contexts enabled seawomen to pity their passengers?
- how did that affect their relationship with the passenger?
- what other emotions might seawomen, and their counterparts, Bedroom Stewards, feel or report?

Maritime historiography has tended to ignore seafarers' subjectivity (particularly women's) and seldom discusses the meanings of their mobility and motility, or their relations with passengers. And when tourism sociology turns, rarely, to hospitality workers it usually focuses on food delivery workers (e.g. Urry 2002). This chapter, therefore, exposes a category of women worker-travellers and hospitality staff whom few know about. They can usefully be read as an interesting early counterpart to the air cabin crew whose emotion work was studied by Arlie Hochschild (1983) (and Whitelegg 2007 and this volume); or as seaborne exemplars of the carers in institutions ashore – whose emotions and emotional control of elderly residents is explored by Geraldine Lee-Treweek (1997).

I was alerted to the surprising existence of pity as a recurring emotion when I read a vignette by Edith Sowerbutts, a Red Star Lines conductress and later a stewardess. She was one of the hundreds of seafaring women whose lives I have studied, particularly using thick detail (Geertz 1988) and seeking to turn up the muted channels (Anderson and Jack 1991) that are available through oral testimony. Sowerbutts' story related to impoverished women without English, the dominant language of the ship. But as a result I began to notice how often the word 'poor' or 'poor things' appeared in women's stories of relationships with passengers, even those who were privileged.

In the 1920s Edith Sowerbutts was a conductress (a sort of travelling almoner for women without men) working with Poles, Ukrainians, Yugoslavs, Hungarians, Greeks, Italians, Germans and Irish, on the *Zeeland*, sailing from Belgium to North America:

> I always made a point of being present on bath nights and at general delousing sessions. There was a tendency to hustle women along and Matron … was not one to stand up to any bullying. I was horrified once when I found the Third Class Steward, a Belgian who had been in the emigrant ships prior to 1914, propelling two girls a time into the bathroom. "Two to a bath" he shouted to Matron. "No," said I, "One at a time." That man was livid – never before or since have I seen a man go pea-green with anger. But my women had their individual privacy in the bathroom. The thought of two to a bath, one lot of salt seawater, was just too much for me, especially as seawater was in plentiful supply! (Sowerbutts 1976, 36/25).

Thus, Edith not only felt pity; she acted upon her emotion in a similar way to the manner in which air cabin crew manage passenger emotions (Hochschild 1983) in order to ensure others (passengers) did not experience distressing emotions.

The Context: Travel as Enviable

Emotions are to some degree socially produced (Fineman et al. 2005; Bendelow and Williams 1998; Harré 1986). Why might pity not be the expected currency between seawomen and passengers? It is difficult nowadays in these easyJet, global-minded days to imagine a time when women had barely loosened the Victorian fetters that confined them to the hearth, or accessed the public sphere, or developed and acted upon motility. Foreign travel was a privilege not available to working-class women. Their inter-war travel involved journeys of only minutes or hours, made to domestic locations, using buses, trams, trains, bikes and walking.

Voyagers' situation was constructed as particularly enviable because they travelled long distances to exotic locations, sometimes in auratic (Benjamin 1936, 224) 'floating palaces' (though underprivileged migrants were cooped-up in smelly and confined lower decks). Such élite sea voyagers were in a location that popular culture held to epitomize glamorous social success. The burnished rails of these grand hotels (connoting civilization and safety), from which to view the sparkling blue ocean (connoting sublime nature), were the background against which Vogue models were proudly posed. And mobility was signalled as freedom. Poems and stories by cultural luminaries such as Hart Crane (1933), T.S. Eliot (1922), Somerset Maugham (1921) and W.H. Auden (1995) acclaimed liner travel as the key symbol of glorious modernity. Auden (1995, 18) tellingly made one of the great shipping lines a byword for modernist glory by writing 'You were a great Cunarder, I was only a fishing smack.' Movies, musicals and literature representing liners at sea as the acme of the desirable included *An Affair to Remember* (1938), *Now, Voyager!* (1942), and Cole Porter's *Anything Goes* (1934). And in these public spaces were women: those who accessed non-domestic space as of right, and those of subordinate classes and 'races' who served them.

Those inter-war women who managed to voyage, even as economic migrants, were generally seen as privileged. And they experienced themselves as lucky. The seawomen who served them were also popularly seen as fortunate, at a time when inter-war women working on other forms of public transport mainly did so as 'clippies' on buses and the category 'airhostess' barely existed.

Sea voyages were gendered experiences where exclusively male workers 'mastered' the technical aspects side of the vehicle. There were segregated sections and cabins. Women passengers who were 'unaccompanied' (i.e. travelling without the aegis of a male relative) were always served by female workers, who were similarly segregated from the main space. This both produced and reproduced a gendered hegemony, mirroring that ashore, with Woman as of special but lower status. Inter-war passengers were largely of two groups: the dominant social group, and the subordinate group, that is, steerage passengers, especially emigrants, whom the (usually upper working-class) stewardesses might be more likely to pity. So class, and 'race', along with gender, determined the power relations in many interactions.

I have argued elsewhere (Stanley 2006) that passenger ships can usefully be seen in several key ways. They function as liminal zones (Turner 1974; van Gennep 1960) for travellers moving metaphorically as well as literally beyond the old and the known. Passenger vessels are marginal spaces where transgressions and carnivalesque misrule might occur (Shields 1991, Bakhtin 1984) and exceptional situations where the high and low might temporarily change places (Stallybrass and White 1986). Ships can also be seen as heterotopias (Hetherington 1997; Foucault 1986a; 1986b) where social arrangements are other than those that inhabitants might expect, given spatial arrangements. While not much emotional response to the vehicle might be expected to develop on a brief bus journey from Penge to Charing Cross, voyages to New York took over five days; crossings to Australia lasted six to ten weeks. Therefore ships could be experienced as temporary homes or portable refuges (like the shells of hermit crabs) (Bachelard 1994).

Although Heide Gerstenberger (1996) has argued against seeing ships as 'total institutions' as Erving Goffman (1968) does, passenger ships do conform in some ways to this model, in that they are worlds in their own right: 'purportedly established the better to pursue some workmanlike task and justifying themselves only on these instrumental grounds: army barracks, ships, boarding schools, work camps, colonial compounds and large mansions from the point of view of those who live in the servants' quarters' (Goffman 1968, 16). Goffman (1968, 73) adds that they are 'storage dumps for inmates.'

Why does such a model matter for a discussion on emotions? It helps us to understand floating, intensive situations that contain a conflict between institutional efficiency and humane standards (Goffman 1968); that produce 'involvement cycles' where passengers and crew developed relations that transgressed against the prescribed ones; that position passengers as 'material to work on ... [with] status in the outside world that must be taken into consideration' (Goffman 1968, 74) and yet incarcerate them and produce conditions that to some extent level them.

In such long drawn-out, cocooned conditions, complex emotional interactions occur between the ships' denizens (those co-shelterers, those turnkeys who were also lags), especially in the case of passengers who were heading towards new lives. And the emotions both workers and passengers alike might experience included excitement, alienation and dread (of the sea and whatever lay at the other side of the ocean), and disorientation in the ship – not least because of its motion and the absence of land, which could have offered travellers a way to find their bearings.

Unenviable Situations

We might not expect the female domestic staff who worked with such women voyagers to feel pity towards their privileged passengers, who could travel apparently at will and without having to work their passage. After all, the very essence of seafaring women domestic workers' position is that they were performing hard, lowly, maid-type work on what are today described as sweatships (Mather 2002). Like maids in hotels, ships' stewardesses served many temporary mistresses as well as the institutions' managers. They performed low-status domestic work, contaminated by the 'primitive dirt' of vomit and urine. The inter-war years were a period characterized by traditional seafaring men's gendered anxieties about the 'demasculinization' of passenger liners into high-tech 'floating chocolate boxes' as Maida Nixson's male shipmates termed them (Nixson 1954), instead of sites of rugged skill in challenging maritime conditions. So women's 90-hour working weeks in these misogynistic confines, where females were usually less than one per cent of the crew, could be lonely and difficult. In addition, seafaring for women and for men on the catering side was an insecure occupation. Each voyage required a fresh contract and turnover was high. Stewarding staff were abjectified by some passengers, some shipping companies and some crew so that: 'On a woman [worker], the effects of sea life was not good. It quickly killed the real warmth of heart and the essential womanliness' (Jessop 1998, 113).

The conditions I have described appear to be such that they might lead to women workers envying, not pitying, passengers. In fact, during my research on thirty-plus inter-war ships' stewardesses, one of the surprising emotions that consistently recurred was pity. Equally surprisingly, it occurred across class, cultural and age divides; it wasn't solely confident or 'motherly' older stewardesses who felt it for 'poor foreigners'. While pity can, of course, mask envy, my informants did appear to be genuinely sympathetic to some (not all) of their passengers. They looked after them with a selflessness and charity that transcended the binary of their oppositional roles: the 'employer' of a kind (i.e. passenger) versus the employee.

Feeling Pity

Pity might be defined as a sense of sympathetic sorrow for the plight of others. It arises from generosity, which enables empathy. It is also produced by a sense of being relatively privileged oneself, and not pitiable. Thus we can infer that stewardesses (who were not enduring quite the difficulties of passage as steerage voyagers) might feel a sense of superiority or dominance.

If we understand emotions as to some degree socially constructed, then we can see that in this gendered time-space, the ship en voyage, women crew's emotions could be composed by the 'local moral order' (Harré 1986, 6), which involves peers, the shipping line's and specific ship's culture, and passenger response. Emotions also result from the stewardesses' own personal histories, lifecourse stages, and predispositions.

In selling a ticket to ride, the shipping line agreed to provide a service to consuming units, whose wellbeing in transit was the good or service being produced by the ship's staff. Women care workers' job was essentially to process units quickly, so they could not afford to be 'be too soft'. Indeed, they had to (at least appear to) adhere to the shipping companies' rule that crew should not become at all familiar with passengers.

The frequent use in stewardesses' testimony of the objectifying terms 'poor souls' or 'poor things' does suggest that the great volume of passenger throughput turned passengers into units to some extent. But I wonder if the use of 'things' and 'souls' was a device produced in retrospect. It may be that in remembering for the record the *thousands* of units (passengers), the *individual* guests' complex and shifting identities became subsumed into a greater (pitiable) whole that is almost metonymic.

Mental disorientation; linguistic disability; physical disorientation – seasickness; illness, loneliness and difficulty, especially within marriage; a potentially tragic future of which the traveller was unaware and tragic histories are all cited by women seafarers as reasons for pity. Perhaps the most pitiable state was the disorientation that came from being literally away from all land, in a vast, sublime space and place that moves, rocks and can sink. 'At sea' indeed. Any voyager might experience themselves as matter out of place. Some were so frightened that they made wills. Stewardess Lena Criddle (interviewed by Howard-Bailey 1990) got the captain to witness it. Major dis-ease was particularly acute for untravelled people who, as Edith Sowerbutts noted:

> have an awful fear of the sea on this, the first time they had ever seen the ocean or experienced what it could do when in the mood. They were sick too, poor wretched souls, and this did not help … If you had the time to think about, how terrible it was for those poor, ground-down peasant types to be storm-buffeted on a rolling ship, knowing little of what they might expect, only that it was a land of opportunity that waited them – a strange land, a better life (Sowerbutts 1976, 62/56).

The problem became even worse when the passenger was dispossessed of her ship/refuge during a sinking. White Star Stewardess Violet Jessop, involved in the iconic sinking of the *Titanic* in 1912, used the word 'pity' twice as she reported that she saw:

> many among those poor, weeping frozen people, murmuring soft prayers in a monotone, nearly died with emotion when they sighted that ship [the Carpathia, that was to rescue them]. One poor soul sitting beside me – thought … that she should soon regain her husband … Alas, so few were reunited (Jessop 1998, 139).

The second cause of pity was associated with the first: passengers' lack of the dominant tongue used on ship. Stewardesses always spoke the language of the country of the shipping line's headquarters (usually the UK or the US). But migrants were often severely socially disabled by speaking a different language to this. And interpreters were not always available, especially in a crisis, as Jessop points out. When faced with the *Titanic*'s sinking

> a few women near me started to cry loudly when they realised a parting had to take place, their husbands standing silently by. They were Poles and could not understand a word of English. Surely a terrible plight, to be among a crowd in

such a situation and not understand anything that is being said (Jessop 1998, 131).

The third cause of pity relates to the acute physical disorientation that is seasickness, something far less common on roads and in the air. However high their social station, all seasick people were pitied because mal-de-mer was so debilitating before remedies such as Dramamine and acupressure wristbands were widely available. Acutely seasick passengers truly believed they would never reach their destination alive. Maida Nixson found 'seasickness, which with the emotional depression it brings, really can cause indifference to the threat of death' (Nixson 1954, 89). Senior stewardesses had witnessed passengers' mal-de-mer many times and a number were themselves turned pea green (Scobie 1990). But they still sympathised with their passengers. Edith Sowerbutts said of her interviews with passengers in mid-Atlantic: 'I found it plain heartless trying to elicit personal details ... when my women were likely to vomit between question and answer' (Sowerbutts 1976, 26/19).

Again relating to being metaphysically 'at sea', another reason for pity was that passengers were often sailing for the supposed beneficial effects, at a crucial lifecourse stage or in a time of major transition, such as bereavement. Stewardesses also pitied the lonely, the elderly, and those travelling with ailing or abusive husbands or troublesome children. As stewardesses spent all their time on just 20 or so cabins each, they were intimately involved in the private life of passengers, especially when difficulties occurred. Sowerbutts was:

> awoken by dreadful shrieking in middle of night ... in a nearby stateroom we found a frantic woman yelling for help. On one of the beds lay her husband, face down, buried in his pillows, completely unconscious. Obviously he had had a seizure of some kind. "Get my friends," cried the shocked and frightened woman ... I sped off ... [but] ... there was nothing for them to do but try and console an elderly lady whose husband had just had a fatal stroke ... [later] only hours before she left the ship she passed me in the main hallway, said "hullo" and fell flat on her back in a dead faint. A sad end to a retirement cruise (Sowerbutts 1976, 189/163).

Mothers were pitied because of the difficulty of managing small frisky children in enclosed and boring spaces. This was especially the case of the mother who was seasick and travelling without helpers.

Passengers were also pitied for the future they faced. Their naivety and potential for disappointment was a cause of stewardesses being upset on their behalf. Women migrants from non-English-speaking, rural, poverty-stricken areas were pitied because they were so ignorant of the ruthless wider world that it was hard to see how they would survive modern cities without being cheated. Others were pitied when authorities turned them back at the doorway to their new life. Cunard stewardess Dora Sweet and Canadian Pacific stewardess Doreen Mather noted this particularly in relation to the subordinate Irish women they sat beside on the 'madwatch'. These would-be domestic servants went insane in the US and were returned home in straitjackets.[1]

Sowerbutts saw official gatekeepers causing distress. Referring to immigration facilities for 'those who might be temporarily held for query, even for subsequent deportation', she wrote:

> This last must have been the final heartbreak for some wretched souls; to come so far to a promised land, to be found unacceptable for some reason, usually medical, and then be returned from whence they came, practically penniless, as these people had always sold up their little "all", their poverty-ridden homes, all their meagre possessions before leaving Europe (Sowerbutts 1976, 19/17).

Heartless bureaucracy was a common cause of pity that extended to dominant class women, and men too. Sowerbutts witnessed:

> the heart-breaking deportation of a woman dying of consumption ... I wondered why the US immigration authorities could not let her die peacefully in the USA instead of deporting her ... she died at sea. I have seen many a funeral in my time but none that upset me as much as this one did. The grieving husband rushed to the ship's rails as the body was lowered into the sea – I thought he would jump overboard (Sowerbutts odd notes 1976, 11).

Having identified the main reasons why stewardesses reportedly felt pity for passengers, I turn to the central interesting question: from whence did stewardesses get the sense of confidence or superiority that enabled seawomen to pity their passengers? Firstly, most stewardesses were caring people, who were in the job partly because they were sympathetic and helpful. This was particularly the case with women in positions of imperial authority (like conductresses and matrons) over those of other 'races' or markedly subordinate classes. Seawomen's official role was to be protective and assist those travelling without authority figures to look after their interests. For many seawomen, it was their gendered personal pleasure and custom to form sympathetic ties, rather than to compete (Baker Miller 1991). Veteran stewardesses were able to identify patterns that occurred (e.g. mail order brides travelling out to marry colonial men who then turned out to be a disappointment: married, poor or alcoholic). Relatedly, travel professionals may have pity for the tourists because professionals have repeatedly seen tourist industry operations and the behind-the-scenes construction of situations that

---

1 Both Sweet (not her real name) (28.12.1987; 22.10.1995; 21.1.1996), and Doreen Mather (not her real name) (6.3.1986; 20.2.1989; 14.11.1992) recalled 'the mad watch' when they sat by such women in confinement. See the fictional 'Mermaid and Madwatch' (Stanley, 1987) based on such testimony.

passengers have not. This is particularly true of new voyagers who imagine they will be the independent travellers with agency featured in brochures.

A second group of reasons for pity being felt and expressible is that there could be a warm general climate in the shipboard world of women (passengers and crew). On P&O's *Malwa*, Violet Jessop's colleagues enabled generosity of spirit. She shared a cabin with two stewardesses who 'proved treasures. The joy in my heart helped to smooth over the rough patches. It helped me ignore the cold snobbishness of the memsahib from India returning from their periodic visits home' (Jessop 1998, 127).

Such feelings could be coupled with a general sense of what was right, be it for passengers or crew. Delia Callaghan, a Cunard stewardess, recalled 'Emigrants, oh the poor things. They way they slept, it was terrible. Our rooms weren't much better anyway' (interviewed by Howard-Bailey 1990). Thus, her pity for the passengers was based on both a sense of justice and common experience.

Expressing Pity

Obviously seawomen's narratives of how they responded to women passengers are a product of the many layers of constraints. These structuring influences include the problem that memories are not preserved intact, like frozen peas or read-only documents. Each time a memory is processed it is 'defrosted and refrozen', rewritten and filtered through changed ideas about the kind of emotions and behaviour it is proper for women of their class and race to express. Narratives are also constructed in a complex 'collaboration' with the contemporary interviewer, as historians problematising oral testimonies' composition, such as Penny Summerfield (1998) and Al Thomson (1994) have discussed (or with seawomen's anticipated readers in the case of written autobiography). Pity is perceived as a gender-appropriate emotion for women (even though 'softness' was a rather despised weakness in the 'dog-eat-dog' wider culture of some ships). Pity can also be a defence against abjectification, a kind of unconscious game of 'I'm OK because I'm choosing to see you as not OK.' But pity was actually evident through interviewees' tone of voice, as well as in choice of phrases like 'the poor things'. The emotion also produced consequential behaviour. Seawomen quietly revealed that their pity was not just a feeling; it resulted in actions, kindly ones. They physically nurtured passengers, gave up their free time to them and encouraged them despite adversity. For example, Maida Nixson created safe spaces for her passengers: 'It would have been unwise for my sick ladies, who included an expectant mother, to leave their cabins or their beds. I wedged them in with pillows and hoped for the best' (Nixson 1954, 207). Nor did stewardesses shirk what might be seen as the distasteful job of holding a dying stranger. Seawomen even suffered in acting upon their pity. Maida Nixson records that in Fremantle:

At the top of the gangway after seeing off some departing people, I came across poor old Sarah Plum the miserress [a female diminutive of miser] in tears because she wanted to go ashore to buy some slippers and no one would be bothered to take her. Visited by one of my unfortunate impulses of philanthropy, I offered to go with her. It was a blazing blustering day of heat and ... I had to support poor old Sarah every tottering step of the way ... standing by shamefully blushing while she tried to beat down the price of slippers in half a dozen shops. Then she decided to get them in Brisbane ... On our return I was hauled before Authority and sharply reprimanded for dragging the poor old lady out, on such a day, in her feeble health (Nixson 1954, 123).

Pity was not the dominant emotion for all stewardesses in all interactions, but it was remarkably present. There was also anger, shame, racialised disgust, pride, enjoyment, curiosity and complicity. Nor was pity consistently felt. Its presence or absence was affected by factors such as the length of the journeys, shipmates, working conditions and passengers' moods. Others felt simply a routine commitment to their role.

Conclusion

Attending to the testimony of seafaring women demonstrates that pity was one of the recurring – and surprising emotions – reported by such crew when speaking of their relations with women passengers. Although inter-war women passengers voyaging in 'floating palaces' might be expected to arouse feelings of envy and admiration in those who cared for them during the trip, in actuality pity was remarkably present.

While historians need to be aware of all the conditions that can affect the construction of testimony many decades after an event, it is still clear to me that their pity was authentic. And it is remarkable that pity was not felt solely by the more privileged stewardesses.

I have argued that the main reasons for the pity included sympathy about the disorientation that sea voyages could bring (including feeling literally 'at sea', seasickness etc); pity for those undergoing difficult transitions, especially if naively; pity for the socially disabled (for instance, the lonely), and the practically hindered (such as sole mothers); and those who would face, or who had already faced, challenges abroad.

The pity was expressed without parade, and through kindly actions. And it seemed to be enabled in seawomen by a range of circumstances, including the cultural climate of the ship; racial 'superiority'; the carnivalesque or upside-down-ness of the ship when the high can become the low, and a sense of common humanity.

Such sympathy is a fascinating example of the way that generosity to strangers – that puzzling and heartening human trait – was a key emotion in these particular women transport workers' itinerant working lives. It illuminates the gendered connections that transcend professional relationships for women experiencing certain types of mobility and motility. Thus it allows us to wonder at an aspect of mobilities history never previously explored.

References

Anderson, K. and Jack, D.C. (1991), 'Learning to Listen: interview techniques and analyses', in Gluck, S.B. and Patai, D. (ed.).

Auden, W.H. (1995), *As I Walked Out One Evening* (London: Faber & Faber).

Bachelard, G. (1994[1954]), (transl. M. Jolas) *The Poetics of Space* (Boston: Beacon Press).

Baker Miller, J. (1991), *Toward a New Psychology of Women* (London: Penguin).

Bakhtin, M. (1984), (transl. H. Iswolsky) *Rabelais and his World* (Bloomington, Indiana: Indiana University Press).

Bendelow, G. and Williams, S.J. (eds) (1998), *Emotions in Social Life: Critical Themes and Contemporary Issues* (London: Routledge).

Benjamin, W. (1936), 'The Work of Art in the Age of Mechanical Reproduction' <www.evans-experientialism.freewebspace.com/benjamin.htm>

Crane, H. (1933), (ed. Waldo Frank) *The Collected Poems of Hart Crane* (New York: Liveright).

Eliot, T.S. (1922), *The Wasteland* (New York: Boni and Liveright).

Fineman, S., Gabriel, Y. and Sims, D.B.P. (2005), *Organizing and Organizations* (London: Sage).

Foucault, M. (1986a), 'Of Other Spaces', *Diacritics*, XVI, 1, 22–27.

Foucault, M. (1986b), 'Other Spaces: The Principles of Heterotopia', *Lotus*, XLVIII, 9–17.

Geertz, C. (1988), *Works and Lives: The Anthropologist as Author* (Stanford: Stanford University Press).

van Gennep, A. (1960), *The Rites of Passage* (Chicago: University of Chicago Press).

Gerstenberger, H. (1996), 'Men Apart: The Concept of 'Total Institution' and the Analysis of Seafaring', *International Journal of Maritime History*, III, 1, 173–82.

Gluck, S.B. and Patai, D. (eds) (1991), *Women's Words: Feminist Practice in Oral History* (London: Routledge).

Goffman, E. (1968), *Asylums* (Harmondsworth: Penguin).

Harré, R. (ed.) (1986), *The Social Construction of Emotions* (Oxford: Basil Blackwell).

Hochschild, A.R. (1983), *The Managed Heart: Commercialization of Human Feeling* (Berkeley: University of California Press).

Hetherington, K. (1997), *The Badlands of Modernity: Heterotopia and Social Ordering* (London: Routledge).

Jessop, V. (1998), (introduced, annotated and edited by John Maxtone-Graham) *Titanic Survivor: The Memoirs of Violet Jessop, Stewardess* (Stroud: Sutton).

Lee-Treweek, G. (1997) 'Women, Resistance and Care: an ethnographic study of nursing auxiliary work', *Work Employment and Society*, 11, 1, 47–63.

Mather, C. (2002), *Sweatships: What it's Really Like to Work on Board Cruise Ships* (London: War on Want).

Maugham, W. Somerset (1921, 1956), *The Trembling of A Leaf* (London: Heinemann).

Nixson, M.M. (1954), *Ring Twice for the Stewardess* (London: John Long and Co.).

Scobie, D. (1990), *A Stewardess Rings a Bell* (Bolton: Stylus).

Shields, R. (1991), *Places on the Margin: Alternative Geographies of Modernity* (London: Routledge).

Summerfield, P. (1998), *Reconstructing Women's Wartime Lives: Discourse and Subjectivity in Oral Histories of the Second World War* (Manchester: Manchester University Press).

Sowerbutts, E. (n.d. but c. 1976) *Memoirs of a British Seaman* (typescript) (Imperial War Museum, Department of Documents).

Stallybrass, P. and White, A. (1986), *The Politics and Poetics of Transgression* (London: Methuen).

Stanley, J. (1987), 'Mermaid and Madwatch,' *Writing Women*, 7, 2, 38–45.

Stanley, J. (2006), 'How did this come to be in Stewardess Scheherazade's Sea-Chest of "Memories": Exploring the Exceptionalised and Auratic Sea Through Inter-war Seawomen's Oral Testimonies', *Diegesis*, 9, 22–33.

Thomson, A. (1994), *Anzac Memories: Living with the Legend* (Melbourne: Oxford University Press).

Turner, V. (1974), *Process, Performance and Pilgrimage: A Study in Comparative Symbology* (New Delhi: Concept Publishing).

Urry, J. (2002), *The Tourist Gaze* (London: Sage).

Whitelegg, D. (2007), *Working the Skies: The Fast-paced, Disorienting World of the Flight Attendant* (New York: New York University Press).

Oral Testimony

Lina Criddle interview by Chris Howard-Bailey, 12 June 1990, no. M0078, Southampton City Heritage Oral History department.

Chapter 20

When Being at Work isn't Work: Airline Cabin Crew, Emotional Labour and Travel

Drew Whitelegg

You are sort of in this isolated world away from reality. You are in this metal thing that is up above the earth and maybe it's sort of an unreal atmosphere and you just, you feel like you are sort of in this together.

Mary, Delta Air Lines flight attendant[1]

Introduction: *The Managed Heart* and Emotion Work

Airline cabin crew have a select place within the field of emotion work (Fineman 2003). Rather like old Labour Party members that would one day find their way to Robert Tressell's socialist tour-de-force novel, *The Ragged Trousered Philanthropists*, researchers and academics in almost any discipline concerned with gender, work and emotion will eventually pick up Arlie Russell Hochschild's (2003[1983]) study of Delta Air Lines cabin crew, *The Managed Heart*. At a twentieth-anniversary tribute held by the American Sociological Association in 2003, Hochschild's introducer claimed the book was the most cited text in social science. I've no idea if this is true, but it easily could be: its core concepts – 'emotional labour', 'feeling rules', 'deep and surface acting', 'the gift exchange' and 'the search for authenticity' have penetrated the academic – and organizational management – lexicon in the way only truly significant and highly original works can. It remains the starting point for any enquiry into the field of emotion and work, especially – given its subject matter – when travel is thrown into the equation.

In *The Managed Heart*, Hochschild (2003[1983]) applies Marx's notions of commodification to a service-industry world. Not only does she lay bare the ways in which companies own and control their workers' emotions, she also warns of the ensuing damage. Just as Marx depicted inchoate, alienated workers, with heads and hearts divorced from the fruits of their labours, Hochschild describes emotional workers who no longer know when or where their 'real' personalities begin or end. 'If we can become alienated from goods in a goods-producing society,' she writes, 'we can become alienated from service in a service-producing society' (Hochschild 2003, 7). 'What, in this situation, should I be feeling?' is a question too many service workers – indeed, too many people, period – are having to ask themselves too frequently, she believes (Hochschild 2003, 22). Increasingly,

---

1 All names of interviewees have been changed to protect anonymity.

she claims, fewer and fewer bewildered emotional labourers – the majority of them women – know the answer.

As an example of the contradictory emotions on the loose, take these two narratives from cabin crew who joined the profession in the 1960s. When Aimée Bratt first started flying for Pan American World Airways (Pan Am) in 1966 she was shocked to hear her work summarized as 'look like a woman; think like a man; work like a horse' (Bratt 1996, 13). Looking like a woman and working like a horse were easily implemented, she felt, though perhaps less easily combined. 'Thinking like a man was something else, though,' she writes. It 'meant especially taking a certain distance from the scene, looking at it all completely objectively, not getting emotionally involved' (Bratt 1996, 19).

Compare this to Colleen, who started flying with Delta Air Lines in 1969 and whose approach seems to be the polar opposite of 'thinking like a man'. 'I am in passenger service,' she tells me, and continues:

> I think Delta benefited from a lot of pride, self pride. Girls would want to do nice service, because it reflected on them. They weren't thinking, "Oh, I hope these people like Delta Air Lines." And when we would have turbulence and you only did half the cabin service, we felt terrible. It was a reflection on us, not Delta.

At first blush, it is difficult to imagine these two women, with such apparently conflicting accounts, actually doing the same job. Of course, their differences could be purely idiosyncratic, yet my research on cabin crew – involving interviews and focus groups with over a hundred respondents – suggests otherwise. It is not the case, I would suggest, that Aimée did not really care that much and Colleen took it all a bit too personally. In fact, rather than having differing philosophies what is striking among cabin crew is that they often exhibit *both* emotions – detachment and involvement – in ways that to an outsider may appear to verge on the schizoid. They have the 'Aimée' approach to the job *and* the 'Colleen' approach. And airlines, if anything, reinforce this literal double-facedness: in training, they tell cabin crew to deliver 'personal' service, yet when passengers complain – and increasingly vent their rage – at workers, airlines tell cabin crew not to take it 'personally'. Cabin crew are reminded constantly that in uniform they 'embody' their company yet when they find themselves on the receiving end of passenger abuse, workers are told that it is not *them* but the uniform that is the target, as if it contained no body at all and was merely an empty shell. No wonder some workers get confused, caught in a mismatch of how they actually feel, how they think they *should* feel, and how they display such feelings (Heuven and Bakker 2003).

Hochschild's (2003[1983]) imaginative argument has spawned a veritable academic industry on emotion and work. Yet her focus is, perhaps unashamedly, production based. We get a very clear picture of how and why airlines want their cabin crew to perform in certain ways; we get less of an idea as to why young women – as most recruits have always been – should want to sign up for such an apparently hellish job in the first place. Though it is fairly obvious what airlines get from employing them – higher revenues and inflated share prices – what workers get out of it remains something of a mystery. And in this absence lies one of *The Managed Heart*'s most egregious problems: in focusing so much on the commercialized aspects of emotional labour, Hochschild (2003[1983])neglects its non-commercial side (Wouters 1989, 96). Work becomes the be-all and end-all, invading the private lives of cabin crew unable to switch off the job when at home, or expropriating notions of home and domesticity in advertising campaigns geared to increase profits.

As Sharon Bolton and Carol Boyd (2003) have suggested, emotional exchanges are not restricted to the commercial nexus. They involve worker-worker interaction as much as they involve worker-customer. At the same time, cabin crew workers perform emotional labour dialectically, not unidirectionally; they shape it as much as it shapes them. Far from a brainwashed and manipulated workforce cabin crew have often found in the shared experience of emotional labour new openings for viewing the world and their position within it (Whitelegg 2002).

My purpose here is therefore to push Hochschild's (2003[1983]) stress on emotion into new areas, framed around two main concepts. Rather than viewing emotional labour as something workers do *when they are working*, I posit it as something that workers do *at work*, which is something rather different. Following Bolton and Boyd (2003) I regard emotional labour as taking place in the entire cabin experience, not solely between worker and customer. At the same time, I think it useful to conceptualize cabin crew not just as workers but also as travellers in their own right. As much as they are part of the production exchange involving profit (or more accurately loss!)-making airlines, cabin crew are also consumers of the flight experience and of the travel experience that goes with it. This point should not be underestimated: one of the reasons cabin crew stay so long in the job is because of the unique and specific travel experience afforded to them every time they go to work. I have elsewhere referred to the job's 'non-fiduciary' rewards as 'spatial remuneration', where the spaces it provides become as – and often more – important than money, and one of the reasons cabin crew stick at it. Travel *per se* is one of these spaces (Whitelegg 2007).

I build my argument in three stages: first, I look at the actual space of the airplane cabin, how this has changed and the implications of such changes. Second, I look at what goes on in that cabin in terms of exchanges not between workers and passengers but between workers themselves. 'Emotional rituals' take place on board, the most important being 'Jump-Seat Therapy', where workers exchange advice and counsel, often with complete strangers. Last, I look at wider implications of travel itself for this group of workers, how they have moved from a fixation with 'destination' – in the traditional tourist sense – to 'post-destination', where spaces they create both in the job and outside it are more important than the consumption of exotic locales depicted in many a paperback cabin crew 'exposé'.

The Cabin Space

The first women cabin crew were hired in the US in 1930 and understandably faced on-board conditions vastly different to today. With pre-pressurized cabins, aircraft could not fly that high and crew therefore spent much of their time attending to 'unwell' passengers buffeted by the clouds. Publicity shots from the time – all smiles and bonhomie – belie the fact that early passengers could find flying an unsettling experience: one of the reasons US carriers began to employ trained women nurses as stewardesses – up to that point airlines had only employed men – was to reassure a still-hesitant public that they would be well-cared-for when aloft. The mothering stewardess figure, adopted by all airlines not long after World War Two, became a staple of advertising up to the 1960s, when it was replaced by one laden with sexual innuendo.

As airplane technology improved, first with the Douglas DC3 in the late 1930s, then with the larger, four-engine propellers after World War Two and leading up to the jet era, cabin crew's relationship with and experience of their place of work changed accordingly. Harriett Heffron Gleeson, a US stewardess between 1931 and 1934, recalls:

> The Boeing B-80A was slow and flew at low altitudes. Air was often turbulent and air-sickness was common among passengers. The wires between the wings would often twang in the wind; it was very unnerving. Ventilation was crude and often exhaust fumes would enter the fuselage. We would turn off the heat and passengers wore their coats and wrapped in blankets (McLaughlin 1994, 20).

Here, flying was a highly tactile experience that intensified workers' relationships with the elements. While inside the tube, fliers were still very much aware that the outside was, literally, just outside: every bump would be felt, cabin crew were instructed to prevent passengers mistaking the exterior cabin door for the lavatory and to remind them not to throw things out of the window. In the modern jet cabin, however, any sense of tactility is lost. Turbulence still lurks – its danger actually exacerbated by the prevailing sense of insularity – but air-sickness is now quite rare. Moreover, the pressurized cabin is sealed from the elements – contrary to airplane disaster movies, the cabin door cannot open in flight due to the pressure – and there is certainly no opening the windows, let alone throwing anything out of them.

Cabin crew more and more inhabit a space in which their relationship to the elements, far from being heightened, is effectively severed. Early crew used to have to keep a rough track on their geographical location in case an impromptu weather delay or mechanical problem forced them to land, in which case they had to accompany passengers to the nearest rail station to continue their journey. Flying at lower altitudes, early crew could identify things on the ground. Modern crew, by contrast, have no clue where they are; in all my time speaking to them, not one mentioned ever having seen anything at all out of the window.

The modern airplane cabin thus differs from the railway carriage on which it was, after the 1920s, increasingly modelled. Amy Richter (2005, 5) has written of the railway carriage's transformative aspects as a venue for a modern public experience, especially for women. 'Many passengers,' she writes, 'boarded trains with the belief that they were entering a space with the power to remake them and all of society'. But part of this experience lay in the relationship between the inside of the carriage and the phantasmagorical rushing-by of outside world.

The kinesthetic thrill of the machine entwined in the environment is a hallmark of modernity. But the modern airplane cabin has almost no relation to the outside world. Only those in window seats can actually see anything at all, and the view is often blocked by cloud. When great scenes do unfold we are so remote from them we could be looking at a satellite photograph. And, besides, with new entertainment systems on board, the blinds are invariably down. It is a weird, disorienting environment, as cabin crew readily acknowledge. 'We travelled on a wave of energy,' writes one, 'spending much of our time in the air – not on the earth – in a timeless kind of space' (Dorger 2004, 23).

As jet aviation increased the sense of temporal and spatial disorientation among cabin crew, and as jets themselves got bigger in the late 1960s, the cabin experience took on a new importance. For a start, there was a clearer demarcation of space. On the old DC3 cabin crew worked in a galley tucked at the back of the airplane in full view and close proximity to the public. There was no escape. On wide-bodied jets – the B747s, L1011s and DC10s – galleys were increasingly cut off from the passengers, either by curtains or by placing them below the passenger deck. These areas became off-limits to passengers, a development that, as Alexandra Murphy points out, actually increased cabin crew power by dint of the fact that, in uniform, they could go anywhere they pleased on the plane. The galley became a kind of 'home base' in a game of tag (Murphy 1998, 60).

Erving Goffman (1959, 112) – upon whom Hochschild (2003[1983]) drew heavily – talks of 'back' and 'front' stage performance where 'actors' prepare and perform respectively. For cabin crew, delivering different emotional scripts – one for the passenger, the other for each other – became increasingly viable once the cabin became geographically demarcated. But what was doubly important about the arrival of the new, wide-bodied jets at the end of the 1960s was that they required far greater numbers of cabin crew on board. 'Back' stage performances are hard enough when you have only got one or two listeners; when you have ten, you have an audience.

As Frieda Rozen argues, there was a direct relationship between the construction of a more solidified, politically aware cabin-crew consciousness and the increase in the number of workers on board individual aircraft. Between 1960 and 1975 flight attendants rose from 6.7 per cent to 13.1 per cent of the total domestic US airlines' labour force (Rozen 1987, 224). No longer did women workers have to seek out male pilots for advice – they could turn to each other. At the same time, a nascent women's movement provided an implicit shot in the arm for flight attendants grappling with 'new' themes ranging from balancing domestic responsibilities with their partners to issues concerning occupational health. The net outcome of these changes was, as Roberta Lessor suggests, a new career identity, in which cabin crew viewed their jobs as permanent and not – as airlines had always maintained and enforced – temporary (Lessor, 1984).

Paradoxically, the more cabin crew were physically and sensually removed from the outside world the greater the space they had to reflect upon that world below. Cabin crew from the 1970s increasingly constructed an 'occupational community', containing its own codes, rituals, discourse and emotional exchanges that took place *only* with other cabin crew. Other occupational communities have been identified in fixed places, such as coal-mining or fishing villages, among people who had known each other all their lives. But this occupational community was formed in the mobile space of the airplane cabin often among complete strangers. Its most obvious expression is Jump-Seat Therapy.

Jump-Seat Therapy

Unbeknown to most passengers, cabin crew – especially on bigger airlines – often fly with people they have never met before, and are never going to meet again. Crew scheduling assigns workers to flights (in the US crew bid for their flights and are ascribed them according to seniority). In short, you have a collection of total strangers, with the only thing in common being that they are cabin crew in uniform. Sarah, who flew with American Airlines comments:

> There is something about the camaraderie with the crew. You meet them the first day and by the end of that day you feel like you've known them all your life and you might not have ever met any of them before. You feel like you've known them your whole life because there's a bond in this business.

That bond comes out 'back' stage in the galley or on the jump-seat, where these strangers often become the most intimate of acquaintances. Again and again in interviews and focus groups, cabin crew would mention Jump-Seat Therapy (its name varies) as an important on-board ritual. Clare, who flies for Continental Airlines says:

> I could write a book. The things you hear at 30,000 feet. People have a tendency to tell you their deepest, darkest secrets. Things you would never hear on the ground. You're in a tube in the sky and you're just like in the twilight zone and they have a way of letting it all out. It's pretty interesting. You would not believe what you would hear. You're a psychiatrist up there sometimes. And an emotional healer. And not a lot of people understand these feelings that we go through. And who better than someone that's going through the same thing that you're going through?

'I've probably heard more than I want to know from some people,' admits Mary, who has flown for Delta since the 1960s:

> Some people who have no compulsion at all about telling you the most intimate details of their life. Their latest sexual experience or those kinds of things and your ears are going like this [wiggling them]. *Who* are you and *why* are you telling me this?

Jump-Seat Therapy is unusual in that it combines the notion of work as a venue for emotional release and counselling with the kind of confidence that comes from the anonymity of strangers. But its importance lies in its undoubted grounding in an emotional experience and exchange that takes place *at work* but does not form part of a commercial exchange. Moreover, it is an emotional bonding ritual where cabin crew are implicitly expected to take part and can find themselves in an emotional display as pre-scripted as those they deliver when asking whether a passenger wants chicken or beef. 'Jump-Seat Therapy gets very personal for strangers, but you are stuck in this environment,' says Linda, another Delta flyer. Yet it is assumed that once the cabin door is open, not only will none of what has been said get repeated, but also none of the participants would dream of carrying on the conversation on the ground. In fact, many flight attendants would not dream of even contacting their colleagues when away from work. As Sheila, who also flew for Delta, says:

> A lot of us never knew last names but we knew first names. We were very intimate yet we were very detached all at the same time. I never talked to any of those people on my off days. I never went to their houses. It was never even suggested, not by any of us.

So Jump-Seat Therapy is not about forming friendships. It is not even necessarily about exchanging advice – though many cabin crew told me about it, none suggested that they, personally, had been helped through the counsel of their colleagues. Jump-Seat Therapy is, more than anything, a bonding ritual in which cabin crew demonstrate their commitment to each other and to their profession.

On the one hand this commitment takes the form of individuation. The best example of this is the 'brag book' – pictures of family and home and cats – that cabin crew exchange during down periods of the flight. 'This is me,' says Susie, pretending to flip open a photograph wallet:

> This is who I am. Otherwise we're all the same people in the same uniform with the same hair and the same shoes and things like that. The only thing that's different is what we are showing you of [our] other life, and that's in these pictures.

This is a chance, in short, for cabin crew to remind each other that they have lives outside of work and that they are in fact individuals. And yet, on the other hand, exchanging stories and personal anecdotes reinforces the sense of cabin crew all being in it together. This is partly illustrated in comments I have heard such as 'no one else understands us' or 'it's us against the world.' Opening up on the jump-seat becomes a rite of passage into this world, as though a worker who does not take part has not quite made it. Not the least factor here is that cabin crew are, above all, safety workers, and divulging personal information is a tacit way of trusting each other with their lives in an emergency.

Though friendships formed on the jump-seat tend not to extend to the ground, the cohesion it illustrates does. For instance, the Employee Assistance Program (EAP) run by trade unions such as the Association of Flight Attendants (AFA), which offer counselling services – most notably after the September 11 2001 attacks – are a 'natural extension of the peer support system that [flight attendants] as a culture have already developed', according to Heather Healy, AFA's EAP director. 'We are leveraging off that cultural dynamic', she says.

Jump-Seat Therapy is therefore an onboard emotional interaction that has nothing to do with the actual work process itself but yet still takes place at work. There is more, therefore, to emotional labour than worker-customer exchange. And there is also more to cabin crew than being workers; they are also travellers.

Cabin Crew as Travellers

The literature of travel has long contained a gendered bias. The archetype modernist urban figure of the *flâneur* – the itinerant stroller of the city streets – has often been viewed as inherently masculine (Jokinen and Veijola 1997). Even if we accept that some women struck out for new geographical adventures it also remains the case that mobility and movement have historically been intertwined with masculinity – from Wordsworth to Kerouac – while stasis and home have been long regarded as feminine (Wolff 1995). Even among dual earning (heterosexual) couples such gendered patterns are evident, with women working in far greater proximity to their home than their husbands (Hanson and Pratt 1995).

What is particularly unusual about cabin crew is that they have historically broken this pattern. There is no other group of mainly women workers that travel as far and as often as cabin crew do on an annual basis. One Pan Am flier, for instance, travelled over ten million miles during her twenty-one years with the airline. Of course, high-powered women executives may also rack up the air miles, but the difference is that they do so as a by-product of their work; for cabin crew, travelling such huge distances *is* their work. My point, in short, is women cabin crew have had their geographical horizons lifted and broadened by the work that they do (Whitelegg 2005).

One useful exercise is to divide cabin crew experience into what I call the 'destination phase' of the job and the 'post-destination phase' (Whitelegg 2007).

The 'destination phase' refers to both an historical period in the job's history and a developmental stage in an individual worker's career path. From the end of World War Two up to the introduction of the large jets at the end of the 1960s, cabin crew joined the airlines largely as a way of 'seeing the world'. Airlines encouraged this in their recruitment policies, first by suggesting that doing so would provide great training for future wives and, by the 1960s, by directly suggesting that young women should do so before 'settling down'.

Women were attracted to the job often as a way of getting out of small towns (United recruited heavily in the semi-rural Midwest, for instance). But airlines made sure that 'seeing the world' was only a short-lived thing, insisting that women leave the airlines should they get married, pregnant, or into their thirties. Some of these restrictions still apply at some of the world's airlines.

During the 'post-destination' phase, cabin crew became less interested in where they were going on the job as opposed to all the other things the job allowed them to do. As civil rights legislation by the late 1960s removed restrictive employment practices, workers found that they could make a full-time career of the profession. With the greater control that they could exercise over their movements – as a product of enhanced seniority – cabin crew began to carve out their own spaces.

The progression from 'destination' to 'post-destination' phase is indicated by changing attitudes towards layovers – time spent in cities away from home. Initially, layovers represented all that was glamorous and exotic about the job. For cabin crew, hanging out in Hawaii, Paris and New York was light years from the experience of most of their contemporaries back on the ground. But along the way, as the glamour wore off, flight attendants came to value the layover as a space in itself, not as a venue for tourist consumption. Mothers, especially, craved the solitude of being alone in a hotel room, where they were able to relax without – as one puts it – 'any little creatures bothering them.' But at a more philosophical level, the space on offer allowed women the kind of anonymous freedom in the city previously ascribed mainly to men. Sally, a Delta flyer, recalls:

> Somehow along the way you get the courage to try things, because there aren't people there that know you and that have expectations of how you will behave. I don't mean getting into trouble morally or anything. It's just people don't know you so it's sort of like you have a chance to start life new. It was like that going to different cities. It was like starting life all over again. You didn't have any baggage.

Notions of self-discovery through both actual and metaphorical travel have an important place in feminist thought (Lugones 2003, 85). But Sally's response here is, more than anything, an emotional one, operating in what Christian von Scheve and Rolf von Luede (2005, 323) call a 'bi-directional mediator between individual action and social structures.' Her reaction – replicated by many other cabin crew with whom I talked – indicates a fluid response and relation between the cognitive awareness of being in another place and a constructivist appreciation of the sociological constraints on her life back home.

Conclusion

I have suggested that, for airline cabin crew, issues of emotion go beyond a framework limited to the exchange taking place between worker and customer. Emotional rituals take place on board, fostered by the camaraderie of safety workers thrown together in a pressurized (in numerous senses of the word) environment. Emotions also come into play when thinking about how cabin crew act and react as travellers in their own right.

The fact that most cabin crew have been and continue to be women means that there is a specifically gendered story at work here, even if it is best viewed through the lens of extremity. In few other women-dominated professions does an occupational community exist quite like cabin crew, where strangers bond with military-style cohesion and where women on a weekly basis find themselves miles from home, with time on their hands to reflect upon their relation to the world around them. A basic tenet of anthropology is that we should study the 'abnormal' to inform upon the 'normal'. Just as Hochschild (2003[1983]) demonstrated with *The Managed Heart*, the experiences of cabin crew continue to be of great relevance to all women workers.

References

Bolton, S.C. and Boyd, C. (2003), 'Trolley Dolly or Skilled Emotion Manager? Moving on from Hochschild's Managed Heart', *Work, Employment and Society*, 17, 2, 289–308.

Bratt, A. (1996), *Glamour and Turbulence: I Remember Pan Am 1966–91* (New York: Vintage).

Dorger, B. (2004), *Turbulent Skies: Run-away Thoughts From a Senior Flight Attendant* (www.xlibris.com: Xlibris).

Fineman, S. (2003), *Understanding Emotion at Work* (London: Sage).

Goffman, E. (1959), *The Presentation of Self in Everyday Life* (New York: Anchor Books).

Hanson, S. and Pratt, G. (1995), *Gender, Work and Space* (New York: Routledge).

Heuven, E. and Bakker, A.B. (2003), 'Emotional Dissonance and Burnout Among Cabin Attendants', *European Journal of Work and Organization Psychology*, 12, 1, 81–100.

Hochschild, A.R. (2003[1983]), *The Managed Heart: Commercialization of Human Feeling*, 20th Anniversary Edition (Berkeley: University of California Press).

Jokinen, E. and Veijola, S. (1997), 'The Disoriented Tourist: The Figuration of the Tourist in Contemporary Cultural Critique', in C. Rojek and J. Urry (eds).

Lessor, R. (1984), 'Social Movements, the Occupational Arena and Changes in Career Consciousness: The Case of Women Flight Attendants', *Journal of Occupational Behaviour*, 5, 37–51.

Lugones, M. (2003), *Pilgrimages/Peregrinajes: Theorizing Coalition Against Multiple Oppressions* (New York: Rowman and Littlefield).

McLaughlin, H. (1994), *Footsteps in the Sky: An Informal Review of US Airlines Inflight service, 1920–present* (Denver: State of the Art Ltd.).

Murphy, A. (1998), 'Managing "Nowhere": the Changing Organizational Performance of Air Travel', unpublished PhD thesis, University of South Florida.

Richter, A. (2005), *Home on the Rails: Women, The Railroad, and the Rise of Public Domesticity* (Chapel Hill: University of North Carolina Press).

Rojek, C. and Urry, J. (eds) (1997), *Touring Cultures: Transformations of Travel and Theory* (London: Routledge).

Rozen, F. (1987), 'Technological Advances and Increasing Militance: flight attendant unions in the jet age', in B.D. Wright et al. (eds).

von Scheve, C. and von Luede, R. (2005), 'Emotion and Social Structures: towards an interdisciplinary approach', *Journal for the Theory of Social Behaviour*, 35, 3, 303–328.

Whitelegg, D. (2002), 'Cabin Pressure: The Dialectics of Emotional Labour in the Airline Industry', *Journal of Transport History*, 23, 1, 73–86.

Whitelegg, D. (2005), 'Places and Spaces I've Been: Geographies of Female Flight Attendants in the United States', *Gender, Place and Culture*, 12, 2, 251–66.

Whitelegg, D. (2007), *Working the Skies: The Fast-paced, Disorientating World of the Flight Attendant* (New York: New York University Press).

Wright, B.D., Ferree, M.M., Mellow, G.O., Lewis, L.H., Samper, M.D., Asher, R. and Claspell, K. (eds) (1987), *Women, Work, and Technology: Transformations* (Ann Arbor: University of Michigan Press).

Wolff, J. (1995), *Feminist Sentences* (Oxford: Blackwell).

Wouters, C. (1989), 'The Sociology of Emotions and Flight Attendants: Hochschild's Managed Heart', *Theory, Culture and Society*, 6, 95–123.

Chapter 21

Ambivalent Journeys?
Some Emotional 'Ups' and 'Downs' of
Service Bus Drivers in England

Gillian Reynolds and Jackie Rose

Introduction

In this chapter we analyze data from a small research project conducted in the midlands and northwest of England. The aim of the research was to explore day-to-day working experiences and their emotional effects upon both male and female bus drivers. The motivation was rooted in our own observations (Mills 1959): we became curious after separately spending a protracted period travelling regularly by bus. Like Kay Milton (2007[2005]), we *felt* emotion was the key to understanding something fundamental about human beings, from the simple observation that emotions define the quality of our own lives.

Although some attempt has been made to explore the historical experiences of long-distance bus drivers in the USA (see, for example, Walsh 2000), little has been written regarding the experiences of UK local bus drivers, despite the job often being described as the 'worst job in the world'.[1] Some research into bus driver training and behaviour has been accomplished (e.g. Garwood and Dorn 2003), and also some psychological and health-based research regarding stress (for a succinct summary, see BBC 2001; also Tse et al. 2006), but there has been little sociological exploration of the influences on emotions among bus drivers.

In English politics and media, local bus networks provide a 'Cinderella service'; over the last decade, bus drivers have seen their earning power drop from just above to around 30 per cent below the national average wage (Commission for Integrated Transport 2004). For most people in Britain, this form of transport is non-existent (except as an irritation for car drivers when following one). Academic theorists perceive it as an ambiguous part of the 'mobility turn' (Urry 2007), liminal space (Cresswell 2006), or 'non'-place (Augé 1995). For some social researchers, it is also a space in which one can observe how different identities are constructed and how they work (Schmucki 2007). For the bus driver, however, the vehicle is far from being such a space: it is, precisely speaking, their place of work. Erving Goffman (1963, 20–21) describes such settings as engendering a 'special type of

---

1 Personal communication by a personnel manager of one bus company.

normative disorganization.' As 'contested' settings (Halford and Leonard 2006), they impact upon drivers' interactions with passengers and other road users. This, along with a range of other external factors, is likely to stir up emotional ambiguity or conflict among drivers, who negotiate the territory as part of their daily occupation. How do they emotionally react to the disorganized norms that appear to govern behaviour within and around their workplace?

Understanding emotions illuminates both the power to affect our environment and the power to be affected by it, as well as the relationship between these two powers (Hardt 2007). Arlie Hochschild (1998) maintains that each culture has its unique emotional dictionary, which defines the predispositions with which we behave over time. Milton (2007[2005]), however, argues that emotions operate and are expressed outside the contexts of interpersonal situations and thus have a pre-social origin. Whichever of these theoretical routes is taken, the fact remains that '[b]ecause emotion is so central to human lives, its understanding is important in virtually every discipline whose focus is humanity' (Milton 2007, 73) (see also, among others, Wulff 2007; Ahmed 2004; Damasio 2000; Bendelow and Williams 1998). Historically in all humanities disciplines, there has been reluctance to overtly present emotion as a source of knowledge, because it 'fundamentally challenges the split between body and mind, reason and emotion, that has crucially set the terms for modernity' (Seidler 1998, 206). It does this because emotion consists of 'both feeling and meaning, as something that combines bodily processes and cultural interpretations' (Milton 2007, 62 original emphasis).

About the Research

We combined quantitative and qualitative methods of postal questionnaires and semi-structured interviews based on a broad range of topics. These were developed around some open-ended themes, including:

- What is attractive in driving service buses for a living?
- What aspects of the job cause identifiable physical, mental or emotional stress?
- What factors irritate but do not produce symptoms of stress?

Respondents were self-selecting: several bus companies – covering inner city, suburban and rural areas – co-operated in promoting the research by forwarding our letters and questionnaires to their employees, but people were invited to respond independently of their employers. Overall, the response rate was low, incorporating in total 50 respondents (less than 10 per cent of the combined potential number of employees). Thus, interpretation of the data is indicative: it raises implications for further research, rather than producing results that can be unequivocally generalized. Among the respondents there was a broad range of bus driving experience, from less than a year to more than 15 years. Only 10 per cent were women, which is representative according to other statistics for women employed as bus drivers in the UK (see, for example, Team First 2005), compared with over 50 per cent in North America. Such statistics perhaps also reflect a peculiarly British stereotype of bus driving as a male-oriented occupation. In relation to our research, the gendered imbalance of respondents does mean that our analyses are themselves necessarily gendered as broadly the emotions of men, but even this bias raises some interesting issues regarding perceptions of masculine emotion.

From the data there is clearly no simple occupational 'roadmap' into bus driving. Respondents cited a variety of previous occupations, including management (the largest group), engineering, manufacturing, truck driving, warehousing, the armed forces, retailing, social work, teaching and self-employment: occupations that largely demand a level of responsible freedom to make decisions. Such experiences spawn a wealth of specific skills: a good transport company will ensure drivers are treated as professional people in their own right, capable of responsible self-management. This may be a difficult concept to grasp in an industry and culture that often stigmatizes service bus driving as a menial occupation in which:

> ... it is often part of an individual's job to accept uneven exchanges, to be treated with disrespect or anger by a client, all the while closeting into fantasy the anger one would like to respond with. Where the customer is king, unequal exchanges are normal, and from the beginning customer and client assume different rights to feeling and display (Hochschild 1983, 85–86).

Some Emotional 'Ups'

Positive emotions identified by the drivers could be categorized as drawing on three areas: individual, social, and environmental. All have an impact on self and social identity, as well as being influenced by the same.

Many of the positive responses about bus driving referred back to individual employment history. Sue,[2] for example, had two different reasons – variety and security – for enjoying driving buses: '[I was] just sick of being in a factory for eight hours a day. I wanted something that was outside, and I love driving anyway so just being out and about ... everywhere I'd worked, I'd been made redundant, and I just thought it's going to be a job where I'm never going to be out of work.' Thus, whilst some reasons for becoming a bus driver related back to previous occupations, others were positive and forward-looking.

Having a sense of control over decisions was important to the well-being of many. Again, this was often connected to previous occupations: 'being your own boss and not being cooped up in a factory' (Tony). For some, being able to use their initiative brought a sense of 'empowerment' (Tom). As Alan

---

2 All names of respondents are pseudonyms.

commented, 'to a large extent I have control over what happens in my working environment – the bus – and can do the job as I judge things should be done.' John described himself as 'being virtually your own boss.'

'Taking pride in careful driving and passenger safety' (John) was an aspect of driving buses that keyed into the simple love of driving, pointed out by nearly a third of respondents. This love of driving may be in relation to 'driving and getting paid for it' (Ben) or, more frequently, the pride and sense of satisfaction that come from being able to 'control a large vehicle on the roads' (Mark).

These drivers see themselves as essentially sociable people. The most often-articulated positive emotion arose from meeting people, mentioned by nearly half the respondents. Many emphasized, however, that it was meeting *different* people that helped to boost their emotional attachment to the job. Others were more specific and guarded about what kinds of people they looked forward to meeting – these were the 'vast majority of passengers you carry around – young and old – [who are] pleasant with a smile' (Harry). As Martin commented, it was about 'meeting the better people who make your journey pleasant.'

Whilst meeting different people helped to develop a positive emotion, 12 per cent said they got a 'good feeling' (Tony) from helping people. This might happen in a number of ways, including providing information about the area and helping people to 'fulfil their daily travel requirements' (Dan). Andy commented that 'on a good day you make someone's day.' Alan said he gained emotional satisfaction from his belief that 'I am doing a useful public service and contributing to local economies.'

The emotional satisfaction gained from helping people was matched by the idea of 'looking after' them; the sense of responsibility for people's welfare, a positive emotion also identified by 12 per cent of respondents. Drivers talked or wrote of 'doing a job with responsibility and having the public thank you for it (most of the time)' (Will). It must be noted here, however, that past occupations can provide differing perceptions of responsibility: as Peter said, 'after a long and quite stressful life in retail management I find driving buses a relaxing and lot less responsible job to do.'

The varied nature of bus driving featured often in drivers' positive emotions. Nearly a third felt this was important. Sometimes it was about 'going to different parts of the city' (Dan) or 'seeing all sections of society and then dropping them off' (Tom). For others, it was that 'two days together are never the same' (Liam). For Carl, the attraction was more sensual – he wrote, 'you meet different people (women) with different perfume smells'!

More specifically than the varied nature of the occupation, nearly a third of respondents mentioned the 'outside-ness' of the job as something that engendered a positive emotion: 'It's good to be out and about, as opposed to being in a building all day' (Will). George felt he *was* 'outside': 'not working in one particular place or site all day ... being outdoors.' Tom found it exhilarating to have the 'freedom from office politics.' But – perhaps surprisingly – both men and women who cited the outdoor aspect of bus driving as bringing out positive emotions related it to the natural world: the weather, the sunrise, or the changing seasons; 'we have some lovely runs ... we go through country lanes' (Sue).

Some Emotional 'Downs'

When exploring negative emotions among bus drivers, we distinguished between 'stressful' and 'irritating' factors. We explained that issues causing stress often have physical as well as emotional consequences (Parker and Edwards 2005). Such consequences might include poor sleep patterns, depression, absenteeism, mood swings or – as acknowledged by some respondents – erratic driving. We found that drivers experienced varied emotional responses to similar themes. We have categorized these themes into passenger behaviour, the urban context (including traffic, town planning, law enforcement) and organizational factors (including management practices, provision of facilities, shift patterns).

Nearly half of the respondents found some passenger behaviour irritating; more than a third reported that it caused physical symptoms of stress. The most frequently cited irritating aspect related to social groups, rather than types of behaviour: it may be that moral attitudes and prejudice play a part here. Thus, as John exemplified, those who irritated were 'the class of passenger – druggies, yobbos, moaning pensioners, unruly schoolchildren.' Several reported feeling significantly irritated by babies crying on the bus. Some bemoaned what they felt was not deserved: 'druggies that come back from the clinic [who] get free travel' (Liam).

Passenger complaints about punctuality were mentioned most often, and seen as unjust accusation: 'passengers assuming my bus is late, when the previous bus was missing' (Alan). The impact of late running is compounded by behaviour of waiting passengers:

> If you are running late it is very irritating to stop at a bus stop for people who looked as though they may have been waiting for you, only to find that they are all waiting for a different bus ... you have now become even later by stopping for them (Will).

As passengers climb aboard, there are irritating issues around fare paying. These might be people who 'can see the bus coming but don't have their fare ready when boarding, then proceed to search to the bottom of their bags for it' (John), or 'passengers who try to pay with large notes such as a £20 note for a 45p fare' (Frank).

The behaviour of onboard passengers was the most often-cited cause of stress among the respondents, 'causing mood swings and fatigue' (George). Sometimes the behaviour of passengers towards each other, rather than towards the driver, is responsible: 'people swearing in front of young children and pensioners' (Frank), or 'yobs ... and young mums with pushchairs arguing about spaces' (Paul).

At other times the behaviour is directed towards the driver personally: 'general aggression towards me for no apparent reason from a minority of the public' (Dan). Jan commented that she gets 'more abuse off females than a man getting on the vehicle.' The 'unpredictability and the low level anti-social behaviour' (Tom) of some schoolchildren can cause significant stress. As Philip's comment exemplifies, they can be:

> ... abusive, you get spat at, you get called all the names under the sun, they just generally misbehave ... I had times when I've been on schools rota only and they were pushing windows out, jumping out of the emergency doors at the back ... they'd open that up on a double decker, so the buzzer's going off, so you've got to go up ... then you have to take everything with you because the little b...s would pinch your money.

Dealing with passenger behaviour, 'particularly drug addicts and drunken people' (Martin) is – predictably – a cause of stress, not just for the drivers but also for their families:

> On occasions I have had drunks on my bus who would definitely have hit me if there hadn't been a screen between them and myself ... I recently had a threat from someone under the influence of drugs who said that if he was to ever meet me in the street he would rip my eyes out. That sort of threat can play on your mind as well as worry members of my family when I'm out at work (Will).

In this context of security, several respondents questioned the need for late-night shifts. Philip, for example, argued that, with declining 24-hour shiftwork patterns in his area, the rationale for late buses had largely evaporated:

> ...then just after 11 o'clock at night, wherever you are, you just get half a bus full of people who think they're talking to you totally lucid, and they're 'out the tree' ... if they can afford to go and get pie-eyed, they can afford to get a taxi to come home.

Anxiety about late night security had gendered implications. Some male drivers expressed concern for women drivers: 'me, personally, I don't think women should do lates because of the anti-social behaviour that does happen then, they're ... vulnerable' (Roger). Jan suggested there was no gender discrimination in practice but felt this was largely because of male colleagues' attitudes:

> There were a couple of women who didn't do lates at the time, they only did earlies or a split turn ... but I used to do lates, and ... the blokes used to say, 'if they want to be employed as a bus driver, which is a men's environment, then they should be able to do earlies *and* lates like everybody else'. That's why

there's no policy on that – 'If *you* want to be a bus driver, you do exactly what the men have to do'.

Additionally, it was recognized that issues of security were not confined to late shifts:

> I was threatened by a drunk, and he was that close off me, and that was in the middle of the day, it was like 2 or 3 o'clock in the afternoon, he came so close to punching me ... with the drunks and the druggies that you get on your vehicle, you have to be on your guard from the minute you get on till you go home ... it's not just lates that's the danger point really (Sue).

A significant proportion of the respondents – both male and female – had experienced being spat at, having their vehicle attacked by missiles (bricks or bullets), or having money stolen:

> I had my takings stolen the other morning ... there's nowhere to put our money, and usually I don't leave me money on the bus anyway but it was half past eight ... there was no-one around, usually it's pretty safe just to run in the toilet and come out, and as I come out the toilet he was on me bus pinching all me takings from the morning (Sue).

Although passenger behaviour was cited as the most frequent cause of negative emotion, the urban context of bus driving ranked second: whereas almost a quarter found it irritating, even more reported that it caused actual symptoms of stress. We have used the expression 'urban context' for issues within the general external working environment, including difficult journey times, other road users, town planning decisions and perceived apathy among law enforcement officers (police or traffic wardens).

The 'state of the bus stops, untidiness of bus shelters and drab conditions of bus stations' (Dan) were singled out for complaint; indeed, scheduled places to stop for passengers were a significant cause of irritation. Sometimes this was because 'it is very common for car and van drivers to park at bus stops with raised kerbs which are needed by passengers' (Will). In this vein, several respondents identified 'blue badge' holders[3] as culprits: 'people with disabled car passes parking on bus stops' (Vaughan). But it is not always other drivers who cause problems at bus stops. Local authorities were also identified:

---

3 In the UK, people with a significant disabling condition are entitled to a special blue disc to display in their vehicle when parked. This permits them to park in some places where parking is normally disallowed, but only at a 'safe place'. Reportedly, some abuse this privilege by parking in dangerous or inconsiderate positions.

> Our local council has spent a massive amount of taxpayers' money over recent years having kerbs built … which are level with the platforms of our buses when we stop at them. Unfortunately many of them are positioned so that we cannot pull up to them without the back of the bus still being on the main highway. They would be ideally placed if our doors were halfway down the bus instead of at the front! But to stop a 40-foot long bus at a safe part of many of our bus stops often means passengers will still be left with a big step down from the bus on to the pavement, or even on to a grass verge. This … has completely defeated the object of the raised kerb (Will).

Drivers were frustrated by road closures or other temporary changes made by the local authority, not least because they bore the brunt of passengers' annoyance. Attitudes of other drivers were cited also as both an irritation and a cause of stress (18 and 14 per cent, respectively). Reasons tended to focus on a lack of consideration or courtesy, such as 'car drivers who think they can pull out in front of buses' (Alan). Perhaps predictably, taxi drivers were singled out by many respondents as 'having their own Highway Code' (Martin).

Timetables and traffic were not simply causes of irritation: they featured also among the causes of stress. Keeping the bus on time was the most-often cited problem: for example, 'tight timetable schedules make me stressed, causing me to drive erratically at times' (Mark). Some suggested that journey times were unrealistic: 'a typical example is to have the same arrival and departure time at a particular stop; unfortunately we could find that it takes over five minutes to unload and load thirty passengers at that stop' (Will).

Some identified an absence of police assistance as a cause of stress. They felt there was a 'lack of help from the police in moving illegally parked vehicles' (Jim), and 'bad parking in the town [that] the police cannot be bothered to book' (Liam). It is interesting to note that the perceived invisibility of police from the urban environment was never cited as an 'irritation'; it was mentioned as a cause of stress only.

A third category responsible for these drivers' negative emotions was organizational: attitudes of management, condition of buses or facilities, or shift patterns. Several felt that organizational 'in-house' bureaucracy caused unnecessary tensions:

> A bus driver has to complete a defect card … [of] any faults with the bus. This is a legal requirement, and bus companies … [threaten] disciplinary action against anyone who fails to sign this card. Unfortunately many points made on these cards by drivers are ignored by the bus companies themselves if it means time and money will have to be spent putting right those problems … I have filled in defect cards making the same notes as other drivers about a steering problem on a bus for example, only to find the same bus still out on the road the next day without the problem having been rectified (Will).

A significant minority of respondents cited as an irritation the quality of vehicles. Issues included the fact that the buses 'may be roadworthy but should not be in service for some reason for example poor heating or destination blinds not working' (Alan). The condition of vehicles can encourage 'messy people [to] throw rubbish everywhere on the floor and sometimes they stink badly' (Steve).

Drivers raised further issues around the provision of facilities. Since deregulation of bus services in the UK, there has been a significant reduction in comfort facilities for drivers, as local authorities have sold off termini to individual companies. Sometimes one company controls the buildings and denies access to the facilities to drivers of other companies. Poor facilities directly affect driver experiences:

> You're supposed to have a break, but ... there's nowhere to go and get anything for your break. Passengers pestering you ... we have to sit on the bus for a break, which by law is illegal – you're supposed to be given somewhere to get off your bus ... But with our company, you've just got no chance (Sue).

> ... it's a council bus station but it's [name of another company] offices and canteen ...This is part and parcel of being a smaller company ... Obviously there's nowhere to eat your food – I mean, I'll go down there to the gardens ... When the weather's bad I'll just sit here [in the back of the bus] and eat my sandwiches (Philip).

The questionnaires had not specifically mentioned the matter of bodily functions. In interviews it emerged that this had been an oversight: a number of interviewees – both male and female – raised the issue of toilet provision and use. For example:

> There's a toilet [at the depot] which is not very clean ... cos it's mostly men that use it you see ... and then in certain places ... I'm dying to go the toilet ... and there's nowhere to go and there's many a time I've had to pull in a lay-by and park the bus right up against some bushes so I know no-one can ... and I've actually had to go at the side of the bus (Sue).

> When you pull into a bus station and you go 'I've just got to go the little boys room' or whatever, the passengers just don't believe that you've got to go the toilet – they think you should just sit there behind the wheel and just go to and fro, up and down all day ... They're not very happy about it ... They huff and puff (James).

> I do a long run now ... I usually get caught short half way between, like, but you've just got to sit there and hold it in, kind of thing, till you get to the other end (Roger).

Negative emotions experienced by respondents resulted also from working shifts. These were more likely to be a cause of stress rather than an irritation. The effects of shift patterns on the human body and well-being are well-known to various genres of health researchers (e.g. HSE 2006). The respondents to this study were no exception. It was the aspect of the job most likely to generate comments that *described* the symptoms of stress: for example, 'sleep deprivation after fast turnarounds' (Frank); 'sleep patterns continuously disrupted because of irregular shift pattern' (Dan), or, connectedly, 'low wages for the shifts and hours that we work makes me depressed' (Mark). Several also mentioned lack of choice concerning holidays as a major cause of stress, especially those who had children and/or partners with limited holiday availability.

When respondents identified shift rotas as a cause of irritation rather than stress, it was most often events that occurred as a consequence, rather than the patterns themselves. Thus, for some drivers the issue was less the rota than 'having to travel to different locations to complete your rota, using different vehicles' (Patrick). For others, it was 'getting a change of rota for no reason at all' (Colin). But for most of this group, the reasons related to their families, such as 'not spending time with my son' (Colin). As Sue described:

> I'm up at 4 a.m. ... At 5.30 I'm leaving here for go to work, then I'm not going to get in till 7 or half past at night. I work 12, 13 hour shifts, but my day is really 16 hours long, and when I get in I'm absolutely knackered ... If it's 8 o'clock, even if I've only seen [partner] for half an hour ... I'll go to bed ... we completely miss each other when he's on a late ... it's mostly text messages isn't it? ... 'Can you get some electric?' – 'If I've got time, I'll get you this'. We just deal with it really.

Reflections: Bus Driving and Ambivalent Emotions

The original aim of the research on which this chapter is based was to explore day-to-day experiences and their emotional effects upon both male and female bus drivers. Although the data have revealed some interesting aspects of gender, the full analysis is itself gendered towards the emotions of men: a future project with a greater proportion of women respondents might produce quite different data. In this chapter, however, we have explored some very ambivalent emotions that suggest a complexity to bus driving not previously addressed. In this 'worst job in the world', drivers experience positive fulfilment, as well as the more anticipated emotions of irritation and stress.

In summary, some of the positive emotions – the 'ups' – come from meeting and helping a wide variety of people. Whilst gaining a sense of satisfaction from such experiences is often viewed stereotypically as a feminine emotion, it can also be interpreted as a consequence of paternalism, a 'masculine trait'. Seeing different places throughout the day, a love of driving, and a sense of greater freedom are also often perceived in the UK at least, as feeding the positive emotions of men, although here the women felt the same.

The negative emotions, on the other hand – the 'downs' – come from the behaviour of passengers, the urban context that often played havoc with planned journey times, the attitudes of other road users, unpredictable shiftworking patterns, poorly maintained vehicles and attitudes of management. All these factors can be interpreted as barriers to the drivers' perceived need for a sense of control over the job, a stereotypically masculine emotion. For some drivers, such experiences caused irritation, but for others they caused stress, with observable physical symptoms.

The fact that a sense of paternalist control and freedom featured so strongly in the positive emotions of these drivers provides a key to understanding also why negative emotions occur in the way they do. Aspects of the job that are more likely to merely irritate tend to be those over which the driver can exercise some partial control – such as passenger behaviour and the actions of other road users. Even if there is no opportunity for control, passengers will soon get off the bus, and other road users will move away. Aspects of the job that cannot be controlled by the drivers – the inaction of law enforcement officers, shift patterns or the urban context – are more likely to cause emotions relating to stress rather than simple irritation.

Hochschild (1983) argues, in the context of air cabin crews, that the job is not the same for a woman as for a man; that men are accorded greater awe and respect, and are less likely to be challenged than the women. This means that they do not, on average, have to work quite so hard in their emotional labour. We suggest that this is less the case for male bus drivers, in part because the job itself is far less glamorous, less respected, and far less well-paid than the job of aircrew.

In the years subsequent to Hochschild's (1983) ground-breaking work, many social scientists have used her analysis to explore emotional labour, especially among healthcare professionals. Despite the fact that bus driving is not generally perceived as a 'profession', in terms of emotional labour the job probably has more in common with aircrew cabin staff than do the so-called 'caring professions' such as nursing or policing. This is particularly true in terms of the *commercialization* of emotional work, which creates the concept of emotional labour (Hochschild 1983). Whereas nursing and policing are a public service, organized on a non-profit-making basis (although this assumes a specific and narrow definition of the concept of profit), bus companies in Britain operate very much on the basis of profit. Emotional labour is a dimension of bus driving work that is 'seldom recognized, rarely honoured, and almost never taken into account by employers as a source of on-the-job stress' (Hochschild 1983, 153).

As Margot Lyon (1998, 53) notes, emotions are central to the understanding of the communicative and associative functions of the embodied person: they 'activate bodies in ways that are attitudinal and physical and that have implications for the way individuals together create a common (though ever-changing) design, purpose or order.' Emotion may be a tool, a reaction, a defence, or a response: what an emotion means 'will depend upon what it signifies in a particular situations and what it does, and its value that we attribute to what it is doing' (Crossley 1998, 32). Like Nick Crossley, we suggest that the causes of emotional reactions and responses we have explored here broadly reflect a perceived need to exert a sense of order and rationality in situations where such rationality or order is challenged.

References

Ahmed, S. (2004), *The Cultural Politics of Emotion* (Edinburgh: Edinburgh University Press).

Augé, M. (1995), *Non-Places: Introduction to an Anthropology of Supermodernity* Trans. John Howe (London: Verso).

BBC (2001), *Stress: The Effects* (dated 25 June), www.news.bbc.co.uk/1/hi/health/1406880.stm, [accessed 25 March 2008].

Bendelow, G. and Williams, S. (eds) (1998), *Emotions in Social Life: Critical Themes and Contemporary Issues* (London: Routledge).

Clough, P.T. with Halley, J. (eds) (2007), *The Affective Turn: Theorizing the Social* (Durham: Duke University Press).

Commission for Integrated Transport (2004), www.cfit.gov.uk/docs/2004/busindustry/02.htm [accessed 3 March 2008].

Cresswell, T. (2006), *On the Move: Mobility in the Modern Western World* (Oxford: Taylor and Francis).

Crossley, N. (1998), 'Emotion and Communicative Action: Habermas, linguistic Philosophy and Existentialism' in G. Bendelow and S. Williams (eds).

Damasio, A. (2000), *The Feeling of What Happens: Body, Emotion and the Making of Consciousness* (London: Vintage).

Dorn, L. (ed.) (2003), *Driver Behaviour and Training* (Aldershot: Ashgate).

Garwood, L. and Dorn, L. (2003), 'Stress Vulnerability and Choice of Coping Strategies in UK Bus Drivers' in L. Dorn (ed.).

Goffman, E. (1963), *Behavior in Public Places* (New York: Free Press).

Halford, S. and Leonard, P. (2006), *Negotiating Gendered Identities at Work: Place, Space and Time* (Basingstoke: Palgrave Macmillan).

Hardt, M. (2007), 'Foreword: what affects are good for' in P.T. Clough with J. Halley (eds).

Hochschild, A. R. (1998), 'The Sociology of Emotion as a Way of Seeing' in G. Bendelow and S. Williams (eds).

Hochschild, A.R. (1983), *The Managed Heart: Commercialization of Human Feeling* (California: University of California Press).

HSE (2006), *Managing Shift Work: Health and Safety Guidance* (Sudbury, Suffolk: HSE Books).

Lyon, M. (1998), 'The Limitations of Cultural Constructionism in the Study of Emotion' in G. Bendelow and S. Williams (eds).

Mills C.W. (1959) *The Sociological Imagination* (London: Penguin).

Milton, K. (2007), 'Emotion (or Life, The Universe, Everything)' in H. Wulff (ed.).

Parker, J. and Edwards, P. (2005), Surveys on Stress and Attendance Management. European Foundation for the Improvement of Living and Working Conditions. University of Warwick, www.eurofound.europa.eu/ewco/2005/09/UK0509NU02. htm [accessed 25 March 2008].

Schmucki, B. (2007), 'Gendered Spaces – Gendered Places. Women, Urban Transport and Walking in the 19th and 20th Century', Paper presented to *Gender, Emotion, Work and Travel: Women Workers and Passengers Past and Present* Conference, Greenwich Maritime Institute (GMI), University of Greenwich, London. 22–23 June.

Seidler, V.J. (1998), 'Masculinity, Violence and Emotional Life' in G. Bendelow and S. Williams (eds).

Team First (2005) *Corporate Social Responsibility Report*, www.firstgroup.com/corpfirst/pdf/11_TEAM.pdf [accessed 8 July 2008].

Tse, J., Flin, R., Mearns, K. (2006), 'Bus Driver Well-Being Review: 50 years of research', *Transportation Research Part F*, 9, 89–114.

Urry, J. (2007), *Mobilities* (Cambridge: Polity).

Walsh, M. (2000), *Making Connections. The Long-Distance Bus Industry in the USA* (Aldershot: Ashgate).

Wulff, H. (ed.) (2007), *The Emotions: A Cultural Reader* (Oxford: Berg).

Section 4

Introduction: Making the Journey – Travel and Travellers

Gayle Letherby and Gillian Reynolds

Background Issues

Arguably, we could identify those sharing a train, bus, plane or other journey as a 'community of occasion' – 'last[ing] no longer than the emotions that keep them in the focus of attention and prompt the pooling of interests – fleeting, but no less intense for that – banding together and adhering "to the cause"' (Bauman 2003, 34). Norbert Elias and John Scotson (1994, xvi) argue that in any community there is an 'established' group (in terms of a given territory, or over a longer period of time), who will tend to 'close ranks' and stigmatize others as 'outsiders': they 'look upon themselves as the "better" people, as endowed with a kind of group charisma, with a special virtue shared by all its members and lacked by the others.' In addition to the significance of 'communities of occasion' on passenger vehicles, driving a car, riding a bike or walking in public spaces also necessitates not only attention to one's own place in the journey but involves interaction and negotiation with others that are passed.

Thus, enjoyable and tense journeys are often shared experiences that promote emotions and emotional experience between individuals who would otherwise not come into contact with one another. With reference to the relationships between strangers, Zygmunt Bauman (1997, 25) argues that:

> [the] difference which sets the self apart from the non-self, and 'us' apart from 'them', is no longer given by the pre-ordained shape of the world, nor by command on high. It needs to be constructed, and reconstructed, and constructed once more, and reconstructed again, on both sides at the same time ... Today's strangers are 'by-products, but also the means of production, in the incessant, because never conclusive, process of identity building'.

The meaning and status of relationships constructed and reconstructed through meetings on regular journeys may change of course – in the first instance from stranger to acquaintance. As David Morgan (forthcoming) suggests that:

> Acquaintances are ... part of the 'given' of the numerous overlapping social fields within which individuals are involved. ... Whatever field we are concerned with

– neighbourhoods, workplaces or, to add a third, professional client relationships [or travel relationships] – there appear to be some sense of a balance between acquaintances; all that is required is a sense that they share the same social field and have some small, although distinct, knowledge of each other. ...

He continues: 'Acquaintances may provide some sense of ontological security. The neighbour walking her dog, the man in the corner shop, the manager or the union representative at work become part of the familiar temporal and spatial landscapes.' This suggests that in addition to our relationships with family and friends (some of whom we might even have first met on a journey (for examples see Letherby and Reynolds 2005) and strangers (see Bauman 1997, 25 above) acquaintances too are significant in the 'process of identity building'.

In 1969 Erving Goffman reminded us that our very ability to engage in social life depended upon managing our bodies in both time and space. Almost 40 years on, Sven Kesselring (2008) and Sven Kesselring and Gerlinde Vogl (2008) reflect on the particular 'mobility management' necessary today. Arguing that spatial mobility is a key indicator for modernity Kesselring (2008) adds:

People need to deploy strategies to cope with a new mobility regime that demands mobility and flexibility from everybody. ...

Deep-going changes within the constitutional settings of modernity occurred over the last twenty years. Today, the risk society is a world risk society; and it is a mobilized society – spatially as well as socially. The time-space structure of the world risk society is based on the functionality, efficiency and the effectivity of large-scale infrastructures of transport and communication (Kesselring 2008, 78/79).

In addition, managing mobility also has implications for both the doing of gender and the display and control of emotion in any journey (Letherby and Reynolds 2005).

Making the Journey

In each of the three chapters in this section of the book the authors reflect on relationships between self and other whilst engaged in travel activities. The travel encounters we have are of course structured by the time and space in which they occur (Sheller 2005; Letherby and Reynolds 2005). Writing specifically with reference to automobility, Mimi Sheller (2005, 227) writes:

Driving can be included among the active corporeal engagements of human bodies with the 'sensed' world. Like other modes of mobility, such as walking, bicycling or riding trains, modes of driving also arise out of 'a specific' time and place. ... Driving, then, suggests many different kinds of affordances between varied bodies, cars and spaces.

The considerations of cycling (McBeth), walking (Nicholls) and travelling on Victorian railways (Stevenson) presented here starkly highlight the significance of space to past and present travel experiences. Mike McBeth in 'Long Live the 'Velorution'! Cycling, Gender and Emotions' (Chapter 22) considers the (gendered) body/machine relationship in a similar way to Sheller (2005). As John Urry (2000, 55) notes:

> The stagecoach, the railway, the bike, the motor coach, the motorcycle, the plane and especially the car have generated newly fast mobilities that have mostly reduced the pleasures and usefulness of walking and strolling.

From McBeth's chapter we can see that the bicycle too has been affected by the growth in travel technology and as a result cyclists are perceived as other to more 'normal' travellers. Although McBeth is concerned in his chapter with cycling for pleasure, cycling as a sporting activity and commuter cycling, Phil Nicholls in his auto/biographical piece 'A Walk in the Park' (Chapter 23) concentrates on walking as leisure and pleasure. As you read Nicholls' piece you might 'walk' with him as he describes the walk, the encounters he and his companions have and the surrounding environment. Until recently:

> The dichotomy between the social and the natural has been most pronounced in the case of sociology. The other social sciences have enjoyed a more messy and confused relationship with the facts of nature. In sociology this academic division between a world of social facts and one of natural facts has been regarded as largely uncontentious (Macnaghten and Urry 1998, 5).

Yet, auto/biographical reflection on cultural understandings of nature demonstrates how emotion (and emotional management) is relevant not only within travel relationships but also in terms of the engagement we have with the nonhuman things in our environment (Milton 2007).

Both McBeth and Nicholls are concerned to some extent with the 'good' and 'bad' behaviour of others; with manners and etiquette, which are, states Norbert Elias (1978), a significant aspect of 'civilization'. The way in which we define civilization is historically specific, and – to some extent – there is a commonsense view of what is, and what is not, appropriate behaviour in any historical period (Letherby and Reynolds 2005). Forty years ago, for example:

> In a train compartment ... individuals may be asked by a fellow-passenger if it is all right if he smokes, or if he opens (or closes) a window. As these opening engagements are patently in the interests of those whose comfort might be affected, the offense or injury the individual might create by his inclinations thus

exposes fellow-passengers to solicitous inquiries in advance (Goffman 1963, 128).

In Chapter 24 "Women and Young Girls Dare not Travel Alone': The Dangers of Sexual Encounters on Victorian Railways', Kim Stevenson draws on her analysis of nineteenth century newspaper reports to explore the gendered implications of 'good' and 'bad' behaviour on trains at that time. Most women today will have experienced the difficult negotiation for space within a railway carriage (or on a bus or aeroplane) especially in the tendency for men to colonize the middle arm of a twin seat, or spread their legs apart when seated, thus 'claiming' a larger space for themselves. Women cannot compete with such practices without running the danger of being seen as 'flirting' by pushing against the man's arms or legs to force a larger space for themselves (Letherby and Reynolds 2005). Stevenson is concerned with historical expectations of appropriate female and male behaviour and how public transport was (and we would suggest still is) 'appropriated more comfortably and 'naturally' by men' (Letherby and Reynolds 2005, 188).

References

Bauman, Z. (2003), *Liquid Love* (Cambridge: Polity).

Bauman, Z. (1997), *Postmodernity and its Discontents* (Cambridge/Oxford: Polity/Blackwell).

Canzler, W. Kaufmann, V. and Kesselring, S. (eds) (2008), *Tracing Mobilities: Towards a Cosmopolitan Perspective* (Aldershot: Ashgate).

Elias, N. (1978), *The Civilizing Process, Volume 1: The History of Manners* (New York: Basil Blackwell).

Elias, N. and Scotson, J. (1994), *The Established and the Outsiders* (London: Sage).

Featherstone, M., Thrift, N. and Urry, J. (eds) (2005), *Automobilities* (London: Sage).

Kesselring, S. (2008), 'The Mobile Risk Society' in W. Canzler, V. Kaufmann and S. Kesselring (eds).

Kesselring. S. and Vogl, G. (2008), 'Networks, Scapes and Flows – Mobility Pioneers between First and Second Modernity' in W. Canzler, V. Kaufmann and S. Kesselring (eds).

Goffman, E. (1963), *Behavior in Public Places: Notes of the Social Organisation of Gatherings* (New York: The Free Press).

Letherby, G. and Reynolds, G. (2005), *Train Tracks: Work, Play and Politics on the Railways* (Oxford: Berg).

Milton, K. (2007), 'Emotion (or Life, The Universe, Everything)' in H. Wulff (ed.).

Macnaghten, P. and Urry, J. (1998), *Contested Natures* (London: Sage).

Morgan, D.H. (forthcoming), 'Acquaintances: Their position within webs of relationships' in E.D. Widmer, A-M. Castren, R. Jallinoja and K. Kaisa (eds).

Sheller, M. (2005), 'Automotive Emotions' in M. Featherstone, N. Thrift and J. Urry (eds).

Urry, J. (2000), *Sociology Beyond Societies: Mobilities for the Twenty-first Century* (London: Routledge).

Widmer, E.D., Castren, A-M., R. Jallinoja and K. Kaisa (eds) (forthcoming), *Families as Configurations* (New York: Peter Lang).

Wulff, H. (ed) (2007), *The Emotions: A Cultural Reader* (Oxford: Berg).

Chapter 22

Long Live the 'Velorution'![1]
Cycling, Gender and Emotions

Mike McBeth

Introduction

Cyclists engender strong emotions: those who cycle regularly are passionate about all things bicycle, while non-cyclists are perplexed by such enthusiasm. Cycling fervour is often expressed in terms of the utilitarian role that the bicycle has as a mode of transport (and the bicycle can be the cheapest, most efficient and even the fastest way of travelling). However, many cyclists also express emotional attachments to bicycles and cycling. Cyclists might describe cycling as a 'love', extol the freedom and liberty that comes from cycling, or delight in cycling camaraderie. Cycling is also celebrated as a way to relax, a leisure pursuit, the answer to climate change, a healthy option or a sport. In short, cycling combines utility with guilt-free pleasure.

Cycling as experience

My own experience of cycling began in childhood and learning to ride a bicycle was a significant rite of passage. The confidence gained while turning those tentative wobbles to independent travel was huge. Learning a skill that becomes unforgettable is 'as easy as riding a bicycle' and for me learning to ride led to a lasting love of cycling. The freedom cycling brought offered escape and my bicycle quickly became as much a part of my group of friends as they and their bicycles. Owning a bicycle was an important symbol of belonging and we boys were intensely competitive about our machines – racing geometry was essential, which meant as many gears as possible and drop handlebars. Ideally a make with components associated with cycling glory was important, too. Not for us the trendy fad for low to the ground 'chopper' or BMX-style bikes with heavy elongated frames, high handlebars, extended forks and seats, rather than saddles. Girls used their bicycles almost as much as the boys; theirs without top tubes (crossbars) and often brightly painted with contrasting handlebar grips and some even had tassels

---

1 Vélorution is a radical bicycle organization based in Paris. Their main objective is a city free of cars.

hanging from the bar ends. In the late 1960s and through the 1970s more modest levels of car ownership meant that we children were fairly casually monitored and could ride freely. Bicycles permitted adventures to the seaside, countryside, towns and even other cities. Cycling was both our main mode of transport and pastime. It would not have occurred to any of us to ask to be driven somewhere and I imagine any such requests would have been sharply rebuffed. In any case, an important part of the experiences of being a young cyclist was the shared journey.

As I grew through teenage years the size of the gang of cyclists gradually dwindled, but I never learned to drive and the bicycle remained my most common mode of transport. Now almost 50, my not driving, along with my not being married, not eating meat and not having children all seem to have reinforced my sense of being something of an outsider. But cycling also creates a sense of camaraderie and exchanged glances, smiles, nods or even greetings between passing riders are not uncommon. A bond is created though a shared understanding of the pleasure that cycling brings and a sense that those who do not ride never seem to understand what it is that keeps those of us who do ride on our bikes.

Cyclists tend to have slightly anarchic temperaments and this could be a significant factor in choosing to become a cyclist, or it may develop as someone becomes a committed cyclist. Cyclists' dislike of hierarchy, rules and authority is mentioned by Tim Hilton (2004, 45) when he discusses the pioneering Clarion cycling clubs:

> Clarion clubs have given us two leading characteristics of British cycling: first, cycling is not a political sport, but it does belong to the leftward side of humanity; second, cyclists do not on the whole wish to be governed and are often unable to govern each other. The administration of cycling, from the smallest clubs to the largest, has often been a shambles. That's the way most of us like it.

Following cycle sport has also been a part of the pleasure associated with cycling. Competitive cycling makes relentless physical demands that are almost certainly without parallel in any other sport. Professional cyclists average speeds of over 25 mph and, in fast sprints, over 40 mph. I average about 12 mph and people tell me that I must be fit! Successful team cycling also requires a combination of contradictory traits: collaboration and individualism. Riding behind a cyclist uses about two-thirds of the energy required to ride at the front and cycling etiquette requires riders to take their turn up front. If a rider falls behind, team members usually drop back to take turns pacing everyone back. Persistently riding behind others, 'wheel sucking', is discouraged and offering one's wheel to others is considered polite. Teamwork only goes so far, however, for to win means judging the right moment to 'break away' and escape from the pack without being caught up and 'reeled' back in, or worse, falling behind and being 'dropped'.

The negative approach to cycling in the UK includes the marginalization of cycle sport. For example, Beryl Burton was one of the most successful British cyclists ever who dominated the sport from the late 1950s through to the 1980s, yet her name is hardly known outside of the cycling fraternity. Burton won numerous events including 122 national championships. She was the Best All Rounder champion every year for 25 years, the world 3,000-metre pursuit champion on five occasions and twice the world road-racing champion. Burton regularly defeated male cyclists and cycling folklore has it that on one occasion as she passed the leading man in a race she offered him one of her liquorice allsorts because 'the poor dear seemed to be struggling a bit' (Woodland 2005, 174). As a successful athlete in a male dominated sport, Burton confronted many obstacles: she was blocked from competing in the inaugural Women's Tour de France in 1984 for want of a road racing licence and women's cycling was not included in the Olympic Games until 1988, by which time she was in her late 40s (men's cycling has been included since the Games' inception in 1896).

Cycling transcends class, ethnicity, gender, sexuality and age – it is something that just about anyone can do. A wide variety of bikes is available that are suitable for different kinds of rider, including recumbent bicycles with hand cranks rather than pedals. Part of the emotional attachment to cycling is its connection to the environment. Lance Armstrong, (the only person ever to win the Tour de France seven times and also the only person ever to win the Tour on five consecutive occasions, despite having been diagnosed with testicular cancer in 1996), describes the visceral aspect of cycling:

> Why do I do it? The simple answer is that I love to ride. To me, riding is living. When I was sick with cancer, I thought constantly about riding. I daydreamed about the sensation of moving through the countryside on a bike, the wind against my face. … I rode to prove I wasn't dying. Now I ride to prove that I'm alive. … I ride to prove that, in a mechanised era, the human body is still a marvel.

> In cycling, there is nothing to protect you from the elements and this makes it a sport as sensuous as it is severe. The cyclist experiences gre.at beauty – sublime views, the swooping exhilaration of a mountain descent – but there's a penalty on the body for cycling, too: a physical toll to remind you that you are human (Armstrong 2004, 1).

Cycling gave to the English language the term 'free-wheeling', meaning to be carefree and happy. Sometimes a strong bond is formed between the cyclist and the machine. The interplay between bicycle and rider may mean that the bicycle can be treated as an extension of the self – its imperfections and idiosyncrasies overlapping or bound up with any perceived limitations that the rider may feel about their own body. Equally, however, it is hard to think of any experience that delivers such a strong sense of personal satisfaction as completing a journey while riding a smooth-running, well-fitted machine on a clear still day. Charlie Woods describes the interplay of bicycle and rider:

When Enzo Ferrari, the famous racing-car builder said that 'Between man and machine there exists a perfect equation, 50 per cent machine and 50 per cent man,' he spoke more truly perhaps of the racing bike. You get on it, pedal up the road and immediately feel the silky, effortless motion that it provides. But go a few miles, confront a hill maybe, and the bike begins to call on your 50 per cent. Are you fit and strong enough to do it justice? ... You have to balance the equation, you have to live up to those sublime mechanics ... if you do rise to the challenge ... you can become equal partners in a wonderfully fulfilling discovery of both body and mind. You can touch upon a sense of life which is freer and more abundant; a transformation of consciousness which inspires cultivation. Such is the secret that all keen cyclists share and generally keep to themselves, for it cannot be taught, only picked up for oneself ... (Woods 2001, 35–35).

Bicycles may be anthropomorphized by their riders, given a personality, named, spoken to, cajoled, coaxed, pampered and caressed. This 'bond' between individual and conveyance is not unusual, but with other forms of transport such as aeroplanes or boats, the gender of the machine is almost always female. When an attachment is formed between a bicycle and rider the machine tends to take on the gender of the rider. Edward Elgar bought his his first bike, a 1900 Royal Sunbeam, when he was 43. He named it 'Mr Phoebus'. Elgar and 'Mr Phoebus' traversed Herefordshire and Worcestershire on long days out and Elgar composed as he rode. Moor (2004, 77–78) suggests that the typical cadence (pedalling speed) of Elgar's bicycle is matched in the rhythms of his music.

In 1895 Frances Willard, a prominent American suffragist and social reformer, discovered the joys of cycling. Like Elgar, Willard took up cycling relatively late in her life. She fell in love with the bicycle and recognized the significant parallels in her struggle to ride a bicycle with the larger struggle of women. In *How I Learned to Ride the Bicycle* Willard extolled the virtues of the bicycle and revealed that hers was named 'Gladys', because of its 'gladdening effect' on health and political optimism.

Enthusiasm for the bike can be observed in the way *aficionados* are organized. For example, in a poll commissioned by the *Times* in 2004 the bicycle was chosen as the country's greatest invention of the previous 250 years, taking 59 per cent of the 5,500 votes (Henderson 2004). In 2005, in a UK Patent Office/BBC Radio 4 Internet and telephone poll, the bicycle was chosen as the most significant invention since 1800 gaining 62 per cent of the votes cast (BBC News 2005). The bicycle was placed ahead of the computer and vaccinations. Even in an apparently car-obsessed nation like the UK, the internal combustion engine could only collect three per cent of the votes. In 2007 the National Lottery conducted an online and telephone poll to allocate £50 million. Of the 286,285 votes cast, Sustrans, a cycling charity that promised to build cycling and walking routes, secured the money with 119,348 votes, over 40 per cent of the total (Big Lottery Fund 2007).[2]

The solidarity of cyclists can be understood as a reaction to, or a defence against, the evident hostility to cycling in the UK. To be a cyclist involves negotiating the physical environment, but the biggest threat to cyclists comes from motorists who pass too close, too fast, exit junctions and collide with cyclists or open doors into cyclists. Cyclists are physically vulnerable to motorists, but cyclists also encounter the opprobrium of motorists. Like bullies who dominate but insist on more, drivers often overtake cyclists then brake suddenly, engines are noisily revved from behind, horns are blared at cyclists and vehicles frequently park in cycle lanes. Cyclists even report abuse from occupants of passing vehicles. The Automobile Association (1993) examined the attitudes of motorists to cyclists and found that 30 per cent of motorists considered cyclists to be a 'nuisance' while 65 per cent of motorists agreed with the statement: 'Most drivers would rather cyclists were not on the roads at all.' Ten per cent of motorists believed that cyclists are too poor to have a car; yet the report also found that pro-cycling attitudes were concentrated among higher socio-economic groups and that 'committed cyclists' were better paid than 'committed motorists', a reversal of what drivers tended to believe. Eighty-three per cent of motorists said that nothing would entice them to ride a bike again. The report conceded that 'Some motorists are inconsiderate and have negative attitudes towards cyclists' and concluded:

> Cyclists are often the underdogs of the road – seen as such by both motorists and cyclists themselves. Some motorists don't like them because they feel they hold up traffic; pedestrians don't like sharing paths with them because they travel too fast. This gives the impression that cyclists are unwelcome on the roads and off the roads (AA 1993).

Cyclists are criticized for running red lights or riding on pavements, but their motivations are more complicated than detractors might imagine. As cyclists feel vulnerable on the roads, seeking refuge on the pavement or riding through a red light makes sense. Cyclists also perceive that the rules of the road in the UK are biased in favour of motorized transport. In a motor vehicle it is no real hardship to wait at red lights, be forced around one-way systems or to frequently stop and start. But cyclists use considerable energy starting and stopping, are exposed to the elements and find it rather galling to be cajoled or bullied into obeying rules that were not devised for cyclists. Since cyclists tend not to regard themselves as 'traffic' in the conventional sense, there is a tendency to do whatever it takes to complete journeys as quickly, efficiently and as safely as possible – even if this means violating rules.

---

2 The results of these 'popularity' polls are controversial because the outcomes seem to be determined by the extent to which a highly motivated discrete group of pro-cycling voters and their supporters rig the results.

The gulf in understanding between cyclists and motorists seems wider in Britain than in other European countries and this may be related to the comparatively high levels of car ownership. In 1986 Margaret Thatcher is reputed to have said that a man, aged 26, who finds himself travelling by bus can count himself a failure (Fenton 2006). The dominance of the car distorts perceptions of drivers and non-drivers alike. For example, retailers in Bristol overestimated the importance of car-borne trade by almost 100 per cent, believing that 41 per cent of their customers arrived by car, whereas it was only 22 per cent (Sustrans 2006, 2). Such retailers often oppose restrictions on cars even though it would benefit their trade.

In Britain cycling is regarded as a childhood activity with driving and owning a car considered another important rite of passage. Adult cycling is often associated with the faintly comic and bike riding signifies eccentricity and/or stupidity in television light entertainment. In mainland Europe more people cycle and motorists treat cyclists with respect. By law, motorists in France must allow at least one metre clearance when overtaking cyclists and in many other European countries motorists are always liable in accidents between motorists and cyclists, a powerful incentive to drive safely. Segregated cycle provision is more common in mainland Europe too and coherent separate provision is important in attracting people to cycling. Research shows that a larger number of cyclists in a given area will disproportionally increase the number of women who cycle:

> ... where cycling is uncommon, it is mostly done by males; larger cycling populations are more evenly balanced between the genders. As cycle flows approach critical mass, as they have in Central London recently, sharp growth may be observed in the proportion of cyclists who are female (Smith 2005, 2).

History of Cycling

The history of the bicycle and its relationship to gender is closely coincident and connected to the rise of the labour movement and women's emancipation. In the 1820s bicycles were essentially gentleman's playthings that relied on treads or pedals directly attached to a drive wheel for their operation; the bigger the drive wheel, the more effort was required to turn the pedal, but the faster and further the machine would travel with each pedal turn. For this reason the front drive wheel grew larger while the rear wheel shrank leading to the development of the Ordinary bicycle, nicknamed the Penny Farthing, which was popularized by young men from the 1870s to about 1885. The larger front wheel delivered more speed, but the Ordinary lifted the rider away from the ground, on a machine that was less stable so there were considerable risks associated with it. Nevertheless, travelling at speed, competing with others and taking risks were part of the allure of cycling, especially for men. For women, riding the Penny Farthing was considered indecorous as well as potentially harmful to health.

The Rover 'safety bicycle', with a transmission system consisting of pedals connected to a chain and gearing to drive the rear wheel, became popular after 1885. The introduction of the pneumatic tyre in 1888 improved rider comfort. The recognizably modern bicycle with a diamond frame, equal-sized wheels, pneumatic tyres and straight or drop handlebars has remained basically the same from around 1890, when something of a cycling 'craze' took place in western Europe and north America.

Women were discouraged from cycling and concerns were raised about the effects on their more 'delicate constitutions', with doctors suggesting that cycling could potentially harm women's reproductive systems and lead to racial decline. There was considerable unease about the potential for cycling as a method of masturbation that would (over) stimulate women as they rode. Despite, or perhaps because of, the concerns, women took up cycling in ever larger numbers. In her book about growing up in Oxfordshire in the late 1880s and 1890s, Flora Thompson (1973, 477) observed:

> Soon every man, youth and boy whose families were above the poverty line was riding a bicycle. For some obscure reason, the male sex tried hard to keep the privilege of bicycle riding to themselves. If a man saw or heard of a woman riding he was horrified. 'Unwomanly. Most unwomanly! God knows what the world's coming to,' he would say; but, excepting the fat and elderly and the sour and envious, the women suspended judgement. They saw the possibilities which they were soon to seize. The wife of a doctor in Candleford town was the first woman cyclist in the district. 'I should like to tear her off that thing and smack her pretty little backside,' said one old man grinding his teeth with fury. One of the a more gentle characters sighed and said: ''T'ood break my heart if I saw my wife on one of they,' which those acquainted with the figure of his middle-aged wife thought reasonable.

For both men and women, bicycles afforded an unprecedented degree of personal freedom of movement. Indeed, the bicycle is credited with extending and improving the human gene pool, as it was possible to travel further to meet sexual partners. Mass production of an affordable safety bicycle was particularly significant for women, coming at a time when many were engaging in struggles for emancipation. Bicycles came to represent all that was modern, futuristic and even symbolized the 'New Woman'. For Susan Brownell Anthony, a pioneering US feminist and suffragist, the bicycle was a significant part of the campaign for women's rights:

> Let me tell you what I think of bicycling ... I think it has done more to emancipate women than anything else in the world. I stand and rejoice every time I see a woman ride by on a wheel. It gives woman a feeling of freedom and self-reliance. It makes her feel as if she were independent. The moment she takes her seat she knows she can't get into harm unless she gets off her bicycle, and away

she goes, the picture of free, untrammelled womanhood (interviewed by Nellie
Bly for *New York World*, 2 February 1896, cited in Willard 1991, 4).

Most outrage was reserved for what women should wear when they rode a bicycle.
Cyclists have always worn special clothes and early bicycles such as the Penny
Farthing were impossible to ride while wearing skirts. Tricycles could more easily
be ridden in skirts and they allowed women to ride without wearing bloomers,
which at that time had sexual and politically radical associations. Following the
introduction of the safety bicycle, women's enthusiasm for cycling led to the
development of 'rational dress' – a divided skirt, which helped liberate women
from corsets, ankle-length skirts and other restrictive garments. In 1897 Cambridge
University undergraduates demonstrated against a proposal to admit women as
full members of the university by hanging an effigy of a woman wearing bloomers
and, of course, riding a bicycle.

The mass development of the bicycle also coincided with a growth of light
industrial manufacturing. Many small engineering works diversified into producing
bicycles and technical innovations that were to become crucial to the development
of that bane of cyclists' lives, the motor car, emerged from cycle manufacturing.
Indeed, many well known car manufacturers began in bicycle production, for
example Peugeot, Rover, Humber, Triumph, Morris and Škoda. Components are
not the only thing that cars owe to bicycles – it was the widespread use of bicycles
that created the impetus to surface many more roads in the early twentieth century.
In the 1890s, fast fixed gear bicycles were particularly favoured by young men
and they were known as 'Scorchers' because of their higher speeds. Orville Wright
was a keen racing cyclist and was nicknamed 'the Dayton Scorcher'. Orville and
his brother Wilbur ran a bicycle sales and repair shop and in 1896 they began
manufacturing their own brand of bicycles. Their knowledge of how best to
maintain stability and steer an inherently unstable machine such as a bicycle was
transferred to their prototype flying machine. Thus the bicycle played a part in the
design of the first sustained heavier-than-air human flight.

The early democratic nature of bicycling is not only demonstrated in its
appeal to women. Marshall Walter 'Major' Taylor was only the second black
athlete to become a world champion in any sport and he held seven world cycling
records by 1898. In 1899 he also won the world 1-mile championship. Inevitable,
Taylor had to fight considerable bigotry and determined hostility to succeed in
cycle racing, which was one of the most popular athletic events at the turn of the
century. Taylor's devout Baptist brand of Christianity prevented him from riding
on Sundays and given that so much competitive cycling took place on Sundays,
Taylor's achievements are all the more remarkable, especially as it is clear that
key races were deliberately rescheduled to Sundays to exclude him (Richie 1996,
85–111).

Cycling, Gender and Emotions

Bicycles are something that perhaps most children – at least in the rich West – can expect to have and both boys and girls seem equally likely to enjoy the pleasures that self-propelled two-wheeled transport affords. However, a gender disparity in cycling is evident from an early age. In 2006 'bicycle use by boys was more than double that of girls, (although this still accounted for only three per cent of trips)' (DFT 2007, 19). In the UK cyclists, particularly those that commute and those engaged in cycle sport, are overwhelmingly male. Department for Transport research suggests that on average men cycle more than three times the mileage of women (DFT 2003, 1). About two thirds of all those cycling to work are men (DFT 2003, 2). In a survey by *Cycling Weekly* (2007, 41), which proclaims itself 'Britain's biggest-selling cycling magazine' and which largely covers cycle sport, 98 per cent of its readership is male.

Matt Seaton's (2002) memoir *The Escape Artist* describes the dogged determination that drives the cycling obsessive; he also reflects on the way that cycling enabled him to deal with the onset of illness and death of his wife. He suggests that either there is something in men's psyche that needs solitary time and that some men turn to cycling because it affords an opportunity for time alone, or that cycling encourages such secluded reflection and having taken it up, the cyclist learns to enjoy the experience:

> Riding solo always had a pleasant melancholy aspect for me. Some days I was happy to be alone with my thoughts, and for the sights and sounds and scents of those lanes to belong to me, in that moment, and to no other ... By the time I had turned for home, though, I always found my mood lightened. Somehow, the familiarity of those roads, and the rhythm of pedal revolutions, and the measured stress of physical exercise, had eased something inside. Riding my bike exorcised the demon (Seaton 2002, 163–4).

The reasons why women cycle far less than men is puzzling, partly because the differences are not so marked in other countries such as the Netherlands, where facilities for cycling are far superior (CTC 2007, 36). But in the UK where women are less likely to have access to a car (DFT 2007) and where public transport costs have continued to increase, more cycling makes more sense for women. It is true that until recently most bikes tended to be manufactured for men and it would have been difficult for women to buy a bicycle that was comfortable to ride for any length of time. Now women-specific frames are widely available. For women with childcare responsibilities the fact that cyclists are perceived as vulnerable on the roads is bound to mean that women on bikes with kids might feel that they are regarded as irresponsibly putting their children's lives at risk. However, bicycles with trailers or tricycles with two wheels at the front to accommodate a child's seat or space for shopping are now available and these are commonly used in places like Holland, Germany and Denmark.

Fears about safety clearly impact on people's decisions not to cycle and although cycling fatalities have declined as a proportion of cyclists and cycle journeys the perception of cycling as dangerous is strong. Recent data suggests that women are more likely than men to be involved in a cycling fatality involving a Heavy Goods Vehicle or a bus (Webster 2007). Explanations for the discrepancy have tended to focus on the different levels of assertiveness that women and men cyclists display when riding. Anyone who cycles needs to have a certain self-confidence to negotiate their way through a public space that is overwhelmingly occupied and dominated by 'privateer' motorists. Cycling timidly is more likely to lead to accidents and keeping to the very edge of the road and cycling in the gutter, which women are more likely to do, renders the rider less visible to motorists. To be more certain of being safe on the road a cyclist must be noticed by drivers and for this reason it is necessary to assertively occupy the road with assurance, keeping to the centre of the lane rather than the edge, even though this often results in impatient abuse from other, larger road users. At T-junctions and roundabouts cyclists quickly learn that it makes sense to try and catch the eye of the occupant of the motor vehicle that is approaching from the side. Making eye contact guarantees that the cyclist has been noticed and makes it less likely that the motorist will pull out in front of the bicycle, or even into it. Women may feel less comfortable with being so obviously assertive towards other (especially male), road users or fear that direct eye contact might be misinterpreted.

Concerns about appearance might also explain wider gender differences in commuter cycling in Britain. Women pedestrians are occasionally sexually harassed by passing men and abuse from (mostly male) motorists is directed at women as women, as well as women as cyclists. So women may well avoid cycling to escape harassment as much as because they fear for their safety. Furthermore, arriving at work sweating after a ride is less likely to provoke comments for men than for women.

Conclusion

Cycling in the UK has experienced a revival recently; concerns about obesity, global warming, congestion, energy costs and public transport safety have all contributed to a resurgence in numbers. London has experienced a 91 per cent increase in the number of people cycling since in 2000 (TFL 2008) and the London Tour de France prologue was the best attended UK tourist event in 2007. British cycle sport lottery funding has recently produced a string of world-class champions such as Mark Cavendish, Victoria Pendleton, Chris Hoy and Emma Pooley. Central government and local council investment in cycle infrastructure and training, with subsidies in some workplaces to buy bicycles, is also helping. There remains a long way to go. The *London Travel Report* (TFL 2007, 2) suggests that only two per cent of all journeys in London are made by bicycle. Research in Darlington, Peterborough and Worcester (Sustrans 2004, 12) highlighted persistent negative attitudes to walking and cycling with respondents preferring cars for local trips because they over-estimated travel times by public transport by around two-thirds and under-estimated travel time by cars by one third. Travelling by car offered little or no time benefit over cycling yet few people choose to cycle. In Holland and Denmark a quarter of all journeys are made by bike (*Cycling Plus* 2008, 10). A high and sustained level of investment in cycling and a concerted effort to change the perceptions of cycling in the UK is required along with a determination to tackle the 'car is king' culture. Whether the resources and the political will exist for this remains to be seen. Whatever the future holds, those in the know will continue their love affair with the beautiful machine.

References

Armstrong, L. (2004), 'The Noblest Invention: an illustrated history of the bicycle', *Bicycling Magazine/Lance Armstrong* (Emmaus, PA: Rodale Inc.).

Automobile Association (1993), *Cycling Motorists and How to Encourage Them* (Cheadle: Automobile Association), www.thebikezone.org.uk/thebikezone/campaigning/attitudesresearch.html

BBC News (2005), 'Bicycle chosen as best invention.' 5 May, www.news.bbc.co.uk/1/hi/technology/4513929.stm.

Big Lottery Fund (2007), 'Sustrans' Connect2 wins £50 million prize', www.biglotteryfund.org.uk/prog_the_peoples_50_million.htm.

Burns, K. (1989), 'Playing Dirty', *Bicycling Magazine's Cycling for Women* (Emmaus, PA: Rodale Inc.), www.mothernature.com/Library/Bookshelf/Books/51/1.cfm.

Cycling Plus (2008), 'Bristol Bags Biking Millions', *Cycling Plus*, Summer.

Cyclists' Touring Club (CTC) (2007), 'Going Dutch: can we, should we, learn from the Netherlands cycling success story?', *Cycle Magazine*, October–November, 36–39.

Cycling Weekly (2007), 'Readers' Survey', *Cycling Weekly*, 19 June.

Department for Transport (DFT) (2007), *Transport Statistics Bulletin, National Travel Survey: 2006* www.dft.gov.uk/pgr/statistics/datatablespublications/personal/mainresults/nts2006.

Department for Transport (DFT) (2003), *Cycling in GB, Personal Travel Factsheet 5a –* January. www.dft.gov.uk/pgr/statistics/datatablespublications/personal/factsheets/19992001/factsheet5acyclingingreatbritain.

Fenton, B. (2006), 'What is blue, green and pale all over? A good Tory.' *Daily Telegraph* 10 April, www.telegraph.co.uk/news/uknews/1515281/What-is-blue-green-and-pale-all-over-A-good-Tory.html.

Henderson, M. (2004), 'So is it the computer? Electricity? No, pedal power makes the bicycle our favourite invention.' *The Times*, 27 November, www.timesonline.co.uk/tol/news/uk/article396050.ece

Hilton, T. (2004), *One More Kilometre and We're in the Showers: Memoirs of a Cyclist* (London: HarperCollins).

Moore, G.M. (2004), *Elgar, Child of Dreams* (London: Faber).

Richie, A. (1996), *Major Taylor: The Extraordinary Career of a Champion Bicycle Racer* (Baltimore: Johns Hopkins University Press).

Seaton, M. (2002), *The Escape Artist: Life from the Saddle* (London: Fourth Estate).

Smith, A. (2005), 'Gender and Critical Mass: do high cycle flows correlate with a high proportion of female cyclists?', *London Analytics Research Journal*, 1, www.londonanalytics.info/research-journal/issue1.

Sustrans (2006), *Shoppers and How They Travel*. Liveable neighbourhoods information sheet LN02, www.sustrans.org.uk/webfiles/liveable%20neighbo urhoods/Shoppers.

Sustrans (2004), *Travel Behaviour Research Baseline Survey 2004: sustainable travel demonstration towns*, www.sustrans.org.uk/webfiles/travelsmart/ STDT%20Research%20FINAL.pdf.

TFL (2008), 'More than Half a Million Cycle Journeys Now Made Every Day in the Capital', Transport for London press release 16 June, www.tfl.gov.uk/ corporate/media/newscentre/8631.aspx.

TFL (2007), *London Travel Report 2007* (TFL), www.tfl.gov.uk/assets/downloads/ corporate/London-Travel-Report-2007-final.pdf

Thompson, F. (1973), *Lark Rise to Candleford: A Trilogy* (Harmondsworth: Penguin).

Webster, B. (2007), 'Women Cyclists 'Risk Death' by Obeying Traffic Lights', *The Times*, 24 April, www.timesonline.co.uk/tol/news/uk/article1695668.ece

Willard, F. (1991), *How I Learned to Ride the Bicycle: reflections of an influential 19th century woman* (Sunnyvale: Fair Oaks Publishing).

Woodland, L. (2005), *This Island Race: Inside 135 years of British Bike-racing* (Norwich: Mousehold Press).

Woods, C. (2001), *Bikie: A Love Affair with the Racing Bicycle* (Edinburgh: Mainstream Publishing).

Chapter 23
A Walk in the Park

Phil Nicholls

Introduction

As John Urry (2007, 86–87) notes:

> A ... distinction surrounds whether walking should or should not be performed
> on one's own. Some emphasize the virtues of private solitary walking, being
> alone and individually reflexive (at home with one's thoughts) ... Others
> emphasize how walking should entail sociability as a result of being with others
> and indeed bonding through the shared achievement of covering a certain 'walk'
> or getting to a particular viewpoint

In this chapter I reflect on my own experience of sociable walking.

Like many other people, I find some time during most weekends for walking –
that is for walking for leisure rather than as an activity involved in some other task
like shopping or gardening. At about the same time on most Sunday afternoons,
my friends will ring my doorbell and suggest that some exercise might be a good
idea. I invariably concur with this proposal and we then cross the road that runs at
the bottom of my drive and proceed up a short lane to the local country park. Our
park is popular, since it abuts a National Trust property, a hospitable pub, and a
growing local community. Nevertheless, our walk is pleasant and companionable
– a time uninterrupted by unwanted visitors, telephone calls, voice or e-mails.

Our Sunday afternoon walk gradually assumed the status of a welcomed
regular activity not long after I had moved to my home town in 1987. It became
an important way of creating some space protected from busily competing
professional and personal demands, for reflection on the events of the past week,
and as a way of preparing for those to come in the new. What has resulted, over
time, has been the gradual accrual of a set of experiences which I am now able to
use auto/ biographically, and as a way of making clear my own role as author, in
'constructing rather than discussing the story/knowledge' that follows (Letherby
2003, 141; on auto/biography as a research methodology more generally see, for
example, Stanley 1993 and Introduction: Moving Off this volume).

Once in the park my friends probably look to others, slightly quaint, slightly
old fashioned: two middle-aged people ambling arm-in-arm along the well-
trodden footpaths that texture the space of the park, occasionally stopping to point
out a view, or the antics of the resident squads of grey squirrels, or to appreciate

the changing displays of seasonal colour. What the casual on-looker does not see, however, is that my friends' arms are linked as much for instrumental as for affective reasons, since one of them is usually more confident in walking with some support. An unintended but happy consequence of this practical arrangement is that they 'pass' – to use Erving Goffman's (1963) terminology – as a couple enjoying a walk together in much the same way as any other visitor to the park.

Although the park is large and its paths could guide people in many different ways through its landscape of trees, lake and meadow, we always take the same route; not because of a lack of imagination, but simply because habit has a high return in terms of efficiency (Young 1997). As we all know the route so well, we know how long it will take us to complete the walk, and every convenient resting place. These are important considerations for my friends. Moreover, we also know every patch of mud, every stretch of uneven surface, and the nature of every incline, obstacle and step. We do not have to work out every time how to negotiate each difficulty afresh. It is a well-rehearsed routine which we can accomplish without interruption to thought or speech or enjoyment.

Sunday afternoon is a popular time for many to visit the park, and we pass and are passed by numbers of different kinds of walkers. Many of them are in family groups, with protective parents often pushing buggies, or coaxing children as yet unsteady on their feet along the more friendly pathways. Tumbling noisily through the undergrowth, older children busy themselves with their own games and imaginaries. Teenagers, proud fathers bearing infants on their shoulders, and the more or less recently retired, meander or strut or stroll according to inclination, ability or (I suspect) the soporific effects of the hearty Sunday lunch served at the nearby pub.

Feeling the Walk

> Nature is both a concept and all those physical things to which the concept refers. It's a complex concept, not just because it refers to many different entities ... but because it also has multiple meanings (Castree 2001, 1).

Embodied movement flows through the park in a variety of ways. 'Nature' (in the form of anatomical and physiological difference) and 'culture' (learnt ways of moving, clothing and managing the body) interact in ways which produce peculiarities of gait and locomotion that are laden with meaning. Age, gender, dis/ability, class and ethnicity are all identities which, to a greater or lesser extent, become constitutive of, and can be read from, the ambulant body.

In much the same way, we are also expert at decoding the emotions, dispositions and intentions which become inscribed on the apparently simple act of walking. We recognize the way in which sadness, anger, abstraction, impatience, determination and infatuation achieve physical expression. We read the mood easily from the movement. Where bodies touch, and move in synchrony, we are usually in little doubt that we are in the presence of lovers exploring their private landscape of shared emotions. In contrast, a quick-stepping, hunched isolation signals anger and argument. Body language, then, represents another narrative. It sits alongside that told by the natural features of the landscape itself. Both can be decoded and appreciated at the same time, and reading the way in which they interweave produces an engaging, and ever-changing, set of stories (Hockey and James 2003).

In enjoying our country park, its visitors are engaged in what is undoubtedly the most popular of contemporary leisure pursuits (Edensor 2000, 81). It was not always thus, of course. Walking has been transformed from an activity that was seen, before the industrial revolution, primarily in instrumental terms – as a means of getting from one place to another, or as a necessary adjunct of agricultural labour, and walkers were regarded as necessarily poor, mad or criminal (Urry 2000) – to something which is now mostly enjoyed 'for its own sake', as physical effort that is 'affectively involving' (Urry 2007; Parsons et al.1953) and as an end in itself. Walking, then, is not merely seen as both relaxing and as healthy. It is also regarded as a way of remaking the self through encounters with the natural world, and as a way of reconnecting individuals, through landscape and architecture, with the past (Edensor 2000, and see also Macnaghten and Urry 2000).

This transformation was the product of the dramatic impact of nineteenth-century industrialization. Once capitalist manufacturing had begun to 'tame' nature, 'wilderness' increasingly came to lose its aura of threat and hostility, and the Romantic movement, in verse and in painting, could engage with landscape via a new sensibility and a new aesthetic – as a way of sustaining the self through connection with a natural world whose apparent purity and history contrasted so strongly with the despoliation of ingénue industry and urbanization.

Countryside walking also came to hold increasingly obvious attractions for the new and growing class of factory workers: the prospect of roaming freely across open, peaceful and unpolluted spaces was an enticing chance to refresh minds and bodies wearied by the exactions of wage labour. The working class had, in fact, begun to take up these opportunities as early as the 1830s (Hill 1980) while, by 1905, the popularity of walking as a leisure activity among industrial labourers had resulted in the formation of the national Federation of Rambling Clubs (Bunce 1994).

For different, albeit complementary, reasons, then, both proletarian and bourgeois sensibilities were drawn to the countryside because it seemed to stand in pristine, natural opposition to the engineered world of factory and town. However, though it is hard to deny the sanctuary offered by rural landscape to those whose lives are more usually bounded by the encroached vistas of urban space and time, the contrast of 'natural' countryside with 'artificial' town was, of course – and remains – very much overstated.

Walking in Manufactured Space

> [Landscape] is a place of memory and temporality ... interpretations of past,
> present and future revolve around the practices or the 'taskscape', of any
> environment. It is this taskscape which introduces the social character of a
> landscape. Such a taskscape only persists as long as people actually engage
> in the manifold tasks and practical activities of dwelling within, and moving
> through, that particular environment ... [L]andscapes are felt through the senses.
> They come to be incorporated into our bodily experiences ... People imagine
> themselves treading the same paths as countless earlier generations that have
> lived there or thereabouts (Urry 2000, 134–35).

To a very significant extent, the countryside is a worked and constructed
environment which, for centuries, has been purposefully contoured by agriculture
and by networks of transport and communication. Since Neolithic times, it has
been used as a source of building and other raw materials and fuel. The Forestry
Commission continued this tradition by covering hillsides with swathes of
conifers – while, more recently, the Woodland Trust endeavours to redress the
balance by planting new broadleaved woodland. Even moor and hillside are
products of previous deforestation, and are maintained by continuous grazing and
the demands of different kinds of countryside pursuits. There is, in short, nothing
much 'natural' about rural space at all – unless we travel, perhaps, to the far north
of Scotland, where remnants of the ancient forest that once covered much of the
country still remain.

The 'enculturated' nature of rural landscapes – see, for example, David Matless
(2000) for an interesting discussion on the cultural production of 'nature' regions
– is well captured by the special characteristics of our national parks. These, like
that of the Peak District, which borders my home town, are specifically managed
environments, where local materials, and local styles of building and farming, have
left indelible imprints on the countryside. Park Authorities are tasked to preserve
this legacy – but at the same time to render it visible and accessible to visitors. Both
walkers and car drivers must therefore be catered for – the one (despite the recent
'right to roam', arguably important only to a minority of countryside walkers) with
clearly waymarked and managed paths, the other with car parks.

My own country park exhibits all these features of a non-natural environment
in high concentration. Yet this does not lessen my appreciation of it, since for
all its artificiality it remains an attractive space for a companionable walk, and
for promoting well-being. Indeed for many people who use the park the fact
that it represents a comfortable and well-groomed rural enclosure is its primary
attraction as a space for walking. The reconnection with the natural world, and the
refreshment of the self which results from this process are, of course, real enough
for those who use the park, but this reconnection and refreshment are actually
products of interaction with an environment in which 'nature' has largely been
designed away.

This pruning of the natural from nature is achieved in a variety of ways. Nesting boxes, for example, designed for different kinds of birds, are attached to conveniently visible trees. In woodland shade, picnic tables are dotted across the more open spaces, while around the lake the shoreline is neatly divided into enclosures cleared for anglers. More obviously, of course, are the security conscious car park facilities, and the pattern of maintained and signposted pathways, complete with urban style litter bins, which allow visitors to choose the length and nature of their walk, and to clean up after themselves in the process. The paths, for the most part, are family and wheelchair friendly and, to this end, all lead back to the Visitor Centre, where the ranger resides and refreshments, toilet facilities and disabled parking are also on hand.

The Visitor Centre, apart from its selection of beverages and confectionary, also hosts maps of the park and its pathways, accounts of its history, and a mini exhibition of the flora and fauna visitors are likely to encounter on their walk. In this way, the animate and inanimate textures of the park are neatly shrunk, displayed and accentuated, opening up the possibility, for those so inclined, of consuming the park experience without the more demanding task of acquiring the experience itself.

The Park Ranger also organizes a variety of activities. Visitors, for example, can join guided nature walks, while volunteers can learn to repair the miles of dry-stone wall which mark the perimeter of the park, or plant trees, or maintain pathways. The clearing of unwanted species – most particularly the ancient tangles of rhododendron which, long ago, escaped from neighbouring gardens stocked by Victorian plant hunters – is one of the more arduous and recurring tasks, but one regarded as essential to maintain the quality of the visitor experience. Important here, too, is the preservation of an appropriate balance between young, mature and older trees, and those which, in various stages of decomposition, must be arranged (neatly and safely, of course) on the ground to act as hosts for fungi and for many different kinds of insects and their larvae.

In sum, then, the park is a specifically manufactured space. Its rationale is to provide a service experience for its consumers, where its 'natural' constituents are actually artefacts cosmetically produced, arranged and disciplined to make the act of consumption palatable. In this way, the park is produced and reproduced across space and time through its visitors, while at the same time the experience of the park helps to remake and refresh its visitors through an artificially constructed engagement with landscape, nature and history.

Negotiating the Walk

> Walkers and walking … give shape to how places are dwelt in and used … Space is thus a performed place … Such performances generally involve conflictual tactics and uses of space by various social groups (Urry 2000, 53).

For the most part, the park is used by family groups or couples who will often bring pets, balls and frisbees to add variety of activity to their time in the open air. Sometimes, however, the park's usual clientele of casual walkers is bisected by those who 'mean business' when they walk. Distinguished in terms of muscular attitude, clothing, footwear and navigational aids, serious walkers will often work (I use the word advisedly) alone, and operate in economising mode: what matters is route, destination and strides per minute. In the park, they are the ambulant equivalent of the speeding motorway driver whose headlights are a signal to give way. Casual walkers, sensitive to the symbolism and signs of serious locomotive intent, readily come to appreciate their status as mere dilettantes by comparison and will usually move aside, ceding the centre of footpaths to those for whom the mission is disciplined movement.

Given that the country park abuts moorland which is on the margins of the Peak District National Park, the numbers of 'serious' walkers using the park as access to more challenging terrain is significant.. Their presence in the park, however, highlights the complexity and variety of the interrelations that are forged between ambulant bodies and leisure environments.

George Kay and Norma Moxham (1996) make a useful distinction between two broad groups of walking practices. In the first group are strolling, ambling, plodding, sauntering, promenading, wandering and roaming. The commonalities binding these kinds of walking together are that, in each case, the activity requires little, if any, physical preparation, and is relatively spontaneous and casual. Most people can accomplish these kinds of walking without thought. A second group of walking practices, however, is more challenging in a physical sense and requires planning, the acquisition of particular skills and the use of more or less specialised clothing and equipment. Included here would be marching, trail-walking, trekking, hiking, hill-walking, 'yomping' and 'peak-bagging'.

Most users of my local country park — including myself and my friends — fall, very definitely, in the first group. What is peculiar about the second group of walking practices, however, is that they are very much 'learnt' activities. Serious walkers need to know how to read Ordnance Survey maps, use a compass and navigate. They need to know how to plan a route, and read the weather. They need to know how to cope with certain kinds of emergencies. They need to know how to dress — which in turn means knowing the properties of different kinds of fabric and waterproof, and the labels of the manufacturers whose products denote quality (as well as sign value). Walking boots become an area of passionate research in their own right here (Michael, 2000). Rucksacks need to be assessed for comfort and capacity, and what needs to be in them for what kinds of walking carefully calculated. The merits of other 'serious' accessories, such as walking poles, need to be understood and assessed, and their use practised.

To engage in serious walking, then, is to engage in an activity whose successful accomplishment requires planning, the acquisition of new skills and knowledge, and training. It requires, in short, an immersion into a new 'habitus' (Bourdieu 1977) — the learning of a new 'style of life' and identity, with its own ways of acting, thinking and feeling. It produces a new self, given shape in terms of its antithesis to the ephemeral identities constitutive of fashion conscious cosmopolitan lifestyles. Serious walkers become to themselves, and are represented to others, as 'natural men or women', a repository of skills which effect a symbolic connection with the past – a past where people's survival depended much more intimately on their knowledge of landscape, weather and wilderness.

Ironically, however, this identity is of course as 'artificial' as those it purports to reject, since it too is constructed in part from the myriad opportunities for consumption presented in the shopping mall and by urban affluence. A convincing display as a serious walker is as much an effect, in a way, of the labels on clothing and equipment as are the identities crafted by other consumers. Even an attempt to achieve 'authenticity' through the *avoidance* of labels becomes a proclamation of identity and style since 'unfashionability' itself becomes a fashion statement. In this way the negation of signification becomes, ironically, potent signification in its own right.

Yet the serious walker nevertheless remains more than a sum of mere sign values. Walkers who 'mean business' must necessarily subject themselves to an internalized discipline of bodily surveillance and control (Foucault 1980) in order to produce and reproduce themselves as accomplished hikers. The appropriate clothing, footwear and equipment – however convincingly branded – need to be part of a performance where the body itself has been sculpted through training and exercise. Labels are no substitute for fitness, and cannot in themselves haul bodies to the end of long-distance trails, or yomps, or bag peaks.

Sensitivity to the variety of walking practices also begins to open up the issue of countryside access: 'access for whom' and 'access for what purpose'. What counts as 'acceptable accessibility' for the family group visiting a national park for an afternoon in the fresh air, or a wheelchair user in a country park, is very different to that required by the serious walker. In the former case, well-maintained, easily navigable and signposted paths that allow people to walk in companionable groups, and which are buggy and wheelchair friendly, are needed; in the latter, the issue is not merely one of a right to walk inhospitable trails, or paths that cross private land, but a 'right to roam' where there are no trails at all. As Kay and Moxham (1996) point out, local authorities, in promoting a successful countryside access policy, need to remain constantly sensitive to the complexities of demand that arise from the different needs and proclivities of many different kinds of countryside user.

All walkers, however, whether tackling moor or mountain or signposted pathways through visitor friendly country parks, are always engaged in an ongoing process of negotiation with their environment (Urry 2000). This is, in fact, a multi-layered activity. At one level, it involves the negotiation of sociability, space, time and movement among those walking as friendship or family or activity groups, or among different kinds of walkers sharing the same terrain. At another, it involves the ongoing management of a personal environment of clothing, footwear and equipment. Both of these activities, in turn, are mediated by the geological features of the terrain through which movement is organised, as well as by variation in botanical and meteorological conditions. Bog, scree, or moorland; bramble, bracken or nettle; ice, rain or wind – all demand, for example, their own peculiar responses. Finally, walkers must also be prepared to reach satisfactory accommodations with both the wildlife and the domesticated animals that either choose – or are forced to share – their routes and spaces.

Walking on Two and Four Legs

> In ... disorganised tourist spaces ... contact with vehicles and with animals is also unavoidable. The trajectories of visitors will co-exist with, and criss-cross, local pathways (Urry 2000, 54).

Long neglected by sociologists – probably because of the artificial distinction between 'nature' and 'culture' established in classical theory – human-animal interaction is now attracting deserved attention as a topic of sociological interest (see, among many recent examples, Hobson-West 2007, Irvine 2007, Jerolmack 2007, Franklin 1999). Where walking is concerned, the interaction between the many non-human inhabitants of the countryside and the subjective experience of walkers themselves is, as Edensor (2000, 101) notes, of considerable importance. Animals, after all, can either serve to enhance or disrupt this experience in quite major ways. Indeed, a key aspect of any enjoyable walk may turn on how well individuals have succeeded in the development of strategies for negotiating and responding to the often unpredictable encounters which occur between people and animals.

Using two variables (potential to harm and degree of domestication) it is useful, in exploring this issue, to group animals into four broad categories – benign domesticated and benign undomesticated; harmful domesticated and harmful undomesticated. Any kind of walker in the UK is likely to encounter animals in all four categories, and not unusually within the compass of a single journey.

In the first group (benign domesticated) are animals such as sheep, cows and horses. Even the most inexperienced of countryside walkers may feel some confidence in attempting a footpath which crosses land where these animals are free to graze. A head briefly raised from the preferred herbivoral activity of grazing is about as much as anyone is likely to find by way of recognition of their presence. On the whole, the only significant thing to avoid with these animals is their droppings – although, on occasion, evasive action from a herd of inquisitive steers may need to be effected (Edensor 2000).

Benign wildlife comprises the second group. These are wildlife – such as birds, small mammals like squirrels or rabbits, amphibians, fish, butterflies, dragonflies, and the legion of other insects and invertebrates – which add unpredictable pleasure and variety to most walkers' experiences. Indeed, the chance to observe animals, birds and so on, especially where they have become known as 'rare' or 'spectacular', may provide the rationale for the walk itself. Many animals in this category, however, being primarily nocturnal of habit (such as badgers, bats, owls and foxes) would normally be encountered only by dedicated nature watchers rather than walkers.

If animals in these first groups are either non-disruptive of walkers' experiences, or serve positively to enhance them, the same cannot be said unreservedly of animals in the second two categories. In both cases, physically invasive and distressing consequences can easily ensue.

Harmful undomesticated animals with which walkers in the UK must contend are largely drawn from among the invertebrates, such as bees, wasps, hornets, flies, tics, mosquitoes, gnats, midges, fleas and ants. Bodily impacts can vary from the merely irritating (a sock full of red ants or an obstinate cloud of flies) to the maddening (an unrelenting attack by hungry mosquitoes) to the frightening and vicious assault of bees or wasps whose nest has been unwittingly disturbed by boot or arm. Some anticipatory action can be taken – through the use of protective clothing or creams for example – but these tend to be fairly innocuous against a determined attack – and, anyway, may well not have been anticipated as precautionary measures.

Probably, however, the most frequent negotiation walkers need to manage successfully is with dogs. People have domesticated, especially with the fashion for more and more exotic pets, a whole variety of potentially harmful animals within their homes but, fortunately, do not tend to let them roam the countryside. Owners of dogs, however, take them for walks. Owners tend to do this religiously and frequently. And that, for some walkers, is where the problem starts. Rather ironically, of all the animal hazards that can irrupt into the embodied experience of walking, the most frequent and frightening is reserved for that most unambitious and unprepared of countryside users – those who come to their local country park to amble, stroll or saunter away a leisurely hour or so in pleasant recreation. For this really is the domain of urban 'Dog' – and that equally difficult-to-manage species: 'Dog Owner'.

Such phenomena are much less frequently encountered by those whose walking predilections are for wilder places and longer marches. The odd sheep dog may be seen at work in the distance and warning barks may come from tethered canines in farmyards, but those whose aim is to bag peaks, trek or trail-walk can more often than not pursue their activities without having to negotiate encounters with Dog. Not so for the walker or family in the park. Indeed, 'family in the park' sometimes includes Dog (or Dogs), which means that 'family' not only has to manage Dog (or Dogs), but also Dog's (or Dogs') potentially explosive encounters with other Dogs, Dog owners or (and this is usually some way down the list of interactions worthy of owners' surveillance and control) the Dogless.

The ways in which 'Dog' refashions the environment in a variety of unpleasant ways is unquestionably the number one issue for many of those who use my local country park (District Council 2005). This refashioning goes on through a continuous but essentially chaotic reclassification of space, the outcomes of which have constantly to be negotiated and renegotiated by walkers: what was clean can be instantly transformed into something polluted through excrement and urine, while what was polluted can be made clean through the hygienic work of rangers, or dog owners themselves or, failing this, through time and weather. Bins for dog excrement symbolically pollute the more popular walkways, and the sites of pollution change as the bins are moved. The absence of bins, however, ensures the real pollution of the more remote paths (as our Park Ranger tells us, emptying bins of dog excrement is a cost, and the cost is greater the further away the bins are in the park – so some paths remain bin-less and consequently are always polluted).

At a more frenetic and entirely unpredictable level, 'Dog' reshapes space and time in the park by closing off routes, and by forcing walkers into delays, detours and other avoidance tactics. These reconfigurations are experienced more frequently by people who belong to the more physically vulnerable groups (for example, older or disabled people, parents with toddlers, pregnant women or those who are generally nervous of dogs or who simply find them offensive). The reshaping of time and space by 'Dog' is further accelerated by size, and by the reputation of the breed for aggressive intent. When on the loose, Bull Terriers, Dobermans, Rottweilers, Wolf Hounds, Great Danes and Alsatians can easily turn what might have been a wary pause by a walker into a rapid retreat to the Visitor Centre.

Avoidance tactics, however, are not always available to walkers. Confrontation with Dog at some point – something equally likely for runners (see, for example, Sutton this volume) and cyclists – is bound to occur in the environs of any country park. The 'Dog Frisk' is the usual form taken by such encounters. Here, the prescribed role for the victim is to remain passive and still while Dog uses its nose to undertake an intimate personal investigation of shoes, feet and genital areas. Sometimes this ritual will be followed by Dog rearing on hind legs and planting soiled paws on jackets or coats, frenzied barking, and an attempt to slime face and hands with spittle.

Anthropomorphism, and a willingness to blame the victims of canine assault, are both characteristics of owners' perspectives which are nicely revealed in the stock phrases used in encounters with the Dogless: 's/he's only playing' or 's/he's only being friendly' or 's/he won't hurt you'. A response from the victim to the effect that he or she was 'not to know that', or an inquiry as to whether owner of Dog might like to get a jacket or trousers soiled by muddied paws and saliva cleaned, is usually met with incomprehension. After all, if Dog is really just a boisterous child, how could it be possible that their intentions be misinterpreted as malevolent, or expected that they should be clean? The victim is being unreasonable – and owners of Dog are quite justified (of course) in taking affront at such suggestions.

Oddly, then, the disruption to walkers' experience of space and time, and to their enjoyment of the series of other narratives, negotiations and recuperative processes intrinsic to walking, is most frequently encountered in that safest and most 'manufactured' of green spaces – the country park – since this is the realm of Dog unleashed. Nevertheless, my friends continue to call on a Sunday afternoon,

I continue to agree to accompany them for 'a walk in the park', and we continue (mostly) to have a good time.

Conclusion

This account helps to underline a point which can be made in relation to travel more generally: any journey, quite unavoidably, involves degrees of risk. For some travellers, risk itself may by the whole point and enjoyment of the journey; for others, risk is something we expect others to minimize or 'design out' of our journey, or is something which, through the adoption of various preventative strategies, we try to manage ourselves (Murray 2008, Forstorp 2006).

The perception of risk, and the strategies employed to reduce it, tend to vary quite significantly by age, gender, class, ethnicity and disability (Jones and Raisborough 2007, Lupton and Tulloch 2001). Sometimes this will mean that some journeys for some people – such as the young child walking home from school alone – are deemed too dangerous even to be attempted. The sense of vulnerability, then, whether real or imagined, will tend to close off certain kinds of journeys for certain groups of people. In the nature of the case, however, risk can never be entirely eliminated from any journey, even one as humble as 'a walk in the park'.

Acknowledgement

With warm thanks to Geraldine Nicholls for her contribution and comments.

References

Böhm, S., Jones, C., Land, C. and Paterson, M. (eds) (2006), *Against Mobility* (Oxford: Blackwell).

Bourdieu, P. (1977), *Outline of a Theory of Practice* (Cambridge: Cambridge University Press).

Bunce, M. (1994), *The Countryside Ideal: Anglo-American Images of Landscape* (London: Routledge).

Castree, N (2001), 'Socializing Nature: theory, practice and politics' in N. Castree and B. Braun (eds).

Castree, N. and Braun, B. (eds) (2001), *Social Nature: Theory, Practice and Politics* (Oxford: Wiley Blackwell).

District Council (2005), 'Visitor Survey Feedback', *Country Park News*, 7, 1.

Edensor, T. (2000), 'Walking in the British Countryside: reflexivity, embodied practices and ways to escape', *Body and Society*, 6, 3–4, 81–106.

Forstorp, P-A (2006), 'Quantifying Automobility: speed, 'Zero Tolerance' and democracy' in S. Böhm, C. Jones, C. Land and M. Paterson (eds).

Foucault, M. (1980), (ed. by Colin Gordon) *Power/Knowledge: Selected Interviews and Other Writings 1972–77* (Brighton: Harvester Press).

Franklin, A. (1999), *Animals and Modern Cultures: A Sociology of Human-animal Interaction* (London: Sage).

Giddens, A. (ed.) (1997), *Sociology: Introductory Readings* (Cambridge: Polity Press).

Goffman, E. (1963), *Stigma* (New York: Simon & Schuster).

Hill, H. (1980), *Freedom to Roam* (Ashbourne: Moorland Publishing Co.).

Hobson-West, P. (2007), 'Beasts and Boundaries: an introduction to animals in sociology, science and society', *Qualitative Sociology Review*, 3, 1, 23–41.

Hockey, J. and James, A. (2003), *Social Identities Across the Life Course* (Houndmills: Palgrave).

Irvine, L. (2007), 'The Question of Animal Selves: implications for sociological knowledge and practice', *Qualitative Sociology Review*, 3, 1, 5–22.

Jerolmack, C. (2007), 'Animal Archaeology: Domestic Pigeons and the Nature-Culture Dialectic', *Qualitative Sociology Review*, 3, 1, 74–95.

Jones, J.S. and Raisborough, J. (2007), *Risks, Identities and the Everyday* (Aldershot: Ashgate).

Kay, G. and Norma M. (1996), 'Parks for Whom? Countryside access for recreational walking', *Leisure Studies*, 15, 3, 171–83.

Letherby, G. (2003), *Feminist Research in Theory and Practice* (Buckingham: Open University Press).

Lupton, D. and Tulloch, J. (2001), 'Border Crossings: narratives of movement, 'home' and 'risk'', *Sociological Research Online*, 5, 4, www.socresonline.org. uk/5/4/lupton.html.

Macnaghten, P. and Urry, J. (2000), 'Bodies in the Woods', *Body and Society*, 6, 3–4, 166–82.

Matless, D. (2000), 'Action and Noise Over a Hundred Years: the making of a nature region', *Body and Society*, 6, 3–4, 141–65.

Michael, M. (2000), 'These Boots are Made for Walking ...: Mundane Technology, the Body and Human-Environment Relations', *Body and Society*, 6, 3–4, 107–26.

Murray, L. (2008), 'Motherhood, Risk and Everyday Mobilities' in T.P. Uteng and T. Cresswell (eds).

Parsons, T., Bales, R.F. and Shils, E.A. (1953), *Working Papers in the Theory of Action* (New York: Free Press).

Stanley, L. (1993), 'On Auto/biography in Sociology', *Sociology*, 27, 1, 41–52.

Urry, J. (2007), *Mobilities* (London: Sage).

Urry, J. (2000), *Sociology Beyond Societies: Mobilities for the Twenty-first Century* (London: Routledge).

Uteng, T.P and Cresswell, T. (eds) (2008), *Gendered Mobilities* (Aldershot: Ashgate).

Young, M. (1997), 'Time, Habit and Repetition in Day-to-Day Life' in A. Giddens (ed.).

Chapter 24

'Women and Young Girls Dare not Travel Alone': The Dangers of Sexual Encounters on Victorian Railways

Kim Stevenson

Introduction

The development and expansion of the railway system was a defining factor of Victorian modernity delivering technological and commercial success. By the 1850s and 1860s the speed with which the rail network increased, moving goods, information and people, transformed the lives of the middle classes. Mass travel transported commuters to and from work, permitted holidays and excursions, conveyed newspapers, luxuries and other essentials and, significantly, allowed women a much greater degree of freedom and independence. But the railway also provided new sites and opportunities for crime and bad behaviour from the petty (pick-pocketing, fare evasion) to the spectacular (serious assaults and even murder), bringing elements of the Victorian underworld into close proximity with law-abiding citizens. Crowded stations, the sheer speed of travel and anonymity of the system emphasized to both genders their vulnerabilities to personal threats and violence.

For women especially, separate carriages and darkened tunnels were dangerous territories presenting considerable risks, not just to their physical and personal safety, but also, as the perfect locale for romantic encounters, possibly their reputations. Victorian society expected women to vigorously guard their honour and virginity; exposure to masculine sexual advances, permitted or unsolicited, could seriously undermine their respectability. Women travelling alone needed to be alert, not only to the dangers of those wishing to indulge in more than acceptable familiarities, but also the fact that any subsequent court case could easily turn on whether her conduct and behaviour satisfied the prevailing stereotypical norms. Feminine emotion and vulnerability expressed at the time of any attack was necessary to secure a conviction; but any display of feminine passion or 'hysteria' in the courtroom would be seized upon by the defence. There was also the suspicion that men travelling alone could be susceptible to the unwarranted advances and false allegations of 'certain types' of women. Drawing on cases reported in the printed press in the 1860s and 1870s in this chapter I highlight the invidious position of women travellers and how their emotional and physical responses to sexual violations were publicly perceived and portrayed.

Abominable Outrages

The 1860s witnessed a spate of violence on the railway system where numbers of male and female passengers were physically assaulted (*News of the World* 10 September 1861). Women were more likely to be sexually assaulted but the incidence of such offences is hidden as these tend not to be reported in the official crime statistics. Until the Prosecution of Offences Act 1879 when a woman was subjected to a sexual assault it was normally incumbent on her, or her family, to initiate criminal proceedings in the courts to bring the offender to justice (Stevenson 2004). This would incur financial costs and could diminish her reputation because of the fact that she had been violated; also, because her reputation and conduct would be tested against the reputation of her assailant (Stevenson 2000). The precise nature of sexual assaults during the Victorian period is difficult to ascertain as substantive sexual offences, such as rape or sexual assault, were not clearly classified in legal terms and in the public discourse were suffused by ambiguous language such as 'crimes of moral outrage' or 'abominable outrages' (Stevenson 2005).

The expansion of the railways provided the ideal environment for men intent on perpetrating such moral outrages. Carriages were self-contained without corridors or alarms. Poor lighting and darkened tunnels not only facilitated such assaults but made it difficult for victims to convince the courts of their allegations as any visual evidence could easily be disputed. Some women were even assaulted when accompanied by their husbands or male protectors. In July 1860, Jane Harrison, who was sitting next to her husband, claimed that Edwin Courtenay, sitting opposite, indecently assaulted her as the train passed through a tunnel. Courtenay, described in the newspaper report as 'a gentlemanly looking man', denied any involvement. The judge advised the jury to consider whether or not they believed him, taking into account his 'high moral character.' Clearly persuaded by his reputation, they acquitted him and accepted his testimony over Mrs Harrison's, despite the fact she was chaperoned (*The Times* 16 July 1860). Another case that month concerned a young lady travelling with her brother-in-law to Chatham to see her husband. She accused Stephen Holman of the 'grossest indecency', a Victorian euphemism for sexual assault which could cover anything from lifting a skirt to touching private parts. The defence claimed it was a fabricated charge as another lady travelling in the same compartment testified to the 'vulgar levity of the complainant' and that she had engaged in indecent familiarities with Holman. Such conduct therefore suggested that she was neither respectable nor a lady and, as there was no other corroborating evidence, he too was acquitted (*The Times* 14 July 1860).

To confirm their respectability it was imperative that female victims reported any violations immediately and made every effort to extricate themselves from compromising situations. In July the following year, Louisa Haven, aged 14 years, was travelling with her mistress from Surbiton to Shanklin on the London and South Western Railway; Louisa alone in a second-class carriage, her mistress and family in the adjoining first-class carriage. Robert Littleton, a bank clerk, entered her carriage and 'made some familiar overtures' which were properly 'treated with becoming indignation.' As they went through a tunnel near Botley, Littleton allegedly committed rape despite Louisa's resistance. She exited the carriage at the next stop and refused to re-alight, telling the porter that she had been 'insulted'. She then proceeded to her mistress' carriage to report the occurrence and that she was 'unwell'. At Shanklin, Littleton made a statement to Louisa's mistress confirming his guilt and was later sentenced to 12 months' hard labour at the Hampshire Quarter Sessions. Louisa was not required to attend and give evidence, partly because she was unwell but also because she had conducted herself in a manner appropriate to that of her position as a respectable ladies' servant (*News of the World* 2 July 1861). As might be expected, women travelling in third-class compartments were more vulnerable but their assailants were often respectable gentleman as illustrated by two cases reported in the *News of the World* on the same day. Joseph Ingram, a master at Dr Morgan's Endowed School, Bridgewater, climbed over an intervening carriage to indecently assault a young woman and then cut off the feathers on her hat and shook them in her face. He was fined 10 shillings and costs at Bristol Police Court. Meanwhile, at Durham County Magistrates John M'Adam, a clerk from Stockton, was convicted of sexually assaulting Mrs Lackenby who was travelling to the funeral of her brother. He was fined five pounds and one pound eighteen shillings costs (*News of the World* 14 January 1872).

Not only were women attacked in the carriages but the whole infrastructure associated with the glorious age of steam presented dangers. William Hill, a railway carriage builder from Birmingham, was committed to York Assizes in 1865 for the 'most atrocious outrage' (i.e. rape), committed upon farmer's wife Mrs Stoker. As she walked past Copmanthorpe Railway Bridge where Hill was working, he grabbed her. She struggled and managed to escape but he caught up with her and 'despite her utmost resistance and screams for help' threw her over some rails onto the embankment and 'effected his purpose' (*News of the World* 12 November 1865).

These assaults and other similar ones led to something of a social panic. In 1864 *The Spectator* acknowledged that 'indecent assaults on ladies in railway carriages are said to becoming frequent' (9 January 1864). Newspapers fuelled the public angst by deploying the oft-used by-line 'Abominable Outrage in a Railway Carriage', exemplified in the *News of the World* in November 1865. Two respectable ladies, Mrs Blackburn and Miss Robinson, each riding in separate carriages, took advantage of an evening excursion train on the North Eastern Railway. Between Scarborough and Pateley Bridge, Robert Agar, a farmer, entered Mrs Blackburn's carriage. She told the East Riding Sessions that he approached her, 'expressed his intention and conducted himself in a most brutal manner, hurting her so much she was ill for a week', suggesting at least the likelihood of some sort of attempted penetration. When the train stopped at Malton, another passenger (who had a key) managed to lock Agar out of their carriage but he then proceeded to enter Miss Robinson's compartment, attacking the younger lady and using 'the most disgusting language.'

The case illustrates the real physical dangers for both sexes; as it was dark outside and the carriage unlit, the other passengers found it difficult to physically restrain Agar. Both women were so traumatized that they refused to enter any other part of the train while he was still aboard. Agar was prosecuted by the railway company under its byelaws but offered no defence, merely stating he felt 'rather fresh.' The magistrates declared the case to be one of the most brutal they had heard and expressed concern that they could not impose a higher fine than the requisite byelaw allowed. If the women themselves had successfully initiated a criminal prosecution for sexual assault it is likely a custodial sentence would have been imposed. The newspaper records that Agar left the court laughing (*News of the World* 12 November 1865).

Men who committed such sexual assaults were usually prosecuted by the railway company responsible for that part of the network, but not for rape or any other sexual offence. Instead they were charged under the company's private byelaws which regulated passenger behaviour, including anyone who interfered with the comfort of another passenger. The companies employed their own police officers to investigate such transgressions and often women who had been sexually assaulted would press the company to initiate a prosecution, avoiding the need to instigate a private prosecution. This would not only protect their reputation as it was less confrontational, but meant that no costs were incurred as the responsibility for finding witnesses and gathering evidence fell on the company.

Another case from the *News of the World*, headlined 'A Shameful Assault on a Young Lady in a Railway Carriage', details the prosecution process. Charles Thorpe, a paper-stainer, was summoned by Southwark police court for unlawfully interfering with the comfort of passengers in a first-class carriage at London Bridge terminus. Police Superintendent Carpenter of the Brighton Railway Company testified that as Miss Fanny Winehurst entered a first-class compartment, Thorpe jumped up and said, 'Come along dear, I am waiting for you.' Not liking his manner she tried to leave the carriage but he caught her by the waist and pulled her back. As she struggled to get away from him, 'he tore her dress and most grossly insulted her.' Fanny managed to enter another compartment but by now was 'in an almost fainting state.' She reported the assault to the guard on the train's arrival at Sydenham. He then informed the stationmaster who forwarded an account to the general manager at Brighton, who then laid all the facts before the Board at their fortnightly meeting, which then instigated the proceedings. Thorpe argued that all he had done was to help Fanny into the compartment and that he had been prejudiced by the company's delay in bringing the case. The jury was sympathetic to the claims of damage to his reputation and returned a verdict in his favour, albeit the proceedings were considerably expedient by modern standards (*News of the World* 15 October 1865).

The use of byelaws as a means of disposing of sexual offences is significant. Many less serious assaults would not have been prosecuted but for companies taking such action. *The Spectator* applauded the Great Western Railway Company for prosecuting a case against William Whitehead with 'commendable earnestness' as the 'danger to ladies travelling alone is very considerable.' The defendant, a gentleman from Wexhead Rectory, somewhat tipsy, flourished his stick at the ladies in his carriage; then pulled one down onto the floor, 'roaring out an obscene offer', and 'grossly assaulted her.' His friends managed to persuade her not to prosecute but the company went ahead and instigated proceedings (9 January 1864). The paper also suggested that railway companies should be compelled to fit sidewalks outside the carriages to allow the guard to pass at regular intervals but this took some years to achieve.

Death Defying Escapes

It was crucial that any woman subjected to a sexual assault reacted according to the stereotypical standards of the day to protect her virginity, or – if married – her honour, whatever the cost. The requirement that victims do everything in their power to evade their assailants has been romanticized in the images of women engaged in death-defying escapes out of carriages, clinging onto doors and windows; but in fact such expectations were very real. An editorial, 'Indecent Assaults, Railways' in *The Spectator*, conjures up the stereotypical image of the female damsel in distress. Risking life and limb to retain her modesty after being assailed with improper questions and afraid her clothing might be thrown up and revealed by her alleged tormenter, a young girl 'was only saved from death by a fellow passenger, who held her up at risk of his own life for 5 miles.' The case was initially heard at Hampshire County Magistrates where the defendant, Nash, resided, but the offence was actually committed in Surrey as the train passed the limits of their authority. Nash was discharged and the case ordered to be re-tried in Guildford demonstrating the jurisdictional limits of local justices where the violation is a moving one (The *Spectator* 16 July 1864).

A similar case of female bravery reported in 1869 describes how Jenny Stevenson, the wife of a machinist travelling from Manchester in a second-class carriage, reacted. George Makinson, a farmer, engaged her in conversation as soon as the train moved off. She tried to open the window but he touched her hand. Alarmed, she falsely told him that she was meeting some friends at the next station but when the train failed to stop he assaulted her 'in a very indecent manner.' She resisted and started to climb out of the carriage window, he seized her foot and begged her not to go further as she would be killed. She managed to climb out onto the footboard and passed from carriage to carriage until she was taken in by a gentleman. Makinson was convicted of aggravated assault and fined five pounds, disguising the true nature of the act; a minor physical assault became 'aggravated' if committed *against a woman*, not because it was sexual (*The Illustrated Police News* 30 January 1869).

Genuine victims were expected to raise the alarm by calling out for assistance. William Lyell, a 42-year-old seaman who had been drinking, indulged in some familiarities with Annie Griggs in a carriage in East London. She told him to stop. He agreed but then 'laid his hands upon her most improperly.' On arrival at Poplar, Annie complained but made no formal charge. Her uncle subsequently heard of the affair and informed the railway police. The magistrate, Mr Benson, said she was partly to blame as the train had stopped at two stations before Poplar and she had raised no alarm, nor called out for assistance. However, he did acknowledge that females travelling on trains needed to be protected and that Lyell's conduct was highly immoral and without justification. Lyell was also convicted of an aggravated assault and fined ten pounds (*The Eastern Post* 26 December 1869).

Another case concerned a railway inspector accused of rape and subsequently acquitted because the woman gave 'no alarm audible through a communication which existed at the top of the compartments, and she and her husband contradicted each other grossly.' This again emphasizes that victims needed to prove they had attempted to raise the alarm and that it was quite possible her husband was unaware or did not comprehend what had happened (*The Spectator* 16 July 1864). Unfortunately it was not always feasible to alert the authorities as not all railway companies provided a means of communication with the guard as highlighted in a contemporaneous discussion in the House of Commons that month. Mr Baillie Cockrane MP recommended that legislation should be enacted requiring corridors to be built into all compartments so that passengers could contact the guard. Milner Gibson for the government acknowledged the recent outrages but was unwilling to introduce a Bill and so the opportunity was lost (*Hansard* 12 and 14 July 1864 col.1384).

Female Monsters

These snapshots highlight some of the difficulties in prosecuting and proving sexual violations but, more significantly, they demonstrate the dangers encountered by women permitted to travel in public (read 'masculine') space. As a result the perceived potential for false allegations started to enter the public consciousness. In October 1864 *The Spectator* led with a strong editorial on the general incidence of indecent assaults, questioning their veracity: 'the manufacture of charges of indecent assault seems to becoming a mania ... no less than three have been detected this week' where the defendants were acquitted:

> the great number of unfound charges of indecent assault seems to have produced something like a panic ... [placing] every man at the mercy of every woman who

happens to be five minutes alone with him. The temptation to turn mere broad joke into a criminal charge needs to be very carefully watched.

Two possible causes are suggested: 'the lack of direct evidence in such cases and the freedom of manners existing amongst certain classes' (*The Spectator* 15 and 22 October 1864). Thus, periodically, the media fanned the flames of social panic. The front page of *Town Talk* in 1879 proclaimed 'Indecent Assaults on Women – How Cases are Trumped up. The Dangers of Travelling.' The article categorizes female passengers as either potentially vulnerable victims or as 'female monsters'. It reassures the former that they need never be afraid of men who assault them in public places or in the presence of others, as direct and independent evidence can be amassed to corroborate their story. The anonymous author, Our Own Traveller, even advises that they might usefully carry a stick and not 'to hesitate in laying it across the head of any dastardly coward who may insult them.' But it also warns men of the risks from female monsters laying a trumped-up charge or manipulating them unknowingly into a compromising position and then making false charges seeking to extort payment in return for an assurance that their reputation will not be tarnished:

> Just as there are men who perambulate the platform in search of a compartment containing a pretty and lovely girl or woman, so many a female monster is on the alert for a carriage wherein a man sits who looks as though he would dread an exposure such as that which would rise out of an indecent assault (*Town Talk* 2 August 1879).

The author estimates that 20 out of every 100 indecent assault charges are trumped up for the purpose of extortion and advises that any concerned gentlemen should take refuge in a smoking carriage, as any woman seen smoking would automatically be stereotyped as a prostitute. Even judges might be caught unawares and subjected to unwarranted advances. Sir William Hardman recollects he 'was caught in a beastly funk the other day by a woman' with short curls and wearing no gloves (hence disrespectable), who entered his compartment while travelling alone to Wandsworth:

> She first of all sat in the opposite seat, then she moved to the opposite corner, then to the middle, three seats in as many minutes! I began to speculate as to where she would sit next – perhaps on my knee and then would charge me with an indecent assault. Happily she got out at the next station, but … I assure you I was "much exercised" (as the Methodists have it) by this little adventure. These unfounded charges of indecent assault have been very common of late, and I have determined to object in future to the entry of any unprotected female into a carriage where I may be alone (Ellis 1930, 153–4).

Hardman was a true Victorian hypocrite. His letters reveal that he was very taken with the new crinolines women were wearing as they allowed the girls 'to show their legs' and another part of the female anatomy subsequently excised by his editor! He continues somewhat disingenuously, 'it pleases them and does no harm to us: I speak for married, not single men' (Crow 1971, 123).

Women-Only Carriages?

The answer to these travelling dilemmas was a more pragmatic alternative suggested by 'an indignant husband' who wrote to the *Daily Telegraph* in 1870 after his wife was approached by a man while travelling in first-class, who asked if he might have the pleasure on calling on her, even though he knew she was married. Why not compel the railway authorities to provide a carriage for ladies only? (*Daily Telegraph* 18 June 1870). This idea had first been mooted in 1845 but dismissed on the basis that women 'could not be completely defended by any process of shutting up' and that they would have to purchase more expensive tickets (*The Railway Chronicle* 22 November 1845). The London and North Western Railway was one of the first to reserve separate compartments for females but generally they were not well received. In 1888 the Board of Trade advised railway managers to introduce separate compartments for female passengers but it was not a compulsory measure. An article entitled 'Lady Travellers' published in *The Railway Times* was scathingly dismissive that this would be an over-protective and unnecessary response. Trials on the Great Western found that, despite the provision of 1,000 female-only seats just 248 had been utilized whereas 5,114 female passengers occupied the smoking compartments (3 March 1888).

Most companies introduced byelaws to enforce any separation zones: for example, the London and North Western Railway prohibited any male aged eight years or over from travelling in ladies-only carriages on penalty of a 40 shilling fine. Unfortunately it is impossible to ascertain whether the incidence of sexual offences diminished as a result, because of the dearth of any official statistics. Women-only compartments were finally phased out in 1975 but, interestingly, have been reintroduced in Tokyo, Shanghai and Taipei. Railway operators in Japan offered women-only compartments at night for a while but have recently extended these to the morning rush hour. The possibility has also been raised in the UK because of the increasing number of sexual assaults committed against women travellers in the last seven years: in 2004 there were 864 sexual offences reported, an increase of 13 per cent on 2003 (Railway Travel Group 2005).

Heroes and Heroines

The most famous case, which illustrates the vulnerability of male and female travellers, is that of Colonel Valentine Baker VC of the 10th Hussars, survivor of the

Crimea and friend of royalty: 'a heroic man of valour and proven moral capacity'. On a hot Bank Holiday in August 1875 Baker appeared at Croydon Assizes charged with an attempt to ravish, indecent assault and common assault. On 17 June 1875 Miss Kate Rebecca Dickenson had boarded a first-class compartment at Midhurst. Her family escorted her onto the train and arranged for her to be met at Waterloo by her brother-in-law, ensuring she was not travelling 'independently'. Baker entered her carriage at Liphook and, according to Kate's deposition, sat opposite engaging in light conversation. Unusually, the full deposition was published in the *Daily Telegraph* under the by-line 'Assault on a Lady' (19 June 1875).

At Woking, Baker suddenly shut the window and asked Kate her name which she refused to give. He then sat next to her and asked for permission to write to her. She pushed him off saying, 'I won't have you so near.' He then put one arm around her waist and kissed her saying, 'You must kiss me darling.' Kate tried to call the guard but the emergency bell was broken. She leant out the window and screamed but he forced her back and put his hand under her dress 'on my stocking, above my boot', and then pleaded with her not to say anything as 'You don't know what trouble you will get me into.' Kate managed to escape and stand on the footstep outside the carriage for five miles until Waterloo where she complained to the officials. She made no formal charge but her three brothers (a doctor, lawyer and subaltern) 'felt they had no alternative' but to protect the family name and so instigated proceedings on her behalf.

Baker was arrested, suspended from duty and brought before the Surrey County Bench without any time to prepare a defence. The Prince of Wales asked George Lewis, a well-known Victorian solicitor, to act for him. Lewis enlisted two eminent barristers, Serjeant Ballantine who notoriously believed that women were incapable of telling the truth, and Henry Hawkins, later Judge 'Hangem Hawkins'. Committed to trial, Baker neither confirmed nor denied the allegation, believing a gentleman should not question the word of a lady. An apology was offered but refused.

The masses travelled to watch the trial, fired up by a leader in *The Times* commenting on this 'brutal assault inspired by animal passion, cowardly and unmanly' (3 August 1875). Kate gave her evidence 'in a calm, firm and modest way' befitting a 'respectable young lady.' Baker had kissed her many times, 'his body was on me and I was quite powerless.' Witnesses confirmed that Kate had been clinging to the open carriage door and, on alighting from the train, Baker's 'dress was unfastened and trousers unbuttoned.' A guard testified that he had heard Baker try to persuade Kate not to report the full story. Baker refused to allow Kate to be cross-examined which was somewhat ill-advised, given that he was not allowed to testify himself. The defence were unable to shake Kate's respectability as the facts were overwhelming, the complainant of a 'pretty disposition' and her 'conduct exemplary' a true 'damsel in distress'. In risking life and limb she had acted stereotypically correctly and, backed by her family, her respectability narrowly outweighed Baker's, even given his reputation and position. The jury, all male and of a 'highly respectable class', had no option but to convict Baker, not of attempted rape as evidence of intent to violate would have been required, but of assault and only common assault at that. Imposing a sentence of 12 months without hard labour and a fine of 500 guineas, Mr Justice Brett advised that 'ladies travelling alone must not forget they do incur a certain risk' cautioning that there had been cases of a 'quite different complexion' and many 'men of by no means weak nerves who dread being shut up in a railway carriage with a young woman' (*The Times* 31 July, 3 August 1875).

Baker was 'permitted to retire' from his regiment but a petition was raised for his reinstatement as there was much sympathy for such a sudden and tragic aberration on the part of so distinguished a gentleman. A counter-petition signed by thousands of ladies, who protested strongly that English womanhood would be insulted, persuaded the Queen that she refuse. After serving his time Baker joined the Turkish army and again proved himself on the battlefield. Kate Dickenson apparently never married and is thought to have led a lonely spinster's life. The case was a true *cause celebre*, dividing public opinion about the possible vindication of the Colonel's behaviour and Kate's ulterior motives. Even in the light of modern interpretations the matter is far from settled; Kate has not fared well from academic discussion and sympathy largely rests with Baker.

Susan Edwards (1981), who makes brief reference to the case from a legal perspective, criticizes the sentence as too harsh compared with similar cases involving middle-class or working-class men. She claims too much emphasis was placed on Kate's respectable position but misses the point that Baker's exemplary reputation was a significant factor; more than anyone else, he should have conducted himself honourably (Edwards 1981, 145). Brian Thompson's (2002) study of the Baker brothers provides a full account of the case concluding that, if the Colonel had allowed Kate to be cross-examined, the defence lawyers would have ensured his acquittal, and that his self-imposed code of silence was his undoing. Baker's biographer and descendant, Anne Baker, is of the same opinion dismissing Kate as flighty, unnecessarily hysterical, and whose day was ruined because 'her hat, perched so deliciously on her head, had been blown away' (Baker 1996, 80). John Juxon, Lewis' biographer, confirms that there is much doubt about Kate's story and the extent to which the whole incident projected her hysteria and frustration, asking 'Who is this Miss Dickenson anyway?' He asserts that Kate was determined to press charges and only wanted revenge revealing a complete misunderstanding of her position and her family's reputation (Juxon 1983, 110–14).

Ivan Bloch (1958) portrays Kate as a flirt and the kind of 'female monster' epitomized in *Town Talk* who, when Baker 'got above himself, and went so far as to say "My Ducky, My Darling" the modest maiden preferring acts of love to words of love, springs up and gives the alarm' (Bloch 1958, 12–13). Perhaps Ronald Pearsall (1969) is the most cynical asserting that Baker gradually came to realize that 'he had actually *kissed* a young unmarried lady without permission', something that had not occurred to the judge as being 'farcical in the extreme.' He concludes that the case was the:

… triumph of Victorian triviality, the cumbrous machinery of law, directed on behalf of a rather smug period damsel against a distinguished fifty year-old man who had a rush of blood to the head and who was destined to be ruined by the most minor of peccadilloes (Pearsall 1969, 398–9).

Despite the ambiguities and opaque nature of the case, such views underline a certain incomprehension about the prosecution and reportage of sexual assaults, reinforcing the fact that historical sources demand a careful examination and sensitivity to the language and expressions used in order to fully understand what is *actually* being represented.

Conclusion

The advent of this new mode of rail travel and the independence women gained from it presented new challenges and problems for law and society, blurring the boundaries between public and private morality and space. Railway carriages could provide an intimate atmosphere and opportunity for cavorting couples, but also a dangerous environment for men and women alike, whether as victims of sexual aggression or, less commonly, feminine deceit. The carriage therefore became a new scene of crime but one that, because of the nature of the crime alleged, it could not always physically confirm beyond all reasonable doubt that a sexual violation had actually taken place. Respectable society had not yet established the necessary conventions to manage inappropriate interaction when forced to travel with strangers in confined and isolated carriages. It was therefore incumbent on complainants, in order to secure justice and see their attackers convicted, to ensure that they acted and portrayed themselves absolutely in stereotypically correct fashion.

References

Baker, A. (1996), *A Question of Honour: The Life of Lieutenant General Valentine Baker Pasha* (London: Leo Cooper).

Bloch, I. (1958), *A History of English Sexual Morals* (London: Arco).

Crow, D. (1971), *The Victorian Woman* (London: George Allen).

Edwards, S. (1981), *Female Sexuality and the Law* (Oxford: Martin Robertson).

Ellis S.M. (ed.) (1930), *The Hardman Papers* (London: Constable and Co. Ltd).

Inkster, I. (ed.) (2000), *Golden Age? Britain 1850–1870* (Aldershot: Ashgate).

Juxon, J. (1983), *Lewis and Lewis* (London: Collins).

Pearsall, R. (1969), *The Worm in the Bud: The World of Victorian Sexuality* (London: Penguin).

Railway Travel Group (2005), *Railway Crime Report February 2005* (London: Rail Safety and Standards Board).

Rowbotham, J. and Stevenson, K. (eds) (2005), *Criminal Conversations: Victorians Behaving Badly* (Ohio State University Press).

Stevenson, K. (2005), 'Taking Indecent Liberties: The Victorian Encryption of Sexual Violence' in J. Rowbotham and K. Stevenson (eds).

Stevenson, K. (2004), 'Fulfilling Their Mission: The Intervention of Voluntary Societies in Cases of Sexual Assault in the Victorian Criminal Process,' *Crime, History and Societies*, 8, 1, 93–110.

Stevenson, K. (2000), 'The Respectability Imperative: A Golden Rule in Cases of Sexual Assault?' in I. Inkster (ed.).

Thompson, B. (2002), *Imperial Vanities: The Adventures of the Baker Brothers and Gordon of Khartoum* (London: HarperCollins).

Afterword
Destinations Unknown

Gayle Letherby and Gillian Reynolds

Where Have We Come From and What Have We Achieved?

In an article in *Walk: Magazine of the Ramblers' Association* John Manning (2008, 37) writes:

> What does a good footpath mean to you? Is it a wild country track offering sumptuous views and a sense of adventure? Is it a historic cross-country trail, with clear waymarks to a fixed destination?

Like walkers on such diverse paths, this collection has, for us, raised questions: questions of gender, emotion and travel that illuminate problems and issues. Our journey has been one of exploration rather than discovery. Destinations remain unknown.

We are certainly not the first (and will not be the last) to invoke the metaphor of the journey when reporting on an academic endeavour; but please indulge us. Editing this book has indeed been a journey on which we have worked with long-standing friends and acquaintances and made new ones. Our journey and the journey of those who have travelled with us is not unique but part of a growing group of people interested in exploring mobility, travel, transport, journeying ... Like others working in the area we find moving across and between traditional inter-disciplinary boundaries challenging and invigorating:

> ... academic mobility across disciplinary borders, [is] a mobility that generates ... "creative marginality". It is this marginality, resulting from from scholars moving from the centre to the periphery of their discipline and then crossing its borders, which helps to produce new productive hybridities in the social sciences (Urry 2000, 210).

Furthermore, given our own interests in the different ways in which academic and other tales can be told we have also enjoyed working with others who wish to break away from more traditional and 'respectable' practices (e.g. Sparkes 2002, Bochner 2001, Cotterill and Letherby 1997). We hope that this collection shows how connections between representation, gender and emotion are as significant as those between belongingness and travel, gender and emotion:

> The narrative turn moves from a singular, monolithic conception of social science toward a pluralism that promotes multiple forms of representation and research; away from facts and toward meanings; away from master narratives and toward local stories; away from idolizing categorical thought and abstracted theory and toward embracing the values of irony, emotionality, and activism; away from assuming the stance of disinterested spectator and toward assuming the posture of a feeling, embodied, and vulnerable observer; away from writing essays and toward telling stories (Bochner 2001, 134–135).

Some readers will not like the multiple styles represented here, not least because 'new writing practices are challenging, and they can appear threatening to more traditionally orientated researchers' (Sparkes 2002, 226). Indeed, not all the pieces in this collection are as we would have written them. Although great friends ourselves, like Danusia Malina and Sian Maslin-Prothero (1998, 13) 'the "we" as editors we present here in the book is false, rendering invisible layers of negotiation, compromise and solidarity' and we have been concerned in this publication, as in others, 'not to subsume each of our individual identities and thoughts into an undifferentiated WE' (Karach and Roach 1992, 307). Inevitably then, the production of this book has been an emotional experience for us and so, too, for chapter authors who have not only spent time thinking about things that make them feel angry, sad, anxious, passionate, exhilarated and so on, but have also had to submit to our particular editorial quirks and failings. Utilizing the travel analogy once more, we compare the emotion work of those involved in this collection to that of the tourist, for: 'Tourism provides us with one of those 'fateful moments' (Giddens 1991: 112), a space and time for both anxiety and opportunity, a point of transition during which reflexivity and attention to the self and focus upon self-actualization are heightened' (Skinner 2007, 339).

Connections Made and Paths Missed

Like the paths that criss-cross the moorland, or the aerial view of 'Spaghetti Junction' (the M5/M6 Interchange at Gravelly Hill in Birmingham) there are many different ways of making connections between the sections and chapters within this collection. Rather than theory, auto/biography, workers, travellers we could for example have included sections on automobility, on public transport and on travel by foot; or possibly, sections focusing around particular emotions – love, hate, fear and so on. So although we have made great effort to arrange the book in a way that seems logical (to us at least), that makes the best of connections between chapters, it is likely that others would have done it very differently. Our main point, however, is that a wide-angle approach to travel is invaluable; not only because it 'enable[s] people to compare and contrast different forms of mobility and begin to see the virtues of slower ways of overcoming the 'frictions of distance' (Urry 2007, 79) but also because it enables us to better observe both how travel 'enables/disables/modifies gendered practices' (Cresswell and Uteng 2008, 1) and provides further evidence that the relationship between the individual and society is an emotional one (Milton 2005).

Inevitably, there is much that we have not covered in this book. One significant omission is the lack of attention to emotion, travel and gender in a non-Westernized context. There is no discussion of developing countries (where walking is often the only means of transport and is done, often by women and children, not for pleasure but out of necessity, for water, food, medical help and so on). In the week that we write this final section, an article in *The Boston Globe* highlights some specific travel problems and concerns in Africa:

> Big cities across Africa suffer maddening congestion, in most cases because they failed to update road networks built decades ago to serve colonial administrations. Lagos, Nigeria – home of the notorious "go-slow" traffic jams – was built in the 1950s to accommodate about 60,000 people. Its estimated population this year? Fourteen million.

> In Nairobi, the population has reached 4.7 million, up from 350,000 at independence in 1963. The number of private cars in Kenya has ballooned to nearly 935,000, with more than half of them in Nairobi alone, according to Simon Ole Kirgotty, Registrar of Motor Vehicles. ...

> There are no subways or elevated trains here to ease the congestion, no bus lanes to help speed commuters to work. The roads are generally two lanes – although aggressive drivers often squeeze four lanes of cars across into the narrow roadways. Jaywalkers make driving even more treacherous, with people desperately sprinting across highways to reach their destination (Muhumed 2008, unpaginated).

Furthermore, our consideration of difference and diversity is limited in that there is little attention given to issues other than gender and a complete political analysis of travel (and mobility more generally) needs to consider other others also. One example of why is provided by Tim Cresswell (2006, 260) who, in his discussion of the aftermath of Hurricane Katrina which devastated New Orleans, notes that those who remained trapped were those with no vehicle to point them away from the flood waters: 'The vast majority of people immobilized in New Orleans were black. The politics of race and the politics of mobility, as so often before in American history, were joined at the hip.' As John Urry (2007, 186) notes: 'Historically much literature on social inequality ignored the complex ways in which the notion of 'space' makes significant differences to understanding economic, political and cultural processes that produce and reinforce social inequalities ...'. In addition to making a small contribution to the growing body of work that analyzes the relationship between social inequality and mobility, this book provides some evidence of positive as well as negative emotional connections of gender with travel.

Are We There Yet?

> It seems to me that I would always be better off where I am not, and this question of moving is one of those I discuss incessantly with my soul (Baudelaire 1962, 211).

Urry (2007, 197) argues that in addition to Pierre Bourdieu's (1986) other concepts of capital (economic, social, cultural),[1] 'network capital' – which is 'the capacity to engender and sustain social relations with those people who are not necessarily proximate' – generates significant and additional emotional, financial and practical benefits for making and remaking social connection for those who possess it. Network capital includes access to documents, money, qualifications and capacities that promotes bodily movement, invitations to travel, access to vehicles to travel in and to technology that enables communication and other resources such as time, safe meeting places and so on (Urry 2007). For Urry (2007, 273–74), network capital, more and more of which is needed in order to 'stand still in the capacity to network' is closely linked to mobility (which includes corporeal, imaginative, virtual and communicative travel of people and the physical movement of objects – see Preface this volume). Thus, he agrees with Bauman (1998, 2) who argues that 'Mobility climbs to the rank of the uppermost among the coverted values – and the freedom to move, perpetually a scarce and unequally distributed commodity, fast becoming the main stratifying factor of our late-modern or postmodern times.' Extending this further through an exploration of how mobility engenders and reinforces social inequality and contributes to global environmental change, Urry's (2007, 2004, 2000) analysis and subsequent predictions are depressing in all sorts of ways – socially, environmentally, even in terms of creative, imaginative, and enjoyable travel experiences:

> The freedom of the car subjects all of civil society to its power. The shortage of time resulting from the extensive distances that increasingly 'have' to be travelled means that the car remains the only viable means of highly flexibilised mobility. Walking, cycling, travelling by bus, steamship or rail may be relegated to the dustbin of history since these are relatively less effective means of roaming the world (Urry 2000, 192).

Perhaps we need to reflect again on Urry's types of mobility that do not involve the movement of bodies or objects – imaginative, virtual and communicative mobility/travel. As he himself says, the growth of new technologies and extended networks supports the growth of an 'interspatial' social life (Urry 2007). Thus:

---

1 Bourdieu (1986) distinguishes between three types of capital:
- Economic capital: command over economic resources (money, assets).
- Social capital: resources based on group membership, relationships, networks of influence and support.
- Cultural capital: forms of knowledge, skills, education, and advantages that a person has, which give them a higher status in society.

Later he adds symbolic capital (resources available to an individual on the basis of honor, prestige or recognition).

> Social positioning in time and space is getting differentiated. Beyond 'classical' forms of integration, social embedding and identity, which are based on locality, presence and face-to-face interaction ... 'connectivity' and virtual mobility become integrative moments of social life ... (Kesselring 2008, 80).

Taking the production of this book as an example, if we had produced it 15, even 10, years ago the process would have been very different. Much of our communication with each other (we live 250 miles apart), with chapter authors and with our publisher has been via email. Indeed, there are a number of authors at least one of us has never met and one that neither of us has met. In the final stages of the process our communication with John Shiels (who is reading through everything for us before we deliver the manuscript) is via email and mobile phone. This one small example both supports and possibly challenges Urry's (2007, 2004, 2000) view that increased network capital leads to a 'bleak future' for all of us. We accept of course that there are network inequalities (see also Golding 2000) but maybe, just maybe, the increasing use of mobile technology both for communication and virtual travel, and the fact that places all around the world are becoming more and more like each other through processes of homogenization and globalization (e.g. Molz 2007, Holmes 2001), will lead to less corporeal mobility. Maybe ...

Last Words

Of course the journey is not finished and, although we have reached a destination of sorts, in some people's eyes we will only be half way there or maybe even should not have started out at all. For others though, this book will provide food for thought in its contribution to an understanding of the complex relationships between gender, travel and emotion. We look forward to seeing how others will take the journey forward in different directions, and maybe to completely different destinations:

> Every story is a travel story – a spatial practice. ...They [the stories] make the journey, before or during the time the feet perform it (de Certeau 1984, 115–6).

References

Ang-Lygate, M., Corrin, C. and Henry, M.S. (eds) (1997), *Desperately Seeking Sisterhood: Still Challenging and Building* (London: Taylor and Francis).

Baudelaire, C. (1962), 'Anywhere Out of This World', *Petits Poemes en Prose* (Paris: Editions Garnier Freres).

Bauman, Z. (1998), *Globalization: The Human Consequences* (Cambridge: Polity Press).

Bochner, A. (2001), 'Narrative's Virtues', *Qualitative Inquiry*, 7, 2, 131–57.

Bourdieu, P. (1986), 'The Forms of Capital' in J. Richardson (ed.).

Canzler, W., Kaufmann, V. and Kesselring, S. (eds) (2008), *Tracing Mobilities: Towards a Cosmopolitan Perspective* (Aldershot: Ashgate).

Cotterill, P. and Letherby, G. (1997), 'Collaborative Writing: The pleasures and pains of working together' in M. Ang-Lygate, C. Corrin and M.S. Henry (eds).

Cresswell, T. (2006), *On the Move: Mobility in the Modern Western World* (London: Routledge).

Cresswell, T. and Uteng, T.P. (2008), 'Gendered Mobilities: Towards an Holistic Understanding' in T.P. Uteng and T. Cresswell (eds).

Davidson, J., Smith, M. and Bondi, L. (2007), *Emotional Geographies* (Aldershot: Ashgate).

de Certeau, M. (1984), (trans. Stephen Rendall) *The Practice of Everyday Life* (Berkeley: University of California Press)

Golding, P. (2000), 'Forthcoming Features: information and communications technologies and the sociology of the future', *Sociology*, 34, 1, 165–84.

Holmes, D. (2001), 'Virtual Globalization – An Introduction' in D. Holmes (ed.).

Holmes, D. (ed.) (2001), *Virtual Globalization, Virtual Spaces/Tourist Spaces* (London: Routledge).

Karach, A. and Roach, D. (1992), 'Collaborative Writing, Consciousness Raising, and Practical Feminist Ethics', *Women's Studies International Forum*, 15, 2, 303–8.

Kesselring, S. (2008), 'The Mobile Risk Society' in W. Canzler, V. Kaufmann, V. and S. Kesselring (eds).

Malina, D. and Maslin-Prothero, S. (1998), 'Coming Clean: on being feminist editors' in D. Malina and S. Maslin-Prothero (eds).

Malina, D. and Maslin-Prothero, S. (eds) (1998), *Surviving the Academy: Feminist Academics* (London: Falmer Press).

Manning, J. (2008), 'Which Way's the future?', *Walk: Magazine of the Ramblers' Association*, 19, Summer, 36–9.

Milton, K. (2005), 'Afterword', in K. Milton and M. Svašek (eds).

Milton, K. and Svašek, M. (eds) (2005), *Mixed Emotions: Anthropological Studies of Feeling* (Oxford: Berg).

Molz, J.G. (2007), 'Guilty Pleasures of the Golden Arches: Mapping McDonald's in Narratives of Round-the-World Travel' in J. Davidson, M. Smith and L. Bondi (eds).

Muhumed, M.M. (2008), 'Walking is Faster in Kenya', *The Boston Globe*, 3 August, www.boston.com/neews/world/africa/articles/2008/08/03/.

Richardson, J. (ed.) (1986), *Handbook of Theory and Research for the Sociology of Education* (New York: Greenwood Press).

Skinner, J. (2007), 'Emotional Baggage: the meaning/feeling debate amongst tourists' in H. Wulff (ed.).

Sparkes, A. (2002), *Telling Tales in Sport and Physical Activity: A Qualitative Journey* (Leeds: Human Kinetics).

Urry, J. (2007), *Mobilities* (Cambridge: Polity Press).

Urry, J. (2004), 'Connections', *Environment and Planning D*, 22, 27–37.

Urry, J. (2000), *Sociology beyond Societies: Mobilities for the Twenty-first Century* (London: Routledge).

Uteng, T.P. and Cresswell, T. (eds) (2008), *Gendered Mobilities* (Aldershot: Ashgate).

Wulff, H. (ed.) (2007), *The Emotions: A Cultural Reader* (Oxford: Berg).

Index